"Rydall not only breaks down all tl how it's played and don't get kickeᴅ ᴅᴏᴡɴ ᴛʜᴇ ꜰɪᴇʟᴅ — he also lays out the spiritual truths that will help you transcend them, tap into your true power, and fulfill your higher purpose."

— Mark Harris, Producer, *Crash*, Academy Award® Best Picture

"For years we've been conducting business and creating art under assumptions about the entertainment industry that are simply false. Derek Rydall, in his important new book, challenges us to exchange them for a fresh world view whereby we can act and work out of our own true nature, whole and abundant. Read this book, do the exercises. Walk right past that clever detractor and step into a new day."

— Lindsay Crouse, Oscar-nominated actress, *House of Games, The Insider, The Verdict, Places in the Heart*

"Derek Rydall has once again successfully navigated the depths of Hollywood, and this time we are enlightened on our spiritual and emotional path toward success. Any artists working their way through the business will be offered guidance and strength to help build the foundation necessary to follow their dreams and passion to obtain their goals. It all starts with understanding oneself and your emotional connection to the creative journey. Read this book and let it open your mind — as success starts with you."

— Matthew Rhodes, President, Persistent Entertainment, Producer, *An Unfinished Life, Southland Tales, Passengers*

"With this insightful, inspiring and much needed book, Derek Rydall gently and wisely guides you through the entire process of creating art that is true to your own joy and passion, that touches your audience at the deepest possible level, and which holds the power to change the world."

— Michael Hauge, script consultant, lecturer, and author of *Writing Screenplays That Sell* and *Selling Your Story in 60 Seconds: The Guaranteed Way to Get Your Screenplay or Novel Read*

"Derek Rydall's latest sets out the bold notion that you don't have to cut out your heart or sell your soul to work in the entertainment business. It gives encouragement to all of us who want our careers to advance the higher possibilities of human nature. Sometimes we feel like we're crying in the wilderness and it's good to hear a voice telling us to keep trying."

— Chris Vogler, best-selling author, *The Writer's Journey*

"Derek Rydall has written another remarkable book. This time he reveals spiritual secrets that will not only help you connect to your creative unconscious source, they will put you on the path to your full potential and your true destiny as an artist. I highly recommend it!"

— James Bonnet, writer, teacher, story consultant, author of *Stealing Fire from the Gods: The Complete Guide to Story for Writers and Filmmakers*

"Just a quick perusal of the chapter titles and subheadings was enough to make me want to read this book! It's a road map to the creative process that illuminates the game of Hollywood, helps artists reconcile their desire to be successful in the industry without losing their spiritual core, unmasks internal obstacles, and gives you the tools to get out of the box — and out of your own way. Whether you're lost on your artistic journey — or just not making the time you wish you were — Derek Rydall's in-depth exercises and insights will help you master new ways of thinking to keep you on the path, and on purpose."

— Heather Hale, producer, teacher, screenwriter, *The Courage to Love*

"This book will save any artist the frustrations we've come to believe are part of our lot as creative beings. Derek Rydall does a brilliant job illuminating the truth that we are the Captains of Our Ship, and tells us how to take joyful charge of our fate. We're not just creators when we work, we create the opportunities to work — simply from how we *think*, then how we *act* on our thoughts. We are powerful beings who have forgotten our power. This book shows you how to get it back."

— Leigh Taylor-Young, Emmy Award–winning actress

"Rydall's book opens your mind, heart and soul to the new spiritual consciousness growing in Hollywood today. A very hip, enlightening journey for anyone who truly loves movies and making them."

— Katie Torpey, screenwriter, *The Perfect Man, Truth About Kerry*

"If our lives are like movies, Derek Rydall has given our screenplay the structure we'll need to follow our dreams. It's a soulful journey, loaded with spiritual enlightenment and truly a must read for everyone!"

— Eric DelaBarre, screenwriter (*Conversations with God*), author of *WHY NOT: Start Living Your Life Today*

"*There's No Business Like Soul Business* is an invaluable tool for any creative soul who wants to channel material the world is waiting for!"

— Dee Wallace, actress (*E.T., Cujo*), healer, author and teacher

"Derek Rydall understands that true success comes from deepening ourselves spiritually. Many of the concepts and exercises in this book can do just that and be useful, regardless of one's religion or spiritual discipline. They can help the writer become empowered in an industry that often leaves writers feeling powerless."

— Dr. Linda Seger, script consultant, best-selling author, *Making a Good Writer Great*

"Derek Rydall writes as one who truly knows the art of Inner-attainment through entertainment. These tools and insights are the only sane way to be in the 'business.' This book will support and strengthen artists for years to come."

— Tina Lifford, spiritual coach, author, co-star of *Hostage, Blood Work*

"Derek Rydall has just awakened the sleeping giant. In this simple yet powerful book, Rydall has given us the tools to unlock the conscious artist within each of us. This book is our stepping stone to igniting the conscious media revolution."

— Matthew Seigel, producer, *Big Brothers*

"All I can say is 'Oh my God, this is amazing!' Derek has come up with another winner... looking at the often invisible connection between spirit and story, and the potential for divine Inspiration, compelling change and soul growth that film can weave into our lives. Derek has fashioned a how to, go to, find god in one's work. He is the pastor, rabbi and guru rolled into one entertaining book on using god in entertainment. It is really remarkable… transformative and informative. A must read for anyone who is looking at their own creative work to change themselves and change the world."

> — Devorah Cutler-Rubenstein, CEO, The Script Broker; President, Noble House Entertainment, Inc.

"Words cannot describe how impactful this book is! An absolute 'must' for anyone in the entertainment industry who wants to inject some light and positive change not only into traditional Hollywood, but into themselves as well. This is definitely a life-changing read. If you want to go to the next level in your career and personal life, this is it! Derek Rydall clearly guides the reader to move forward on their own unique path with ease and deep understanding. You'll feel a sense of 'finally finding home'."

> — Amanda Robinson, President/Founder, The Institute for Spiritual Entertainment (ISELA)

"In this magnificently inspired book, Derek Rydall shows you the way to the divine muse within your own soul. This book rocks and rolls with passion, joy and enough good will to last through the millennium. You will not be able to put it down — it is truly a blueprint for creating a new paradigm and achieving creative success. Enjoy!"

> — Akuyoe Graham, award-winning actor/writer, *Spirit Awakening, The Little Book of Transformation*

"*There's No Business Like Soul Business* and Derek Rydall is in the Business of the Soul."

> — Viki King, author, *How to Write a Movie in 21 Days — The Inner Movie Method*; creative consultant on *Conversations with God*

"At last, a nuts-and-bolts, step-by-step guidebook that teaches you how to survive and prosper in the soul-less business of show and stay positive and spiritually balanced along the way. Amen."

> — Rich Krevolin, author, *Screenwriting from the Soul, How to Adapt Anything into a Screenplay.*

"Derek Rydal has introduced the soul's purpose for storytelling and has shown us how to express this purpose in our work to produce stories that compel and capture audiences and Hollywood alike on a grand scale. He states that the book was written to inspire 'a change of heart. A change of mind. And a change of consciousness.' This is true from the very first page."

> — G. Michael Torres, producer

"This book is a one-of-a-kind treasure map that will reward you and reward the world with your works once you follow it and dig below the surface. The greatest and most successful stories in show business tug at our hearts because they have soul! Derek Rydall guides you on a step-by-step journey bringing forth heart and soul through you to your creative projects. Tapping into this elixir has the alchemical power to turn your projects into gold and light up the world along the way."

> — Bill Lae, writer/director, *SuperGuy: Behind the Cape*

"Derek Rydall's new book is a sparkling example of what happens when we take the best of the new thought/evolutionary consciousness movement and mix it with a full career as a creator and facilitator of pop culture. This book is chock full of exercises, meditations, tools, tips, tricks and processes that will help you on your journey to become a more conscious filmmaker, conscious human, and conscious creator of everything and everyone around you. If you've wondered 'What the Bleep' and are in on 'The Secret,' I invite you to stew in the cosmic juices of Derek's ideas and insights, then step back and enjoy what comes alive in you."

> — David Brownstein, Hollywood career coach, author, *The Cosmic Mission of Hollywood, A Course in Hollywood Miracles*

"Having been a working actor, talent agent, talent manager and producer for more than 25 years, I must say that I found Derek's book to be a refreshing approach to a profession that can beat you up and shoot you down. Reading chapter after chapter not only brought me a greater understanding of self and why I am in this business, but it showed me how to have a sense of amusement about things that I took so seriously in the past that I just felt like giving up many times. Stick with it and remember who you really are. Acting isn't pretending... acting is telling the truth. And attitude is indeed everything."

> — Kate Romero, President-CEO Guardian Angel Ent; host of Spiritual Hollywood Radio Show; Author, *The End of the Anonymous Actor*

"All those books on your nightstand — visualizing success, meditating for serenity, writing the great script, breaking into Hollywood, contributing to the growth of the planet — put them away and replace them with this! It's a spiritual guidebook, an inspiration for artists, a business handbook — all this and more. Calling upon his own experiences as a Hollywood professional, Derek Rydall offers insight, inspiration, and practical advice to anyone wanting to contribute their creativity to the enlightenment of the planet, through entertainment — and get well-deserved rewards and recognition for it. So take *There's No Business Like Soul Business* in hand and start creating those wonderful stories we all long to enjoy."

> — Pamela Jaye Smith, author, *Inner Drives: How to Write and Create Characters Using the Eight Classic Centers of Motivation* and *The Power of the Dark Side: Creating Great Villains, Dangerous Situations, and Dramatic Conflict*

"*There's No Business Like Soul Business* couldn't have come at a better time, because the entertainment industry makes a huge difference in shaping the world and its thinking. Derek Rydall has created a blueprint to inspire those in the industry to create from their spirit. Every artist should inhale this book and all those thinking about being a creative artist need to devour this great read. Congratulations to Derek for being a trailblazer in merging a spiritual life with a creative life!"

> — Paul Ryan, TV host/producer, author of *The Art of Comedy...Getting Serious about Being Funny*

"I am absolutely awed and inspired! Derek Rydall has written the definitive practical spiritual manual on how to be consciously 'in this business but not of it!' I found so many practical tools and rich revelations here — all of which can assist any individual in becoming unstuck in every area of our lives. With this powerful book we can free ourselves to express our true Divine nature — with ease, grace, impeccable authenticity and unbridled joy! This book is on my list of recommended 'must read' books."

> — Chemin Sylvia Bernard, president , Casting Society of America

THERE'S NO BUSINESS LIKE SOUL BUSINESS

A Spiritual Path to Enlightened Screenwriting, Filmmaking, and Performing Arts

DEREK RYDALL

MICHAEL WIESE PRODUCTIONS

Published by Michael Wiese Productions
3940 Laurel Canyon Blvd. – Suite 1111
Studio City, CA 91604
(818) 379-8799, (818) 986-3408 (FAX).
mw@mwp.com
www.mwp.com

Front cover by agdesign.com
Interior design by William Morosi
Copyedited by Paul Norlen
Printed by McNaughton & Gunn

Manufactured in the United States of America

Library of Congress Cataloging-in-Publication Data

Rydall, Derek, 1968-
 There's no business like soul business : a spiritual path to enlightened screenwriting, filmmaking, and the performing arts / Derek Rydall.
     p. cm.
 ISBN 10 1932907246
 ISBN 13 9781932907247
 1. Performing arts–Religious aspects. 2. Performing arts–Moral and ethical aspects. I. Title.
 PN1590.R45R93 2007
 791.023–dc22

                        2006032909

Contents

Part III: Character Development 79

Chapter Five: Reclaiming Your Power 81

Chapter Six: Developing a Practice 103

Chapter Twelve: Becoming an "Enlightened Entertainer" 227

About the Author 236

Foreword

For me, *conscious entertainment* is about making film and television that has something to say about humankind and what right action is. It shows us where we're living and, hopefully, how we can live better, live together, and, ultimately, love one another.

It's not always about having a "message." If you can find the right material and create something that matters, that's great. That's what I always try to do. But at the very least, it's about doing good work, good filmmaking, going for excellence. What conscious entertainment *isn't* about is getting on a soapbox. You need to find a metaphor to carry the message. If it's a current issue, it's better to use a past event, like *Good Night, and Good Luck,* or put it in the future, like *Star Trek* or *Star Wars,* or use comedy, like *Dr. Strangelove.* Bottom line, you need to show, not tell.

In this book, Derek Rydall clearly explains what conscious entertainment is and what it isn't. He also reminds us that the word *entertainment* is actually defined as both "to amuse" and "to contemplate." In a powerful story, the "entertainment value" keeps our senses distracted and our judging mind preoccupied, while the deeper meaning slips in. As Derek says, it's like the spoonful of sugar that helps the medicine go down. The problem arises when you go too far in either direction. Too much sugar without any medicine and you're left unchanged — or at least unfulfilled. Too much medicine without enough sugar and you'll spit it out — or walk out.

The challenge, when you get into a subjective area like art and entertainment, is determining what is "medicine" and what isn't. As Derek says, it's a fine line when you talk about "conscious entertainment." It's not about censoring or judging what kind of entertainment people should make — because you don't know what impact a project is going to have on somebody — it's about knowing what your intention is in making it. Why are you doing it? Is it about bringing a little more light to humanity — or at least more excellence — or it just about the money?

The state of mind you're coming from is also important in terms of how things turn out, personally and professionally. If you're doing it for the wrong reasons, from a place of fear or greed, it's usually doesn't work out well. When I've acted out of anxiety and insecurity, I've run into problems — what I call "producer's block." But through my own spiritual practice, I've learned to trust the process, as described in *Zen in the Art of Archery*. You don't look at the bull's-eye, you just feel the bow and arrow in your hand and point it in the right direction. You don't focus on the goal, you stay in the process. Whatever's in front of me at the moment — whatever spirit calls me to do — that's what I try to do.

Sometimes it's frustrating because I have to wait and nothing is happening. And it doesn't always turn out the way I want. But it always turns out the way it should. There's a bigger plan unfolding. The practice is to live in the moment and honor the truth as it reveals itself to you, not force your idea or direction. As the saying goes, "Want to make God laugh, tell him your plans."

In this book, Derek expertly guides you through a process that helps develop these inner senses, so you can live directly from your Spirit, not from fear or worldly pressures. He lays out a step-by-step program of spiritual principles and practices that can help any artist or entertainment professional live more in the process, uncover their creative vision, develop greater confidence in their work, and be in this business more consciously.

One of the biggest challenges in making more meaningful entertainment is dealing with the "bottom line" in this business. Studios are interested in targeting wide audiences. They want to know if they're going to make a hundred million or more on a film. They're about stockholders. Even in the independent world no one wants to put up a dollar to lose a dollar — they want to make two. Films I've been part of, like *Crash, Gods and Monsters,* or *Million Dollar Baby* are no different.

They want names to offset the concept. That's their insurance policy. If the film doesn't make money, they can at least keep their job by saying "hey, we had these names." And many people in a position of saying yes or no to a project have no track record to show that their judgment is based on any real wisdom, talent, or quality. So all these things seem to be stacked against you.

But if you follow your spirit, trust your own judgments — and don't try to adapt to what you think the industry wants — things can still work out. That's how *Crash* happened. When Paul Haggis gave me the treatment for *Crash* and asked if we could get it made, I said probably not. It had no foreign value. But that didn't stop me from trying! I knew it was great and I wanted to see something like that made into a film. Something inside told me to stick with it. And as I stayed in that place of trust, eventually it found its home.

In this book, Derek not only breaks down all the "rules" of the Hollywood game — so that you know how it's played and don't get kicked down the field — he also lays out the spiritual truths that will help you transcend them, tap into your true power, and fulfill your higher purpose. And that's just the first few chapters!

In other words, you're in good hands.

This is *your* life, *your* career, *your* destiny. You have to trust that, listen to your spirit — and go with your heart. I wish you great success and fulfillment on your journey!

Peace,

Mark Harris
Producer, *Crash* (Academy Award for Best Picture)

Acknowledgments

This book is the product of years of praying, playing, and teaching conscious entertainment to hundreds and hundreds of people, all of whom contributed to the insights in these pages. To every client, colleague, and student — especially those who pushed back and forced me to look deeper — thank you!

I probably wouldn't have made it this far if not for the support of my spiritual mentors, Reverends Michael Beckwith and Nirvana Gayle (who facilitated the first conscious entertainment group with me and is a powerful artist himself). In a way, you guys co-authored this book — since so much of what I know you taught me! Words can never express my love and appreciation for you.

To my beautiful wife and children — you are my inspiration, motivation, and greatest teachers. You make life worth living. I love you with all my heart — and appreciate you putting up with my less-than-enlightened ways!

To Michael Wiese and Ken Lee — thank you for believing in me and my work, and for taking a chance on something original in a business that puts a lot of pressure on you to do "more of the same." You guys are visionaries and true creative collaborators. I look forward to blazing new trails!

Thanks to Bill Morosi, designer, and Paul Norlen, copyeditor, for giving the manuscript form and coherence.

Many people took time out of their busy lives to read early drafts of this manuscript and/or offer insights that helped shape it: Tina Lifford, Brett Butler, John Griggs, Matt Seigel, Allan Katz, Jon Stevens, Scott Hoffman, Mario Celestino, German Michael Torres, Kimberly Burns, Jana Collins, Pamela Dearing, Melissa Hall, Sara Siffler — and Mark

Harris for contributing the inspiring foreword. Thank you all *so much* for your incredible generosity, wisdom, and support!

There are many spiritual teachers, artists, and entertainment professionals who have made a powerful contribution to my life and work — too many to mention. I just want to thank all of you who endeavor to grow spiritually and strive for excellence in the arts, entertainment, and all forms of media. You are a source of continued inspiration and motivation to me.

I want to offer a special thanks to my uncle, Don Siegel, who gave me my start in this business of show when he directed me in my first movie as a child. He's now making movies on the "other side," entertaining angels — and no doubt stirring things up with the big Studio Boss in the sky.

Finally, I want to thank God — my source, my muse, my constant companion, the true author of this book and my life. Thank you, thank you, thank you!

The Sacred Storytellers

A Parable

Once upon a time there was a tribe, connected to heaven and earth. They spent their days hunting and gathering, learning and exploring, being born and dying. But there was one ritual that held their village together — storytelling. Whether it was tales of daily drama or nightly dreams, ancient myths or legendary heroes, *story* was the way they interpreted life. Stories were "equipment for living."

While storytelling was common to all, the "professional storytellers" were the spiritual leaders. They knew life's most meaningful problems were solved through stories. And as long as rich stories were woven into the fabric of tribal life, it was nourished and thriving. Nightly, the village gathered around the tribal fire, as the resident mystic spun simple tales or profound plays, with performers, musicians, and special effects (smoke and fire used to go a long way) creating an "entertaining experience" that allowed for the potent — sometimes painful — wisdom to go down more smoothly.

One night, a businessman was shipwrecked on this foreign shore. As he gathered himself, he heard the beat of drums echo through the trees and ventured into the jungle. Through dense foliage he trekked, drawn to the enchanted sounds and, parting a curtain of leaves, saw something that took his breath away. Gathered under the stars, firelight flickering in their eyes, the tribe watched as a thrilling play was performed. The businessman was struck by this communal gathering, moving as One to the rhythm of story. For a moment, he too lost himself in the rhythm of oneness — but only for a moment.

Soon his business mind — one that had exploited vast resources — recognized it was witnessing something special, something that could make him rich, even famous. "If this *experience* could be broken down into a formula," he thought, "it could be packaged and delivered to audiences everywhere. An industry could be created around it, with ancillary products to enhance, supplement, and complement it!" He was dizzy with possibilities.

And in that fateful moment, show *business* was born.

The businessman was only aware of what he saw on the surface — the "entertainment value." He failed to see *why* the stories were being told, *why* the music, dancers, costumes, and special effects were employed. Untrained in the ways of sacred storytellers, he believed that "dazzling the senses" was the purpose of entertainment, rather than just the method by which the *meaning* was delivered. And before he could learn otherwise, he was rescued and headed home to launch his new enterprise.

It was an immediate success and grew rapidly, attracting modern-day shamans who recognized their calling, if only unconsciously. But as the "business of soul" became the "business of show," it lost touch with its true origins. As the "shows" lost their sacred substance, the soul of the larger tribe became malnourished. And as the "hunger" increased, people began finding other ways to feed their inner famine: destructive ways, disconnected from heaven and earth — and each other.

So it came to pass that entertainment became a mass distribution system of diversion rather than the powerful tool of awakening in which it had its roots. (Ironically, the term "entertain" is defined as both "to divert attention" *and* "to contemplate an idea.") And as the soul stirrings became louder, like a hungry stomach growling to be fed, more distracting entertainment was created to drown it out — until the tribe could no longer hear at all. Living in the constant "noise," they became oblivious to it.

Despite the mass-depravation of soul-inspired entertainment — or perhaps because of it — the impulse to be touched in this way still remained. On a daily basis, the tribe continued to gather in darkened theatres, beneath the "stars," as the light of the virtual tribal fire flickered in their eyes and the storytellers wove their tales. Yet what they were given rarely fed that primordial pang.

And they often left hungrier than before.

Introduction

Entertainment Today

You want the "good news" or the "bad news" first?

Okay, the "bad news": our hearts, minds, and souls are rarely nourished by the entertainment we consume. This is no small thing. "A society without vision perishes." The lack of fresh, vital stories, myths, and parables (whether as plays, movies, music, novels, TV, even narrative-driven video games) is a real threat to our humanity. We can have all the food and water we need, but without the sustenance of real story, real art — without the wisdom, insight, and "life instruction" it brings — we will stagnate as a culture and become a swamp where quality life can no longer be sustained.

The "good news" is it's never too late to tell a good story (in any of the above media), to create a new myth that rouses us from our intoxicated slumber, that lifts us above the din of confusion and arms us against the weapons of mass distraction. The good news, from a business perspective, is that the world is so hungry for real entertainment that if you build it, they will buy it.

If you were drawn to this book, it's because you are part of this primordial tribe of Sacred Storytellers. Whether you're a writer, director, performer, producer, executive, video game creator — or any of the necessary artists and craftspeople it takes to make this business of show go round — you are being called to take a stand for a higher vision; to restore *entertainment* to its original purpose, and create an industry that is a tool of education and transformation; a dream machine that awakens individuals to their true potential, and helps build a world that works for everyone.

You might be thinking the entertainment industry could never be such a thing, even if we wanted it to be. You might even be thinking you *don't* want it to be, that it *shouldn't* be — that it's just entertainment! Leave the serious stuff to people doing serious things, like brain surgeons! I have nothing against brain surgeons — in fact, some of my best friends are brain surgeons — but they're just working on the meat of the brain. We're working on what's inside it; those fanciful little things called thoughts, values, and beliefs; the very things that drive a person to create the Sistine Chapel or a concentration camp; the very things that inspire a heart to love and heal or hate and destroy.

Entertainment may not be brain surgery, but the images and ideas we convey do, in fact, operate on the hearts and minds of those we serve — perhaps more powerfully than any other influence in society today. Sure, we have great teachers, therapists, and even some good parents — but who are the kids running around dressed like? We can talk about building a stronger, more influential family culture, so that we can weave greater moral fiber into our kids' character — and that's important — but we can't ignore the fact that what our youth value and believe, what they aspire to be and who they admire, how they dress and what they talk about — is largely influenced by the movies, music, video games, and TV they consume. And this continues, to a great degree, into adulthood. We are what we eat — not only physically, but mentally and emotionally as well.

My goal here is not to debate the adverse effect film and other media can have (or why we're so attracted to the darkness), but to proclaim the *positive* influence it can provide — and to lay out a path of spiritual practice that will help you discover your unique purpose, a higher creative vision, and a plan to fulfill it for the greater good. I won't spend much time trying to convince you of the merit of this mission. But if you're uncertain, let me pose some questions for you to consider (or to ask others who have their doubts):

1. If the industry — or more specifically, the products it produces — *could* have a powerful positive influence on the planet, would that be a worthy goal to pursue?

2. If we could, as artists and entertainment professionals, create inspired works of entertainment that make the global audience laugh, cry, think and, ultimately, become better citizens of the earth, would that be a valuable endeavor?

3. If every time an audience gathers around the virtual tribal fire (whether in a movie theatre, playhouse, concert hall, or living room), the members of the tribe are nourished mentally, emotionally, even spiritually, and sent on their way better equipped to do their part in the global "village," would that be worth the effort?

4. If you could do all of this, while still creating the types of things you love (comedies, tragedies, action, horror, pop, rock, punk, and every genre in between) — and make good money doing it — would you have any reason *not* to do it?

There are already great talents producing meaningful mainstream material — flashes of light illuminating what sometimes feels like a long, dark night. The 2006 Academy Award nominations for Best Picture were, amazingly, all examples of this. *Crash*, which took home the top trophy, was a poster child for conscious entertainment — as was George Clooney, nominated for best actor, writer, and director in two different films of substance, *Syriana* and *Good Night, and Good Luck.*

Was this a fluke or the beginning of something bigger? Time will tell. But one thing is certain. How brightly this business of show can shine, and how soon, will be determined by how many of us join together — if only in consciousness — and commit to this higher calling of enlightened entertainment.

Purpose of This Book

In order to restore Show Business back to its ancient roots of Soul Business, it will require change. A change of heart. A change of mind. A change of consciousness. Any spare change we can manage! In other words, you and I must do the changing. As Gandhi said, "We must become the change we want to see in the world." This is because what's "outside" is merely a reflection of what's "inside." It's all a mirror. And the change starts by taking an honest look in that shiny piece of glass and asking: "How must I be different to allow this higher vision to unfold?" That, finally, is what this book is about — *becoming the change we want to see.*

You might be thinking, "I don't wanna change, I wanna be a star! Or at least pay my damn rent and get this stinking script finished!" I hear you loud and clear. And you're in luck — because an important part of this path is becoming a working, even thriving, professional in the business. As you become a more "enlightened entertainer," we need you out in the field, creating projects that entertain *and* enlighten. We need you to be successful — a living example of how great life, art, and the "biz" can be when you walk this road connected to your Source (whatever your concept of it is).

After all, how can you be a light in the world if you can't pay your light bill?!

If you sincerely practice the principles in this book, you'll be able to pay your light bill (and then some). But the "divine electricity" that moves through you will do more than power your appliances — it will power your purpose and passion as a sacred artist and soulful professional, and light your path to creative freedom. Just a word of warning. This trip is unlike any you've ever booked. On this journey, you *want* to lose your baggage. In fact, I'll do everything I can to make sure *all of it* is lost, so that when you reach the end of this road, you have nothing left to cover your Self up with.

How to Use This Book

Think of this as an "Enlightened Entertainer Manual." A map of the inner terrain artists/entertainment professionals must trek on the journey back to their sacred self. Use it as a book of guiding principles that, when practiced, allow you to walk this path consciously; staying productive, purposeful, *and* prosperous; selling yourself without selling your soul; making a living without losing the joy of life; and getting a "piece of the action" without losing your peace in the act.

PART I
The Foundation

ONE ～

Conscious Entertainment

"The theatre sprang from religion. It is my greatest wish that, somehow, through me — in some small way — they may be reunited."
— Eleonora Duse, *The Mystic in the Theatre*

What Is It? Why Do We Need It?

We think and live in story terms. Just watch your mind during a crisis. Notice how *you* are at the center trying to achieve some goal — like the protagonist in a story — and how there are other voices in your head, pushing, pulling, advising, rooting you on, shooting you down, blocking your path, and guiding you along. Some call this the inner Board of Directors. But you could also call it the Cast of Characters in this drama called your life.

Why do we dream in stories? Why do therapists encourage us to tell our stories? Why do we feel the need to tell them in the first place? Why are we so drawn to stories in all their various forms? And why is the entertainment industry one of the biggest and fastest growing industries on the planet? I believe it's because story is the mechanism by which we live, express, understand, and evolve. Story is more than just equipment for living — it's life itself. When a culture's stories are honest, authentic, and connected to the truth, the culture is strong, productive, and progressive. When a culture's stories stagnate and become derivative, deceptive, shallow, and unconnected to the energy of life, the culture erodes, degrades, and eventually perishes (although the people may not realize they're dead!). Stories are the manner by which we extract meaning out of the fibrous pulp of our everyday lives. And meaning is the spiritual oxygen that allows our soul to breathe. Without stories, life has no meaning. Without meaning, we cannot live.

In his powerful book, *A Whole New Mind*, Daniel H. Pink says that we are moving into a Conceptual Age, where the elements of "story" and "meaning" will become as essential to our evolution as the plow and pitchfork were to the Agrarian Age, the steam engine and factory to the Industrial Age, and the left-brain thinking of the "knowledge worker" to the Information Age. As we reach a critical mass of materialistic abundance, where even "poor people" have TVs, cell phones, and Internet access, we are finding that the more we fill ourselves up, the emptier we feel. Our materialistic fix just isn't getting us high any more. We may not be conscious of this. It might feel like a low-level anxiety, a gnawing hunger, a quiet desperation. No matter how you put it, we're "jonesing" for something to take the edge off. And a new ring tone, iPod, or mindless action flick ain't gonna do it.

While the younger generation may still be able to anesthetize the soul's hunger pangs for more meaning (barely able, as we can see by the growing angst, violence, and depression amongst the youth), Gen-Xers and baby boomers are finding it more difficult to deny.

The more we fill ourselves up, the emptier we feel. Our materialistic fix just isn't getting us high anymore.

Many boomers have done all the things that are "supposed" to make you happy (have a career, make money, raise a family). And now they're left with the one thing often neglected — meaning. Where are they going to find it? As Pink says, they'll start by looking to the products they buy. And as we move into a mass media culture, those products are going to be increasingly entertainment-related. If you need a bottom-line profit motive to buy into this concept — or convince your studio boss to — think about this: *The Baby Boomers are the largest and richest demographic in history.*

Why Entertainment Needs to Be Entertaining

If stories are powerful and necessary when they're consciously created, why do we need the "entertainment" aspect tacked onto them? What is "entertainment" after all? Why can't we just create art, tell stories, and forget about this nonsense of entertaining people? In a nutshell (chocolate covered), "entertainment" is the candy coating, the fancy packaging, the "spoonful of sugar" that helps the medi-

> "Entertainment" is the candy coating, the fancy packaging, the "spoonful of sugar" that helps the medicine go down.

cine go down. Without it, we aren't as likely to "swallow" the message or meaning making up the soft chewy center of conscious media.

Look at the act of procreation. It's something we must do to survive as a species. It's the most fundamental requirement. It's also one of the most "entertaining" and pleasurable acts. Do you think that design was by accident? Imagine if it didn't feel good. How likely would we be to do it? We'd find all kinds of excuses for not "getting around to it," the way many regard going to the gym. We'd probably wait until we were on the brink of extinction before mustering up the muscle to get off our butts and on our backs!

The intercourse we must have with story in order to conceive and give birth to our greater potential is much the same. If it wasn't such an entertaining experience, how likely would you be to drag yourself off that comfy coach, track down a babysitter, fight traffic en route to a crowded multiplex, engage in the Fast & the Furious to find a parking space, wait in a line that gives you flashbacks of a day at Disneyland, dish out a thousand dollars for movie (or concert) tickets, take a second mortgage on your house for snack bar concessions, sit on sticky chairs in a dark box full of strangers spewing god-knows-what pathogens into the air, listen to ear-shattering surround sound that takes years off your hearing, and spend two hours watching people who make a gazillion more dollars than you, living lives more exciting than yours — all so you can be taught a frickin" lesson?!

You wouldn't do it. Not if they paid you. Not without a darn good dose of entertainment value packed into it. And you wouldn't do it for just a couple hours of distraction either. There's something more our soul is seeking in movies, music — whatever the medium. And when done right, it not only touches us deeply, it gives us a mental, emotional, biological, and spiritual response that acts as a surrogate for otherwise untouchable life experiences. It's like "virtual living" that can actually change our lives.

Nevertheless, our egos need some enticement to embark on this adventure. We need to be given a promise of a "good time," whether it's thrills, chills, laughs, or, for some of us, even tears. That's the bait. But it's *only* the bait. Once we're hooked and reeled in, there needs to be a real (or reel) feast. Unfortunately, what passes for entertainment nowadays tends to be all bait — and no bite. And that's why we're so damn hungry all the time!

The aim of this book is to feed you what you're hungering for. But it's also to teach you how to use that bait to catch the big fish. There's the saying, "Give a man a fish, you feed him for a day. Teach him how to fish, you feed him for a lifetime." My intention, however, is not just to make you great fishermen, but to make you great "fishers of men" (and, of course, women). Ultimately, that's what an enlightened entertainer does with her work. She casts her line into the souls of others, hooks their heart, and pulls their greater potential to the surface.

TWO ∼

Spiritual Tools of an "Enlightened Entertainer"

"Highly developed spirits often encounter
resistance from mediocre minds."
— Albert Einstein

very trade has its tools. If this were a traditional book about the
entertainment industry, we'd talk about how to write scripts or
songs, how to act, how to make movies, or raise financing. But
this isn't a traditional entertainment book (as if you hadn't noticed).
As you embark on this journey, you're no longer merely an artist /
entertainment professional — you're a disciple of enlightened entertainment, a sacred storyteller in training (or whatever term works for
you).

You may look like everyone else, but you're on a decidedly different
mission. Your movies, music, performances, and other media may *seem*
similar to others — they'll be entertaining, technically and artistically
proficient, and have all the bells and whistles of mainstream media
(if you desire) — but these creations will carry a profoundly different
vibration, an energy of transformation that will seep into the hearts
and souls of the audience, while their senses are dazzled by the sights
and sounds. You will not be distracting them from their life, but bringing them into a deeper connection with it.

The tools below will help lay the foundation for the work you are undertaking. You can find some version of these tools in just about every great religion or world philosophy, so if you don't like how I describe or define them, and you want to try something different, go ahead — as long as the basic result is the same. However you approach these, in whatever religion, philosophy, or self-help book, you need to practice them regularly, make them a part of your daily lifestyle. That's what a master does.

"I'm too busy for this," you might say. While these exercises do take time, by practicing them you actually create *more* time. Time seems to expand; you get more done in a shorter span. It's like an investment that builds passive income (income that flows in even when you're not working). At first, you have to work hard to build it and you don't always see immediate results. Then momentum kicks in and you begin getting back much more than you're putting in. Another analogy is the Chinese bamboo tree. The first four years, you water and nurture it, and it only sprouts a small bulb and tiny shoots. Your efforts seem futile. Then in the fifth year *it shoots up eighty feet or more*! All that time it was simply building a sufficient root system capable of sustaining its majestic heights.

As you go through these processes, you might think "What does all this have to do with the entertainment industry?" Or "How is this going to help me be more successful?" When you were in school, studying math, you might have thought "Why do I need to learn this if I'm going to be an actor, writer, or studio exec (fuzzy math, maybe)?" And if you decided *not* to learn it, you might be struggling in the area of finances right now. Even if these don't seem directly related to how you're going to get that next audition or writing gig, they are laying a foundation that will allow you to manifest a more prosperous, purposeful, empowered career. They'll also make you much more creative.

I guarantee it — or your baggage back!

Insight Meditation

Meditation in its simplest terms is a tool that allows you to connect with your Authentic Self, Higher Self, Buddha Nature, God-Self (or whatever term you prefer). The form of meditation you use isn't nearly as important as the purity of your intention and the clarity of purpose — to connect with your ultimate ground of being.

I won't get into a whole meditation program here. Suffice it to say that if you decide to master the art of meditation, you might want to take classes or read books dedicated to it. Nevertheless, this will lay out the basics if you're just getting started, and perhaps give you a few new insights if you already have a practice in place.

There are many kinds of meditation, maybe an unlimited variety. Insight Meditation, or Vipassana, as it is also called, is pretty simple. There are no mantras, like in TM (Transcendental Meditation), however, you can use one if you choose. The basic practice here is to close your eyes, follow your breath, and maintain dominion over your attention as you sink beneath layers of mind-chatter, into the exquisite stillness of your spirit — a stillness so profound that even one moment of it can transform your life.

This "stillpoint" is the fountain of all creation. It's like plugging into the Universal Energy Source for a recharge. It has the power to heal, awaken, and deliver works of genius through you. It is the "Ark of the Covenant," the "Secret Place of the Most High," the "Muse," the "Kingdom of Heaven," the "Garden of Eden," the "Land of Milk and Honey," and "Paradise" — all wrapped into one! It is the realm where all great songs, scripts, books, films — all masterpieces — reside. Tap into it and you cannot help but create powerful entertainment products appropriate to your unique purpose.

So how do you do this thing called Insight Meditation? Find a quiet place where you can sit upright in a comfortable position, without distraction for a period of time. You can start out with as little as five minutes, and work up to a full hour or more. Eventually, you won't even need a quiet place. You will gain enough mastery over your attention that you will be able to meditate in the middle of a noisy movie set, stage production, music studio, hectic office — anywhere you feel the "urge to emerge."

Once you're comfortable, close your eyes and begin to watch your breath breathing in and out. Don't control it. Let it do what it wants. It might be shallow at first, then grow deeper or vice versa. There might be moments where it stops altogether, then starts up again with a series of quick shallow gulps. Just let it be and watch it. Watch it going in and out of your nostrils or mouth, or watch your stomach rising and falling. If your mind wanders into fantasy, planning, or other tangents, become aware of what you're thinking, then bring your attention back to the breath. You may have to do this over and over. Your mind will wander off and you'll need to bring it back again — like training a puppy.

When you first begin — and on stressful or "cleansing" days — your mind may sound like a circus. When you're learning to get still inside, your mind may feel like it's spinning out of control. In some respects, that's exactly what it's doing — losing control. But that's a good thing. An untrained mind is usually flailing about in a panicked frenzy; we just don't notice until we get quiet and pay attention. Not to worry. At some point, your mind will relax and you'll find yourself in a state of peaceful receptivity — at least until the next cycle of growth, where you'll wonder if you've made any progress at all!

As you gain some proficiency with the process of watching the breath, you'll be able to widen the focus. You'll be able to watch bodily sensations arising, thoughts unraveling, emotional patterns emerging, and finally even hear the "still small voice" — your intuition, Higher Power, or Authentic Self. The ability to observe your thoughts and feelings without engaging them is a powerful skill that will be important as we get into the work of uncovering the limiting beliefs holding you back from expressing your full potential as an artist / entertainment professional. What's more, just by watching the content of your consciousness, you'll begin to break up these old patterns — literally pull them up by their roots. And what will you find underneath these limited perceptions — a universe of creative genius, wisdom, and freedom waiting to be released into the world.

Visioning

Visioning (originally taught by Dr. Michael Beckwith) is a form of meditation that allows you to tap into an idea and manifest it. It's based on the premise that the full potential of a thing, and the mechanism for its unfoldment, is already present in the idea itself, in consciousness. Just as the entire oak tree is already potential in the acorn, so too is the mighty oak of your own being already within you. It simply requires the right conditions to grow. This is ultimately true of everything.

> Just as the entire oak tree is already potential in the acorn, so too is the mighty oak of your own being already within you.

In the beginning, God (Higher Power, Universal Intelligence, the Unified Field) created everything out of Its own perfection. That means the universe, and all that is within it, is perfect. We can't improve upon it. We can't create something that isn't already potential in it. What we do is "discover" it. In fact, that's the true meaning of "having a vision." A real vision isn't a prediction of a future event, it's a moment when the curtain of the time-space continuum parts, giving us a glimpse of what exists *right now* in the invisible realm. And the very act of "seeing" it starts the creative process of bringing it into form.

Everything we see, every person, place, and thing is an outpicturing of a spiritual idea. If the thing looks "bad" or "destructive" it is an aberrant expression of a perfect pattern. In other words, behind every human aberration is a spiritual aspiration. Or to draw a scriptural reference, "Man meant it for evil, but God meant it for good." Plato talked about this concept in the Allegory of the Cave, where he depicted the notion that there are divine forms of everything outside the cave, in the light, but man lives in the cave, seeing merely shadows of these perfect prototypes — thinking they are the real things. Visioning is a process where we tap into the perfect prototype of something and bring it into form.

Visioning is not to be confused with visualization. In visualization, a person is picturing something they want. If they hold the image in mind long enough, with enough intensity, they can use the law of creation to bring it into form. The problem with this practice is that the thing they're manifesting may not be for their highest good. I once knew a guy who visualized and manifested a Mercedes — then couldn't afford the upkeep and, after a painful period of struggle, had to sell it at a loss! The problem was that he changed his world, but remained the same. He hadn't attained "Mercedes consciousness." I've also known people who visualized their ideal mate, only to meet that person — and end up in a relationship from hell! From their limited thinking, they had a concept of what was best for them, but it turned out to be not at all what they wanted — although it could be argued that it was exactly what they *needed!* I've seen this happen with colleagues in the entertainment industry, visualizing the perfect job, the perfect part — only to end up desperately trying to visualize their way *out of the mess they got into!*

None of these nasty side-effects happen with visioning. In visioning, you're not using your limited perception of life to manifest. You're using your mind for the purpose it was actually created — as an avenue of awareness, a receiving station to pick up the divine ideas being broadcast everywhere. And once you catch this vision, it doesn't just manifest, it changes you, stretches you, transforming you into a person who can handle the higher vibration and larger manifestation. You don't just get the new Mercedes, you get Mercedes Consciousness. You "become the change you want to see."

The process of visioning is really quite simple. While we'll be outlining specific exercises through this book, I'll break down the basics here. Like Insight Meditation, you'll want to get in a quiet place, undistracted for a period of time. Start by watching the breath, to quiet the mind and calm the body. Then once you achieve a sense of peace, you can move to the next stage — setting your *intention.* Like meditation, the most effective intention is a desire for a conscious contact with your soul, a deeper connection to your Self. This is the most powerful purpose to intend every time you meditate, pray, or do any spiritual practice. It doesn't matter what human goal you're going after, whether it be to manifest an acting job, script sale, movie deal, studio contract — whatever — if you consecrate it to having a sacred tryst with your spirit, with unconditional love, you'll be tapping into the greatest power of your being.

This meditation is guided. You will be prompting your soul with a set of questions throughout. These questions can be added to or substituted for different ones, as long as they have the same basic purpose behind them. Once you have become centered and established your intention, you can pose the first question:

1. What is the Vision of my life? What is the divine pattern of potential? What does it look like, feel like, what is its true essence? (You can substitute "my life" for whatever you're visioning on; "this acting job," "this script or film," "the entertainment industry.") You can also ask "What is God's vision of my life?"

Now wait, watch, and listen. Become aware of whatever images, sounds, or sensations arise. Sometimes it will be literal; you'll see specific pictures that relate to what you're visioning on. Other times, it will be symbolic; you may not see any connection at all. Some people see things in Technicolor. Others are more kinesthetic. You might only get a feeling or a vibration. It's all good. Whatever comes up is part of the process. If you find yourself drifting, planning your grocery list, or thinking about what you're going to eat later, gently bring your attention back to the breath. But don't take anything for granted. Even the distractions might be clues from your unconscious.

Repeat the question as many times as you need. As insights come through, you can open your eyes and take notes or wait until after the meditation. In the latter case, however, you might forget what came up — just as you forget dreams moments after you've awakened. Once you've received sufficient input, ask the next question:

2. How must I change in order for this vision to come forth through me? How must I be different? What must I let go of or embrace?

This is probably the most important question. Remember, the thing you want is already here, in the unified field of pure potential. Everything you need to fulfill your greatest desire is already part of your being. But it can't come out until you align with it, let go of the obstructions to it, and raise your vibration to the level at which it already exists.

And the final question:

3. Is there something that I need to do, some symbolic action I need to take, in order to step out on this vision and create the space for it to express?

Remember in *Indiana Jones and the Last Crusade*, where Indiana had to cross an invisible bridge to get some potion that could heal his father? All he saw was a chasm, a certain drop to his death. But this was a bridge of faith. It required stepping out onto the invisible for it to appear. That's what this question and the subsequent action is about. It's not about "making something happen" (because in consciousness it already has), it's about making it *welcome*. Sometimes the actions you'll be told to take won't seem to have anything to do with what you're visioning on. Sometimes they'll seem only slightly related. But when you follow the guidance, you'll often get surprising results.

I remember visioning early on in my writing and consulting career, where I was guided to get cards printed up with my name and the title of president/CEO. It felt so silly getting such cards when I wasn't even an employee of my own company — let alone the president! Nevertheless, I followed through — and was shocked by how much negative self-talk came up. I thought I had cleared most of that, but I was sorely mistaken. There was so much crud still lurking in the swamp of my soul, bottom-feeding off my spirit, sapping my vital energy, keeping me small — and I didn't even know it! Taking this seemingly innocuous action brought it all to the surface where I could process and heal it.

That's all you need to vision. However, there are many other questions you can ask to prompt the sometimes unwilling unconscious, such as: *"If this vision was fully manifest in the world, what would it look like? What would I look like? How would I act? How would I feel?"* This may sound similar to the first question, but it actually brings out a subtly different color. When the first question doesn't elicit much, this one might create a cascade of insight. You could also ask, *"If this vision were a color, what color would that be?" "If this vision were a song, what would it sound like?" "If this vision were an animal, what would it be?" "If this vision were a symbol, what would it look like?"*

You could even ask, *"What other questions should I ask to realize this vision in its full potential?"* or *"Is there anything else I need to see, hear, know, or feel, to allow this vision to unfold in my life?"* That's a good one to finish with. It pretty much covers all the bases. All of these are ways to bypass the intellectual, logical mind, and access the subjective realm

> Not only are all the answers within you, but all the questions as well.

where the real power, substance, and genius reside. Let your heart speak to you, stay open to new and creative questions that allow you to tap into the divine vision. Not only are all the answers within you, but all the questions as well.

Night Pages

If you've read *The Artist's Way,* you're aware of something called the Morning Pages. In that process, you basically dump out whatever is in you for a few pages in the morning before starting your day. Sometimes nothing but junk comes out, sometimes you're ranting and raving, and other times deep insights and creative ideas splash across the page. It's a great process and I highly recommend it. You can even do it before meditating. (But I wouldn't suggest doing it in place of meditating.)

The Night Pages have a different purpose. They are actually composed of a few written exercises, which you can do every night or pick one per night and rotate. The purpose of these pages is to focus on the *good* in your life; what you have, what you're grateful for, what you are accomplishing. These pages are intended to develop an Abundance Consciousness, an "I Have, I Can" state of mind versus "I Don't Have,

I Can't." As the ancient statement goes, "To he who has, more shall be given. To he who has not, even that which he has shall be taken away." A person with a mindset of *having* manifests more *having*, while a person with a mindset of *not having* manifests more *not having*. Another way to say it is "What you appreciate, *appreciates*."

The Universal Computer doesn't judge or question, it just reflects back what you program into it. That's why you don't want to use negative affirmations. A statement like *"I am not an out-of-work actor"* isn't very effective, because the law focuses on the subject — "out-of-work actor" — and magnifies that. The result is that you feel like you're peddling uphill with the brakes on! So our goal with these pages is to build a consciousness that focuses on the good, the abundance, then magnifies and multiplies that.

Appreciation Pages

This is where you write down everything you're grateful for, no matter how seemingly insignificant. *"I'm grateful for that breath I just took." "I'm grateful that I ate today."* If this is your first time doing it, you might want to play catch up, reflecting back on your life and listing *everything* you're thankful for. This could take several nights, but it'll be worth it. You may be walking around thinking your life is seriously lacking. But after doing this process, you'll begin to see just how rich it really is. The ramifications of a perceptual shift like that are huge. This exercise alone can transform your life and career.

"What I Have" Pages

This is similar to the process above, however the focus is slightly different. On these pages, go through the four main dimensions — mental, emotional, physical, and spiritual — and write about all you have. For example, in the "physical" dimension of finances, if you only have two bucks in the bank, write *"I have money in the bank."* The universe doesn't know the difference between two cents and two million. It only knows you *have* — and multiplies that consciousness. If you don't have any money, focus on your money-making talents, *"I have the ability to make money with my writing/acting/musical talents."* It may be hard to find the good in your life sometimes. Keep looking and keep writing. There's more abundance here than you can imagine.

"I Can" Pages

This exercise focuses on the active elements of your life, the proactive choices you can make in any circumstance to move your life forward. Let's say you're living in Wichita with no means to come to L.A. and start your writing career. You might find your mind focusing on all the things you "can't" do. That's human nature. It's also a path to failure. In this process, write down all the things you *can* do, no matter how insignificant. For example, "I *can* write a script; I *can* read books on how to succeed; I *can* send query letters to people in the business; I *can* submit my script after it's finished; I *can* save up money for a trip out West." There are more things you *can* do than you realize. The tendency to focus on what we can't do is usually procrastination in disguise. And behind that is fear of failure. As long as we can be a victim of "I can't," we can rationalize not going for it and risking rejection. But with this exercise, you'll never have that excuse again. What's more, as you focus on what you *can* do, divine guidance and right action will emerge to move you forward in ways you may have never imagined before!

> The tendency to focus on what we can't do is usually procrastination in disguise.

These Night Pages are just a template. There are unlimited ways to achieve the same result. Let your creativity kick in. Maybe you want to draw pictures or create a collage. Maybe you want to write a song about all you have, all you can do, and how grateful you are — and sing it every night. Whatever your process is, trust it — and go for it!

Filling the Well

If you're actively creating, you'll need to regularly refill your creative well. I know you have a lifetime of material to work from, but you'll still need to "sharpen the saw" as it says in *The 7 Habits of Highly Effective People*. You'll need to take time to commune with your inner artist, connect with your spirit, and create a lifestyle that allows you to be fully alive — constantly seeking new insights, ideas, personal growth, and life experience. This can look like many things. But here are a few examples:

1. Study the collected works of Shakespeare, Homer, Plato

2. Learn about World History, Black History, the History of the Letter "A"

3. Take a road trip, hike in nature, go on some adventure that you normally wouldn't do

4. If you don't exercise, start. Join a bowling league, find a tennis partner

5. Go browsing in a used book store, smell the books, join a book club

6. Go to the movies, go to two in a row, have a movie marathon

7. Go to more parties and events if you're an introvert; stay home if you go out a lot

8. Tell your parents how you really feel, give your children permission to do the same

9. Take a different route home, every day for a week

10. Quit a job you hate, get a job you love, take a risk, take a chance, take a leap of faith

As you can see, these ideas cover a lot of ground — and I'm sure there are many more you can think of. It's not just about recharging your creative batteries, it's about breaking out of old patterns, the inertia (and minutiae) of everyday living, getting outside the box, and being open to more and different experiences — setting in motion an alchemical process that can turn the dross of your everyday living into pure creative gold.

~

Those are the basic tools. You can add to your toolbox over time, or take something out. The key is to lay a foundation of stillness and connection (Meditation), clarity and vision (Visioning), Abundance Consciousness (Night Pages), and a fertile creative soul (Filling the Well) — all of which allow you to build your entertainment dreams on solid ground instead of shifting sands.

PART II
The Big Picture

THREE ~

Catching the Vision

"You never change things by fighting the existing
reality. To change something, build a new model
that makes the existing model obsolete."
— Buckminster Fuller

et's talk about the Big Picture. Not *your* big picture, but the
entertainment industry's. By that, I don't mean Hollywood *per
se*, but the whole process of creating and distributing entertainment products — whether inside or outside the studio/corporate
system. You may be thinking, "Why do I need to deal with that?
I just want to get my career going!" The thing is, you (your career
and purpose) are not separate from this industry — any more than a
cell is separate from the body. The cell has a purpose and individual
needs — but it's all in service to a larger organism. The cell's "bigger
picture" is the health and well-being of the body. A conscious artist or
enlightened entertainer's bigger picture is the higher expression of
entertainment and media and its impact in the world.

The "Game" They're Playing

Before we leap into the transcendent vision of show business, it's good
to ground ourselves in its immanent expression. In other words, let's
deal with the way things *are* before we talk about the way things can
be. The entertainment industry is a game, with a rulebook all its own.
Ultimately, you can break these rules, but it helps to know what they
are first. Picasso didn't begin by breaking the conventions of his art.
He learned the rules of drawing realistic portraits before creating faces
with two eyes on one side.

I love the story of Oprah when she was dealing with the Cattle Rancher lawsuit. At the time, her court advisor was Dr. Phil McGraw (before he was *the* Dr. Phil). One night, feeling overwhelmed by everything, Oprah showed up at his room and began to bemoan her fate, basically asking "why me?" "Why is this happening to a good person?" (I'm paraphrasing here.) She had good reason to feel that way. She was being treated unfairly, harassed and threatened. Any average person would be freaking out. But Oprah has never been an average person, and Dr. Phil knew that. So he told her to snap out of it and get in the game these Cattle Ranchers were playing — or she was going to get creamed all over the field. It worked. She stood up, suited up, and kicked their Cattle Carcasses!

You may feel like it isn't fair how the entertainment industry works, that it's "evil," "wrong," "greedy," or "dark." You may think they *should* recognize and employ you because you're a good person, a beautiful person, a talented person — with the next great whatever. You may want to give up, give in, or rail against the dying of the light! But none of that has anything to do with the game they're playing. "They" don't care what you're thinking or feeling. "They" don't care how good or smart or beautiful you are. "They" don't care about you at all! Now before you take a Prozac, take a breath and let me explain. "They" are not a group of people, but a pattern of thought that pervades the business and has gotten so entrenched it's become personified. It's a mass hypnotic spell making many deep-down decent people run around out of their minds (and hearts).

So why is it important to know this "game" they're playing? When you know something is an illusion — just an unconscious agreement that isn't supported by natural law — you stop wasting your energy reacting to it and perpetuating it. Then, and only then, do you possess real power. It's like the story of the master and disciple who entered a dark room and came upon a snake coiled at their feet. The disciple shrieked in terror, grabbed a large stick, and began beating the snake to death. The master let him go for a moment, then turned on a light — revealing the snake to be nothing but a rope! The disciple perceived a danger in the darkness of his ignorance — and became reactionary and powerless. The master knew the true nature of this image and, therefore, was able to dispel the illusion.

This may seem like a simple story. But it holds a powerful lesson. It depicts how a false perception can spiral into a whole paradigm of living. Had the disciple stayed in darkness, he might have devised more strategies for defeating the snake, none of which would have worked. As more people entered the dark room, new ways to combat the snake would be created — all of which would also fail. Soon, a belief system would develop, complete with coping mechanisms that enabled the village to live with, and work around, this undefeatable snake. They might even enshrine the room in which it resides and make sacrifices to it, revering it as some all-powerful deity. But none of these entreaties or tactics would ever solve the problem — because the premise was wrong. *There never was a snake!* All they ever needed to do was turn on the light.

This is, in effect, what has happened in the entertainment industry. The limitations we now perceive are relics of an ignorant belief system that has evolved — and become enshrined — over the years. This has become "the rules of the game." And many of the books, courses, and gurus that teach us how to "break in," "make it," and "succeed against all odds" are just a collection of coping mechanisms on how to defeat the snake in the room. There's just one tiny problem — *there is no snake!* All these things are teaching us how to solve a problem that doesn't really exist. You don't need any more "techniques" on how to win the game or manipulate the players. You just need to turn on the light and see what's really there. And as you "turn on the light" for yourself, you will illuminate the room for others — including those sitting in dark theaters across the planet.

So what is the game? What is the pattern of thought that pervades the studio halls and bustling boulevards? While it doesn't reflect the attitude of all the people, or represent the ultimate "truth" about the business, I believe the primary mindset of the industry is propped up by what I call "The Four Pillars of Purgatory": Pride, Power, Pocketbook, and Preservation. As Tina Lifford, a successful actress and spiritual coach, says, "Our attachment to our idea of survival is one of our

> "Our attachment to our idea of survival is one of our biggest obstacles."
> — Tina Lifford

biggest obstacles." And this isn't unique to the entertainment industry. It sums up the baseline nature of human thinking. In other words, if we really want to know how the industry works — what its rules are — we can look at the machinations of our own "Monkey Mind."

Below are the basic paradigms that pervade the business. They don't all sound "negative" or "limiting." It's the sum total of "group-think" that creates the constrictive consciousness preventing the full potential from being realized. (If you're working in the business, you probably know most of this. But it helps to be reminded of what software is running the operating system, especially if you've fallen asleep inside the Matrix.)

1. Global audiences want to be entertained by something fresh and exciting; something that moves them, scares them, makes them laugh or cry, and takes them on a roller coaster ride. (Many actually want more than that; an experience that transcends and even transforms their lives, but they don't always know this consciously.)

2. The Entertainment Industry (not any one person, but the "collective consciousness") wants product that satisfies a global audience and is profitable, so it can survive and make more stuff. (The underlying need to survive often overrides higher ideals.)

3. To do this, the Entertainment Industry needs product (scripts, books, video games) that attract the elements (star actors, directors) that get things made and get audiences to give up the green (a star is their insurance policy). A core belief is that audiences just want to be "entertained," so our senses are assaulted with F/X extravaganzas and over-produced music. Another core belief is that the surest path to profit is a "pre-sold" idea (something we've already heard of, like a novel, video game, comic book, sequel, TV show remake), or just a rehash of what worked before (which is why much of the music sounds the same, and many movies look the same).

4. The elements (actors, directors) have certain needs as well. Actors mostly want parts that make them look good, showcase their talents, and keep them on top. You can't really blame them. They're the ones with their

proboscis projected two stories tall. Directors want scripts that showcase their talent, give them a strong visual style, something to say and, likewise, keep them on top. Some artists do seek projects that force them to stretch and actualize more of themselves. Some realize that theirs is a shamanic path of awakening, and that every part they play, every song they sing, every project they write, every film they make is an opportunity for personal growth — a chance to be a different person when they're done.

Many people in the business know they're holding back and desperately want to walk this path — but lack the courage to go for it. This might be you. And that's okay. (My hope is that by the time you're done with this book, you'll have the confidence and clarity you need.) There are others who don't want to change, don't want to take the journey, and don't realize they're not only starving their own soul — but withholding a banquet from the rest of us. Don't judge them. Don't be superior to them (because you're not). And don't try to change them. Let them be. And be yourself. If they see how much fun you're having, they might just join the party.

5. The "buyers" (studios, production companies, music companies, some producers, some elements, and financial backers) say they want something "fresh." And they do. Sort of. But they also want something "familiar." Their formula is "Give me the same thing — only different!" If it's too different, if it has no proven track record, it scares them. Ironically, some of the biggest hits are projects that take risks, that break out of the box, that are more "fresh" than "familiar." (This doesn't mean they're completely unrecognizable, it means they have won the war on clichés and found an authentic way to express one of the age-old archetypal patterns.) Nevertheless, this is how many buyers think. It's all about hedging their bets, keeping their jobs — staying alive! I certainly understand that impulse. Many of us struggle between "saving the play" and "playing it safe." But many buyers, deep down, also want a project that innovates, knocks their socks off, has a "voice" — and makes them go "wow!"

6. The buyers in the film and TV industry want projects that can become the "F" word — a Franchise. In other words, they're not just looking for another script or movie — they're looking for a cottage industry. There's so much more risk (and marketing costs) in an unproven product that studios prefer to make pre-sold titles (as already stated). So when they

do decide to create something truly original, they ideally want it to be a new brand that can be spun off into many ancillary markets — sequels, video games, board games, soundtracks, books, comics, graphic novels, TV series, mugs, lunch boxes, cereal, candy, T-shirts, toilet seat covers. (Okay, I haven't seen that one yet, but unfortunately, that's where most of these products belong.)

7. The "brokers" (agents, managers, some producers) want the same thing everyone else wants, because they know what sells — and thus makes them money.

8. Everyone in the business says they're looking for that next "new face," "new talent." And while there's truth to this, what everyone really wants is to work with their friends, have a good time, and play it safe. (There's that word "safe" again. One of the Pillars of Purgatory, "Preservation." It's a thought pattern with a lot of pull in this business.) In other words, relationships are key in the "game." People have to spend a lot of time with each other, often under extreme circumstances, so they want to hang out with people they like. The "likeability" factor has trumped talent many times.

9. What everyone is really looking for is the "buzz." So whatever you do, generate a "buzz," and they will come looking for you. Or so the theory goes.

10. The basic formula for success in the business — from a purely material level — is:

- Have the goods (a great piece of work/talent that attracts elements and buyers)

- Get those goods next to the buyer

- Showcase the goods

- Generate a buzz

- Make the deal

Simple but not always easy.

11. If you put all this together, the "playbook to success" sounds something like this:

"Create a great product that is fresh yet familiar, totally new yet already proven, with a breakout role for a star (that plays on their already proven persona but gives them room to stretch), has mass appeal to the global marketplace (ideally a four-quadrant project that appeals to all ages and genders), and can become a franchise with multiple ancillary products. Make friends with as many industry people as possible, become a really likeable person that they'd want to work with, get the goods next to the buyers, show them what you got, generate a "buzz" — and make a deal! Do not attempt this while operating heavy machinery. Rinse and repeat often."

12. And the final "rule" (at least in this section) is — drum roll please — *none of these rules apply if you break them successfully or, better yet, completely transcend them!*

Playing by these rules doesn't guarantee success. In fact, most of the success stories we hear are of people who have done something outside the box and broken the rules "successfully." They went in the back door, made their own movie or CD, created their own role or showcase, generated a buzz through some unconventional way.

Of course there are many sub-rules, guidelines, and variations on these ideas — but that's basically the "game." Now that you know it, you won't be blindsided by it. You won't need to say "why me?" or take it personally. Now that you know the rules, you can be open to ways to break them and, ultimately, transcend them (realize the snake is just a harmless rope). That, finally, is what the bulk of this book will focus on.

In the final analysis, the only rules that matter, the only ones with real power, are Universal Principles. Live in accordance with these and you will not only play the game with finesse — you'll transform the playing field from a competitive mine field where winning is everything to a cooperative Mind Field where everyone is a winner.

The 7 Myths of Show Business & 7 Truths of "Soul Business"

Let's look at why many of these "rules" are false and what the Truth is behind them. To understand what I mean when I talk about "false" versus "true," let me share what I have discovered the underlying premise of life to be. I didn't invent this; it's what all major mystics, metaphysicians, and spiritual leaders have articulated through the ages:

Life is already perfect. It is a system of wholeness and unity, indivisible, all-inclusive, all-containing. It is inexhaustible abundance, perfect peace, unconditional love, and total fulfillment. It can never be diminished or improved upon. The divine design of you and I, of the entertainment industry and the world, is already perfected — just as the divine design of the oak is already perfected within the acorn. Our job, therefore, is not to make something happen, but to awaken to what already is — the Song, Script, Story, or Performance that the Great Creator created "In the Beginning."

The "false" beliefs are based on a limited premise about life, a premise that says there isn't enough to go around, that we're separate from our good, from each other, from our heart's desires. A false premise says that only some people have what it takes to make it, that they've been given a special gift from God. A false premise says that life is really chaos, that there is no plan — that it's all about the luck of the draw. Any of these false premises can spawn countless false beliefs. As these false beliefs are acted upon, they become the laws of our life, the seeming "rules" of the game called show business (or whatever business we're engaged in). And as these laws, rules, and beliefs are crystallized in consciousness, they become so seemingly solid and "real" that people stop questioning them. They just accept them as fact, as "fate," as the way it is — as the truth.

But the real Truth (what masters and mystics have been declaring for millennia) is that anything which contradicts the fundamental harmony of the universe or denies the fulfillment of your heart is false, has no power, and will be overcome or transcended. As Tina Lifford says, "Play in the realm of possibilities, in every circumstance, no matter how thick the door in front of you may appear, and a way will be shown."

So let's take a look at how the "truth of the ages" breaks down in this business of show:

Myth #1: It's All in Who You Know

This belief or "rule" says you can't make it unless you have major contacts in the business. We've all heard this one, and many of us live and die by it.

Truth #1: The Only Person You Need to Know Is You

While this *is* a people business, the people aren't the ones who determine your success — *You* are. It's true that it's "all in who you know." But the "who" you need to know is *you*. Not the human-ego you, but the dimension of your being beyond the surface chatter of the mind, beyond your childhood, past mistakes, and neurotic patterns — the part of you that is ultimately one with everyone and everything.

In a very real sense, you already know everyone in this business (and the audience) in the most intimate way it's possible to know someone — at the level of the soul. But while this is a *Truth*, you can't experience its *effect* in your life except to the degree by which you consciously *know* and accept it. Then, and only then, does it begin to operate as a law in your life. "A lie believed acts as truth until it is neutralized." The lies you have accepted have disguised themselves as "truths" and become the personal laws of your experience. But a truth *known* neutralizes the lie and

> "A lie believed acts as truth until it is neutralized."

becomes the new law. And once a truth is running your life, no lesser lie can ever take control of you again!

When you contact this deeper part of yourself, you've just done the most important "networking" you can do — you've connected to the divine network of light. You've stepped out of Hollywood and into "Holy-wood." And in that instant, you've begun to attract the right people, places, and opportunities you need to fulfill your purpose. I'm not saying you shouldn't go to parties, make cold calls, or do the foot-work. What I'm suggesting is that when you do the "inner networking" first and foremost, you find more successful and meaningful connections occurring with ease, grace, and dignity.

In *Zen in the Art of Archery*, the student meditates until he realizes he is at one with the bow, arrow, and target. From this state of consciousness, he can shoot in the dark and still hit the target. In industry parlance, you're already connected to the perfect acting roles, agents, managers, script sales, record deals, blockbusters, or executive positions. You just need to contact that place within where you are already "one with the target."

Myth #2: Some Have "It" and Some Don't

This false belief says that some people are endowed with more talent, more ability, more whatever, while others get the leftovers or nothing at all.

Truth #2: Everyone Has Equal and Infinite Potential

This is a uni-verse ("one song'). There's one song playing everywhere and we are all notes in it. There are no "special" or "better" notes. Every note is necessary and contains the whole essence of the music. All the power and substance of the universe is seeking to sing its song through you as magnificently as it has ever been sung before.

This might sound like some pithy, feel-good piece of fluff. The cynic in us (the part that has been burned, that is afraid) wants to write off ideas like this — or, worse, to attack and kill them. But I assure you, as idealistic or "new-agey" as it may sound to the "inner skeptic," this is the Truth. You really do have infinite abundance, talent, wisdom, and brilliance within you — an "imprisoned splendor." And you have as much of it as anyone else in the world — including the world of show business. Don't accept anything less. Don't let yourself die with even one note of your music left inside you.

That doesn't mean everyone is alike. Far from it. How interesting would the One Song be if all the notes were the same? You are a unique expression of infinite potential. If you're an actor, you may have all the ability of Pacino or Streep, but you won't act like them. If you're a writer, you have the potential of Shakespeare, but your works will be *your* interpretation of life. If you're a director, you have the capabilities of a Spielberg, Bergman, Scorsese — take your pick — but your films will bear *your* unique soul-print.

I remember my first demonstration of this principle. I used to do a lot of singing gigs. One day, I was sitting in an audience listening to a singer, and he hit a high note that blew me away. I yearned to achieve such vocal heights, but it seemed like a pipe dream (as in "windpipe"). I felt a moment of doubt and discouragement as I accepted the idea that it would never happen. Then I remembered this principle. I caught myself and began to reclaim my unlimited potential, reminding myself that there was only One Singer — and whatever was possible in any singer was possible in me. It dissolved the doubt. As I continued to affirm it day after day, I began to believe it. And within a few weeks I hit the same note — a note I never would've thought possible before.

An ancient statement declares that "God is no respecter of persons." What this means at the mystical level is that Spirit/The Universe doesn't know or see separate "people" any more than the sun sees separate sunbeams, the ocean recognizes separate waves, or a tree views the branches as separate from each other. All of Life is a unity, expressing fully at every point in the universe. Nowhere is it more or less. Nowhere is it withholding anything. In other words, *the only thing blocking your good is your lack of acceptance.*

Myth #3: You Have a Limited Window, Once It Closes It's Over

This is a scary false belief, because it tells you you're too old, you missed your chance, your ship has sailed, it's just *too late* and you'll never make it. It can compel people to lie, cheat, beg, borrow, and steal in pursuit of an ever-illusive, rapidly receding dream. At the very least, it can make someone an anxious, obnoxious, irritable individual.

Truth #3: It's Never Too Late to Fulfill Your Purpose

I'm aware that these statements can sound like cliches. If the inner skeptic is trying to convince you that this is all "pie in the sky," I urge you to suspend your disbelief just for the journey of this book. You can always pick your doubt back up when you're done (but I doubt you'll want to). While I can't guarantee your outcome, I can guarantee these principles are real. I've seen them proven in my life and many others — many times.

As we've already discussed, there's only one omnipresent power and intelligence governing the universe — One Creator — and whatever It creates is eternal. There is no other power to diminish or destroy it. It created you and your awesome purpose in this divine design called the entertainment industry, and nothing you have ever done or failed to do, nothing anyone has ever said or done, nothing the world or the "biz" says is possible or impossible can ever diminish you and your purpose.

As the ancient sayings remind us, "I will restore to you the years that the locust hath eaten," and "Behold, I make all things new." These are spiritual principles and promises. It doesn't matter how much time you think you've wasted, how many opportunities you think you've missed — it's never too late to live the life you were created for. But you must live according to the fundamental laws of the universe. There is a "Way It Works." When you align yourself with this "Way," you reap the rewards. Just as when a farmer plants according to the law of the farm, he reaps a bountiful harvest.

Myth #4: You Have to Play by the Rules to Win the Game

We've touched on this in the previous section. This lie says that you can only succeed by "their rules." The problem is you can never *really* know what rules anyone is playing by. This might sound like a contradiction of what I've already said. It's not. The fact is, the statements "you must know the rules of the game," "you can never know what rules anyone is really playing by," and "there are, finally, no rules to the game" are all true. Relatively speaking. If this gives you a headache, that's okay. The ability to hold seemingly contradictory ideas in your mind is a high state on the path.

Truth #4: The Truth Within You Is the Only Authority

Once you learn the game they're playing, you can transcend it. There is an "inner authority" that knows everything you need to know and do to fulfill your mission. It's like learning to fly a plane. At some point you are trained in "instrument flying." In this exercise, you must fly the plane using only the instrument panel. It's an incredibly important part of your training, because when you fly into clouds, you can't depend on anything you can see "out there." Likewise, you must learn to navigate your life — and entertainment career — not by what you can see "out there," not by what "they" (agents, managers, producers, partners) are saying, not by what's splashed across the trades or tabloids — but by your *inner instrument panel.* Then when the rough weather hits, you're not thrown off course — or worse, sent hurdling into the side of a mountain!

The challenge with piloting our life and show business career is that we don't always know when we're "in the clouds." We sometimes don't realize we've been turned upside down and are spiraling out of control — until we crash and burn. Learning to live by your inner instrument panel, however, will largely eliminate that danger, because you won't be making decisions based on what you perceive with your senses, but what you *know* in your soul. When you do this you not only transcend the rules of the game, you become the master of your own game, the maker of your own rules. You become an innovator, a cutting-edge creator setting new precedents and blazing new paths — because you're not conforming to "the way it is," but revealing pure potential in the unrepeatable way that is authentically you. As the ancient statement says, "Be ye not conformed to this world, but be ye transformed by the renewing of your mind." That's how to win the game!

Myth #5: You Need to Have the Right Education

This myth says that you can't be successful until you learn a bunch of stuff, go to the right schools, read the right books, and study at the feet of the right gurus. It's a clever way for the ego to keep you stuck (and for the gurus to make a buck), because you can always be tricked into believing you "don't know enough yet."

Truth #5: All Knowledge Is Already in You

I know this is going to sound like a broken record, but if you're going to have a broken record, this is a pretty good song to have playing over and over: There is only one Mind in the universe, and your mind is just your individual use of this source of all knowledge.

Perhaps you've heard of the "hundredth monkey theory." It details an experience where a particular monkey, on a particular island, learned to wash a potato in a new way — and pretty soon other monkeys on the island were doing it. This, in and of itself, wasn't the breakthrough, although it spread faster than the monkeys could've learned it. The real revelation happened when monkeys on *other islands*, with no connection to "monkey zero," started washing their potatoes the same way. A similar phenomenon occurred with the four-minute mile. At one time nobody in the world could break it. Then someone did. And a short time later, people were breaking it all over the planet. How did this happen? If we're separate beings, with separate minds, there's no way it could occur. There must be some medium in which we are all connected and all knowledge is collected. This is the One Mind, the One Consciousness that has been the message of mystics for millennia.

So what does all this have to do with you? All the knowledge (acting ability, writing wisdom, filmmaking genius, musical mastery, business savvy) that has ever been or ever can be known is within you. Natural born geniuses, like Mozart or Shakespeare, don't have anything *more* than you — they have something *less*. What they lack are the self-imposed blocks to the outflow of this infinite creative intelligence.

The fact that you already have it all within you doesn't mean you shouldn't go to school, learn your craft, read books, or go to workshops. Just remember that all you're really doing is using other people and things to *remind* you of what you already know. And you don't have to wait until you know "enough" before you go for it and become successful. Be an "on-the-job training" success. Learn as you go. Don't let your seeming lack of education hold you back at all. Especially don't let the *belief* that you don't have enough education hold you back. If you *believe* you need to know more before you can succeed, you will *experience* that belief as the law of your life — no matter how much you learn!

Remember: *It is done unto you as you believe.* Those are perhaps the most important eight words in all personal growth, success literature, and spiritual texts throughout history. In the final analysis, the only things holding you back are your limited beliefs.

Myth #6: You Have to Wait Until the Conditions Are Right

This false belief says you can't go for it or be successful until all your ducks are in a row, until your stars line up, Mercury gets out of retrograde, it's pilot season or staffing season or duck hunting season! Basically, this lie says that outer conditions have power over you; that they have to look a certain way before you can fulfill your dreams.

Truth #6: Your Inner Conditions Determine Outer Experience

We are not indigenous, like a palm tree that can only survive in certain conditions. We are "indogenous," as Emerson said. We can create whatever conditions we need in our consciousness. It doesn't matter if there's a recession, if you create the inner conditions of prosperity — *that* is what you'll manifest. It doesn't matter if the industry is not hiring your type, buying your type of product, or if all the doors seem closed. Create the

> Create the inner conditions of a successful person and you will manifest a way to succeed.

inner conditions of a successful person (confident, peaceful, abundant, inspired, etc.) and you will manifest a way to succeed. It's the Law! "A way will appear out of no way."

I remember years ago when I was just beginning to practice this path. I was out of work and had "more month at the end of my money." There was no visible resource to make the rent, nothing humanly for me to lean on. So I decided to put this to the test. (We all have initiating moments when we are forced to prove these teachings for ourselves — often more than once.) I sat in my meditation chair and said *"God, either this stuff is real or it isn't. Either way we're gonna find out tonight — because I'm not getting up until I know for sure!"* I guess you could say I laid down the gauntlet, put all my cards on the proverbial table. Then I just sat there in my chair, and sat, and sat… looking within for a glimpse of truth, praying and meditating, sweating and pleading. The sun went down, the stars came up. I nodded off and woke up. Several times. And at some point, late at night, a "click" happened inside, and a sense of peace came over me.

I couldn't really describe it then, but it was a "knowing," a feeling that all was well, that God (Spirit/The Universe) really was taking care of everything. I proceeded to crawl into bed, fall into a deep sleep, and basically forget about it. A few days later, my ex-commercial agent called me "out of the blue" and said that he knew I wasn't doing commercials any more because I had become "spiritual," but he just got a call where they requested me and wanted to know if I could come down from the Mountain Top to audition for Pepsi. I knew instantly that it was "answered prayer" and said yes. I booked the commercial. It was split into three spots, and I made about $30,000. Not bad for a day's work (two days, if you count the day I spent meditating and praying).

Myth #7: People Don't Want "Deep" Entertainment

This is a common refrain from professionals in the business, especially the more "enlightened" ones. There is a real cynicism and skepticism around whether or not the industry or the global audiences want anything of real, lasting quality and depth.

Truth #7: The Audience Is Starving For Meaningful Material

We are all the same at core. If you want to express deeper meaning and better quality, there is an audience out there who wants to pay for it. And there are also studio executives or independent financiers who will recognize it. That's the simplistic answer. On a more mystical level, we are all rays of the One Light, so in our soul we all want to be in the Light (love, truth, peace, joy, abundance). When real Light hits us, those who are ready open their eyes, let them adjust, and see the room clearly for the first time — while those who aren't ready shut their eyes, shout for someone to turn off that damn light, and go back to their habitual routine around the darkened room. (Although the momentary glimpse of light can never be forgotten and will eventually drive them to flick that switch on again someday to see what kind of place they're really living in.)

There are millions on this planet hungering and thirsting for greater meaning and truth. There is a poverty and famine of the collective soul. Look at the news. Look at magazine covers in the check-out line. Listen to your colleagues around the coffee machine. Just listen to your own heart and mind! Many of us are as famished and parched as someone coming out of a long desert trek. Give us a good meal and drink (quality, conscious entertainment), we'll wolf it down without coming up for air — and ask for seconds!

"But what does this conscious entertainment look like?" There is some debate about that, which we'll get into later. (The 2006 nominees for Best Picture are a good place to start, but there are more main-stream examples as well.) Suffice it to say, it doesn't have to "look" like anything in particular. It's more about what the intention is behind it. For now, know that there's a real demand for that which you deeply desire to express. If it weren't so, you wouldn't desire it. If that doesn't make sense, contemplate it for a while. There is a profound truth in that alone. Hint: It has something to do with oneness.

—

The Spiritual Aspiration Behind the Human Aberration

For many people, the "biz" seems like an amoral, superficial, exploit-ative place, filled with greedy, shallow, out-of-control narcissists, offering no lasting value to society. Come on, you've thought some-thing like this before — if not yesterday! You know, like when that "done deal" fell through because the "money guy" absconded with the funds, the writing payment bounced the same day the producer's phone number became unlisted, your boyfriend hired his mistress for the part you were promised, and you discovered you'd lost your executive job — when you read about it in *Variety*! But even to the extent that this describes actual persons and production companies, it's still just a description of the surface, just the "tip of the iceberg." Beneath the seemingly shark-infested waters of Hollywood, a mystical realm is waiting.

As I touched upon in the "visioning" process, behind this "aberrant picture" of the industry is a spiritual prototype trying to express. The problem is that this high vibration is trying to move through a narrow-minded collective consciousness — like a thousand watts trying to shine through a hundred-watt light bulb. That's why we can never judge by "appearances" (our senses), but must instead use "righteous judgment" (our heart and soul). What we see and hear doesn't necessarily tell us the truth, it tells us the relative consciousness of a person, institution, or collective group.

Everyone in the entertainment industry (and the world) is trying to give expression to the higher ideal within them, whether they're conscious of it or not. No matter what their human motivation may be — underneath it is a spiritual impulse trying to emerge. Many people are just so caught in a consciousness of fear, separation, and limitation that only a small amount of the spiritual wattage can move through their inner coil. In their spirit, there's an impulse to build something better, but it comes out as a need to cut down and destroy; in their soul there's a call to reveal abundance, but it breaks through as greed and bottom-line thinking; in their heart there's a cry to express the best in themselves, but it bleeds out as competition and envy.

One purpose of this book is to guide you to an awareness of the "spiritual aspiration" behind the human aberration of the industry and your role in it — then help you put it into practice. Imagine what that would be like. When a group of conscious individuals capture the higher vision of this industry, and begin acting on it — look out! Like the hundredth monkey theory, a whole new paradigm will be created. People everywhere will create more inspiring, life-changing material — and global audiences will line up for it.

The "Divine DNA" of Show Business

So what is the higher vision of this business called show? While I don't claim to have the final answer — not by any stretch of my ego — after years of meditating and dialoguing on the subject, what has been revealed is that the "divine prototype" of the industry is *a mass distribution system of Truth, expressed through all forms of media (film, TV, music, games, etc.), for the inspiration, illumination, and transformation of the planet.*

I'm biased, but I believe entertainment is the most powerful tool of change on the planet. How many people around the world partake of some form of media every day — usually many times a day? Imagine what would happen if the majority of that input was "Conscious Content." That doesn't mean it's preachy or has a "message." It simply means it is content created from a conscious intention to bring people into a deeper connection with their life and world — rather than distract them from it — ultimately transforming them and their environment. And doing it all in an entertaining way!

It doesn't matter what medium or genre you choose to express in. One form is no better than another. The goal of conscious content can be accomplished with equal validity through a high-concept comedy or a serious drama, an action flick or a PBS program, a pop song or a classic concerto. There's a way to express Truth in every form of media, in a way that speaks to every level of audience. Some people will get their dose in movies like *The Matrix*, others will tune into Oprah; some will be empowered playing X-Box, others will find God in a graphic novel. Movie versions of *The Celestine Prophecy, Way of the Peaceful Warrior, Conversations with God,* or *The Passion of the Christ* are no more "spiritual" or "enlightened" than movies like *Crash, A Beautiful Mind, Bruce Almighty,* or *Signs* (all Shyamalan's films are about faith). Reality shows like *The Biggest Loser* have healed thousands and sports programming — when the focus is on excellence instead of excess — are some of the most inspiring experiences one can have. In other words, every level of teacher has an audience for their teaching — and all of it is necessary for the evolution of the whole.

So let's not get caught up in, or held back by, the particulars of our entertainment products. Instead, let's embrace the basic premise that the "divine DNA" of the industry is designed to be a positive force of change on the planet — in whatever form it expresses. Let's also agree that this is its essential nature *already*. We're not going on a crusade to convert it into something it's not. We're not going to put on white shirts and ties and bicycle around Hollywood handing out pamphlets! We're awakening to what the idea of entertainment *has always been*. We're putting all our energy into being *for* something, instead of being *against* anything. We're not fighting a negative perception, person, or institution, we're engaging in an act of deep devotion to the highest form of entertainment — and becoming midwives for the birth of its next stage of expression.

It's crucial that we release any judgment of, or resistance to, the industry in its current form, because all that does is put the brakes on our forward momentum. What's worse, it perpetuates the very condition we're struggling to overcome — because *what you resist persists!* I remember at one seminar I was teaching for entertainment professionals, a woman came up and thanked me for doing this work, saying that it was such a dark and cold place in the business and she was so grateful we were doing something to change it. As much as I wanted to accept that compliment, I had to inform her that I wasn't trying to change any "dark, cold entertainment industry" into a light-filled one — because that would be impossible. She looked at me kind of cross-eyed and said, "Huh?" I explained that as long as she held this limited belief about the business, she could never experience anything better — no matter how many workshops she attended!

Needless to say, she wasn't too happy with my response. She thought she'd found an ally in her fight against the big bad entertainment boogeyman. But that's not me. And I hope it's not you either. Remember, *it is done unto you as you believe.* It's not "I'll believe it when I see it," it's "You'll see it when you believe it." You can't make a demand on life that *exceeds* your belief about it — because you don't experience life as it *is*, you experience life *as you are*. You literally experience the personification of your own perceptions. So if you think the industry is hard, cold, bad, and greedy, you don't even have to tell me your story — I already know what you've been experiencing! That's the Law of Life. We'll get into this more later. For now, begin to contemplate the ways in which you have set yourself up in an adversarial relationship with someone or some aspect of the industry. These are the "walls of Jericho" that must eventually come crumbling down for you to know true creative freedom and lasting success.

The "Acorn Principle"

We've articulated the outer rules of the industry, so we can transcend them. We've touched upon the myths of the biz, so we're no longer hypnotized by them. We've learned that behind every negative human condition or institution is a spiritual idea trying to get out. And we've opened to the possibility that there is an awesome purpose for the entertainment industry, regardless of how it might appear. Now we're going to take it one step further and talk about the "acorn theory" — which is an appropriate metaphor, since this industry is filled with so many nuts. (And I mean that in an endearing way.)

Simply put: Within the acorn, the oak already exists; the entire divine pattern and the mechanics to fulfill it are built in. All it needs is the proper conditions (which nature creates automatically when we let it) and it will become a mighty, majestic tree. I touched upon this in the section on "visioning," but there's much more to this principle. In fact, if we could catch the significance of this concept, that insight alone could set us free.

Likewise, within this divine idea called the entertainment industry, the grand vision of its greatest potential — and everything needed to fulfill it — already exists. And when the proper conditions are met, nothing can stop it from realizing its destiny. Nothing! Not an executive, not a government, not the economy, not even the audience. It is a law of fulfillment. And what are the proper conditions? You and I, together in consciousness, agreeing and acting on this vision with faith and passion. It's a guarantee. Why? Because when you align yourself with the vision of Infinite Intelligence, you are in league with ALL the power, presence, substance, and law of the universe.

The Acorn Principle also applies to you individually. Within the seed of your being is a mighty oak with everything it needs to fulfill itself.

And here's the coolest part — you don't need to change any "outer conditions" to activate it. Remember, you're *indogenous.* You possess the power to create your own conditions, to choose the weather you live in — and bring with you wherever you go. That means you — not an agent, director, executive, star, financier, or casting director — wield the power to fulfill your destiny.

Don't rush past that last sentence. Take a moment and soak it in. Because that's the truth! You really do have the capacity, the power, the substance, the wisdom, the inner weather system — everything you could ever need, want, hope for, or desire — to fulfill your destiny. Not tomorrow, not when you get a better agent, take another class, get better connected, more talented, or say the right prayer. You have it now! Accept this. Affirm it. Give thanks for it. Then let "It" have Its way with you.

Throwing Out the Old Scripts

You've heard of the "Starving Artist Syndrome." How about "You have to be in pain to create good art?" Or, "It's all in who you know?" What are these statements — truth or merely beliefs? Has anyone ever broken these "rules?" Of course. And if they can be broken, they're not based on principles. And if they're not based on principles, they have no real power over you. Many of the limitations we've accepted about the entertainment industry (and the world) are nothing but false beliefs that can be transcended.

Just because it's a false belief, however, doesn't mean you won't experience its painful effects. That's why you can't judge by appearances. The lies feel just as solid as the truths — when discerned through the senses. Remember, "A lie believed acts as truth until it is neutralized." The false beliefs about the business become the personal laws of your life, holding you prisoner until you break your agreement with them. We're going to do that shortly. But first let's discover the false beliefs you've signed off on.

Belief Journal Exercise

Find a place where you can write for a while. How long is up to you. But I would suggest at least a half hour. If you don't have a journal, I encourage you to get one for this work. You can call it your Enlightened Entertainment Journal (or whatever name inspires you).

Take a few cleansing breaths. Close your eyes and allow yourself to become still. When you're ready, put pen to paper and free-write about all *your* beliefs around the entertainment industry and those you've heard expressed by *others*. Things like, "It's all in who you know." "Once you're over 30, you're over the hill." "You can't be a true artist and make a living." "You have to struggle to create good art." "You can't be spiritual and successful." Get the picture? I'll see you in a little while.

—

Were you surprised by what came up? Could you see a pattern emerge? Did you notice some beliefs having a stronger emotional charge than others? Did some anger you, scare you, make you sad? Did some make you happy, hopeful? These may only be beliefs, but they have power. *Your* power. Your belief and attention feeds and sustains them — giving them control over you, allowing them to set the parameters you live under, and determine the experiences you have. This brief anecdote illustrates this truth powerfully:

A baby elephant is trained for the circus by being tied to a heavy chain staked deeply in the ground. No matter how hard it tries, it can't pull free. As it grows, it becomes accustomed to its restraints. And as the conditioning takes it toll, it stops resisting. Finally, the trainer only needs to tie it down with a normal rope that the elephant could rip out of the ground in an instant. *But it doesn't even try.* It believes it is stuck in place as long as it can feel even the slightest resistance of the rope. It believes that this is "just the way life is." The elephant's mind has been trained to think that there are limits to its life beyond its control — despite the obvious fact that it has *all the control.*

A while back there was a story about a fire that broke out in a circus tent full of elephants. They were restrained only by these normal ropes from which they could have broken free, but they thought they were stuck. Not even the fear of death could get them to test their boundaries. And they all died in the fire. They didn't even *try* to escape. They just screamed in pain as their lives went up in flames. Tragic. But a striking example of how conditioning works. (The movie *The Truman Show* is a lighter example of how a person's whole world can be created and controlled by a specific process of conditioning.)

The binds that appear to hold you or this business back — even those you believe with every fiber are unbreakable — are just the byproduct of conditioning (personal and group-think). They're not supported by natural laws and principles. They're not supported by anything real or substantial. There is nothing in this universe that can, or wishes to, hold you back from true fulfillment. In fact, the universe is conspiring to grant your heart's desires. Even if everything in your experience tells you otherwise, whatever obstacle seems to be pinning you down is really as weak as a small stake in the ground.

> The binds that appear to hold you or this business back — even those you believe with every fiber are unbreakable — are just the byproduct of conditioning.

Unlike the elephant, we've been blessed with the ability to think independently of our circumstances and create new beliefs. That begins by releasing old ones. To help with this, I've put together two Belief Sheets to mirror your conditioning. Follow the simple instructions and write down your first impulse. Don't think. In this way, you'll bypass your monitoring mind and gain access to your unconscious thoughts and feelings.

Entertainment Industry "Belief" Exercise #1

Rate the statements from 1-10 (1 = "totally disagree," 10 = "totally agree")

____ Hollywood is a closed system

____ You can't create good art unless you're struggling/suffering

____ It's wrong to create art (write scripts, act, etc.) to make money

____ Actors/artists are flakes/self-centered

____ Writers are low on the totem pole

____ Striving for success will corrupt you/ruin your relationships

____ You have to take a lot of rejection to make it

____ You have to pay your dues

____ It's too good to be true

____ It's all in who you know

____ The business is corrupt/full of greedy egomaniacs

____ I don't want to be a star

____ Stars don't have any freedom

____ It's not important how successful you are, as long as you do your art

____ Realistically, chances are I'll never make it

____ I'm not good enough to make it

____ It takes a lot of luck to make it

____ It's almost impossible to "make it," very few ever do

____ I'm not good-looking enough

____ I'm too old

____ I'm too young

____ I missed my chance — and you only get one

____ I'm too late in the game — you have to start young

____ You have to sell out to make it

____ Most actors/artists are below the poverty level

____ I have the potential to be successful — all I need is a break

___ If I "make it" some people won't like me

___ If I "make it" I'll be stalked, or worse

___ You can't have a family/marriage AND be successful in this business

___ Entertainment people are totally screwed up

___ You can't make it doing your true passion

___ I'm just not talented or smart enough

___ I didn't go to the right school/class

___ If you don't have friends/family in the biz, you'll probably fail

___ I don't like selling or promoting myself/my product

___ Auditioning/submitting my work is too much of a hassle

___ Most of the good opportunities are already gone

___ You need to have a good agent

___ Trying to make it is too much work — it's really not worth the struggle

___ You need something else to fall back on

___ It's much more difficult to make it as a woman

___ It's much more difficult to make it as a minority

___ If I make it, I could get addicted to drugs or alcohol

___ Nobody knows anything in this town

Entertainment Industry "Free-Association" Exercise #1

Complete the following statements:

The entertainment industry is _____

The entertainment industry is _____

The entertainment industry is _____

Being a success in the "biz" is _____

Being a success in the "biz" is _____

Being a success in the "biz" is _____

Artists/entertainment professionals are _____

Artists/entertainment professionals are _____

The reasons I can't or may not become successful in the "biz" are:

Some of the negatives about being successful in the "biz" or going through the process of trying to become successful are:

My greatest worries, fears, and concerns regarding the entertainment industry and my experience in it are:

The worst thing about this business is: _____

How was that? Were you shocked by how you rated certain beliefs and statements? Did you see yourself in some — or many — of them? Were you surprised I knew what you were thinking and how you felt? Did you wonder if I read your journal?!

If you saw yourself and your beliefs in there, it wasn't because I've had a private existential detective following you around — it's because these aren't *your* beliefs, they're the "collective consciousness of the entertainment industry." There are certain limited beliefs floating around and you've just used your unique creative faculties to personalize them, to make them your own. But they don't belong to you. You don't own them. You don't *owe* them. And it's time to tell them to "hit the road, Jack!"

There are many ways to release these beliefs — affirmative prayer, meditation, writing them down, burning the paper in a fire ceremony! You can try any and all. For now, we'll do a simple NLP (Neuro-Linguistic Programming) technique.

Make yourself comfortable. Hold your left hand in a fist. (This is a form of anchoring, which you'll use to release.) Say the limited beliefs out loud (anything above a 3 on your list, and anything else you feel has a charge on it). As you repeat each belief, sense your hand getting tighter, all the restriction of these beliefs imprisoned in your clenched fist.

Now imagine all of these negative beliefs and their constrictive energy have been crushed into a handful of sand in your fist. Picture yourself dumping the sand into the ocean. Brush your hands off. Watch the sand disintegrate into the water and wash out to sea, all the negative energy dissipated into the deep blue, gone... forever. If you feel moved, you can say a prayer, a chant, or meditate — whatever gives you closure and completion.

How do you feel? Lighter? Heavier? Emotional? If you're still feeling the stirrings of limitation, worry, doubt, or fear, that's okay. This is a process. You've spent a long time building up these beliefs, so it might take some time to break them down.

The Master Plan: A Visioning Exercise

All the work we've done up to this point has prepared you to leap into this visioning process. You understand now (whether or not you believe it yet) that there is a divine pattern of perfection within you (the acorn), that you don't have to wait for things to change "out there," you just have to create the right conditions "in here" — and the seed of your potential will grow into the destiny of greatness you were created for.

You're probably eager to do this process on your individual purpose and career, but we're going to start with the vision of the entertainment industry's greater potential. Remember, we're building something here. It has a natural sequence. We could jump right into your career, but there's a possibility that the ego still has a hold on your heart and mind. By doing the work in this progression, we're chipping away at the structures the ego is holding onto, at the grip it may have over your identity, until you are in command, instead of being controlled by it.

Visioning is a transformative process. It's not about making something happen, it's about making something welcome — by becoming it in consciousness — which automatically manifests in form. Dreams don't come true, they already are. But we must be true to them.

> Dreams don't come true, they already are. But we must be true to them.

We must raise our vibrations to the level at which the dream is vibrating in order to be a conduit through which it can express. And, like the acorn, we must be willing to let go of our little self-concepts so that we can become bigger than we ever imagined.

Why do we need to have a vision of the entertainment industry's higher purpose?

In realizing the spiritual prototype of this "business of show," we'll not only change ourselves and be more effective in it, but as a critical mass of individuals align with this new value system, the collective consciousness of the industry will shift. The Hundreth Monkey Theory was an example of this phenomenon (where a certain breed of monkey on one island began to wash potatoes a certain way, and soon monkeys on surrounding islands were doing the same — despite having no physical connection). The "idea" had reached critical mass in "monkey consciousness." Remember the four-minute mile? Nobody could break it. But once someone did, runners began breaking it around the world. Ancient scripture echoes this truth when it says that "Ten holy men can save a city." I just say that if a bunch of monkeys can learn to do things more effectively, so can we.

Okay, let's do some visioning on the entertainment industry, and see what comes through. Later we'll go deeper into your individual role in it. Get comfortable, preferably sitting up, back erect but not stiff, feet flat on the floor, hands resting in your lap. Close your eyes, and take three slow deep breaths, releasing everything that has come before this moment with each exhalation. Just let it all go, all your ideas of who you are, where you've been, what you think the entertainment industry is, and what you think your role in it is. Let it fall away. The past does not equal the present. And nothing in all of history can prevent a divine idea from unfolding when you're willing to tap into it.

The following process can last as long as you want, but at least long enough to pose the following questions, which can be repeated for a deepening effect:

- What is God's/My Higher Power's vision of the entertainment industry?

- What does it look like, feel like? What is its essence?

- If the full potential of the industry were realized, what would it look like? What would its products look like? What would its impact be on the planet?

- How must I change to be an instrument of this vision? What must I let go of or embrace? How must I be different?

- Is there a symbolic action I can take to assist the manifestation of the vision? Is there a project I'm working on, a job I'm working at, a contract I'm negotiating, a relationship I'm involved in — where I can do something to represent this vision?

- Is there anything else I need to see or know at this time to be in alignment with the higher calling of the entertainment industry?

Allow gratitude to well up, give thanks for what's been revealed. As insights or images arise, you can write them down and return to meditation, or wait until afterward.

Please feel free to e-mail me your visions for the industry. I might use them to inspire our growing community. Send them to: *derek@ EnlightenedEntertainer.com.*

Writing a New Script: Affirmation Exercise

The universe abhors a vacuum, and will quickly move to fill in the holes where the old beliefs were. Therefore, we want to install new, empowering beliefs before our old house guests try to move back in. We'll do this through an affirmation process. It's important to remember, however, that the words you speak are not nearly as important as the *feeling* behind them. This is the key to their effectiveness. You need to feel in your innermost being that you already have the thing you're affirming or praying for.

You might be thinking, "If I felt like I already had the thing, I wouldn't be affirming it!" But that's how the Law operates. To effectively manifest, you need to affirm, pray, and set intentions from the "feeling tone" of fulfillment — because that thought-energy is the substance of the thing you're seeking, just in invisible form. And as you hang out in that vibration, like water becoming ice, that liquid energy will solidify into your experience.

To aid you in generating these inner feelings, don't be afraid to "physicalize" your affirmation. For example, if you're trying to be a confident person, stand confidently, hold your head confidently, and speak the affirmations with confidence.

Now pick the top five limited beliefs and create simple, power-packed affirmations to replace them. For example: "I'm too old to succeed in this business," can be replaced with: "*My maturity as an actor/writer/etc. makes my work rich and in demand. The business wants what I have, and rewards me abundantly for my talents.*" Don't worry about getting it right — just write something that inspires you.

In case you have a hard time coming up with your own affirmations, I've created a list of basic ones to get your juices flowing. You can modify them to fit your own unique style:

- I'm an important and necessary part of the "entertainment industry"
- My unique talents and perspectives are needed and appreciated
- I deeply believe in myself and my work, and stand behind it 100%
- My work makes a powerful impact on the industry and across the planet
- I live on purpose every day in every way, and I feel fulfilled
- I am a true and lasting success in the "entertainment industry'
- I support others in their success, wanting for them all that I want for myself
- I'm an Enlightened Entertainer! (Or "Sacred Artist", "Conscious Creator", etc.)

As you declare these or any affirmations, remember to close your eyes and feel the vibration, the tonal quality of confidence, enthusiasm, and expansiveness. Become intimately connected to it. Contemplate it. Breathe it in. Consciousness always clothes itself in form. So as this vibration becomes a permanent part of your consciousness, it *must* manifest outwardly as a more abundant expression of good in your life.

Acts of Courage: "Snap Out of It!"

To anchor the affirmation work, find a rubber band (the thicker ones work best), and put it on your wrist. For the next 21 days, whenever you think these limiting beliefs, snap that sucker hard enough to draw blood! (Okay, not that hard. But it should sting.) This is a "pattern interrupt." Every time you do it, it's like scratching a record until it can no longer play. It sends your brain a message that this belief is painful. Because your mind tends to move away from pain, this trains it to be less interested in this painful thought.

But you're not finished yet. As you break the old pattern and uproot the limited belief, you need to reprogram your mind with the new, empowering belief. The mind doesn't just move away from pain, it moves toward pleasure. So after you snap your wrist, caress it and kiss your boo-boo — as you declare your affirmations. That sends your brain the message that this new belief is pleasurable, thereby drawing it to this way of thinking.

If you associate enough pain with an unwanted behavior or belief, and enough pleasure with the new belief or behavior, your mind will shift. This may seem like a silly exercise, but it can have a powerful impact. Give it a try. See what happens. What do you have to lose, except some limited beliefs — and maybe a little feeling in your wrist. (Kidding.)

Check-In

How are you doing? As part of your journaling practice, answer the following questions:

1. How do I feel about the entertainment industry and its greater possibilities? Do I feel more inspired/empowered than before I started this? Why? Why not?

2. How do I feel about my place and purpose in show business? Do I feel more inspired/empowered than before I started this? Why? Why not?

3. What inner and outer changes must I make in order to achieve my purpose in this business? Am I willing? If so, why? If not, why not?

4. Is there something I know I'm being called to do, but am afraid to do it? Why?

If you haven't already done so, I encourage you to try out the Night Pages at least once this week. It's a powerful practice that will grow your consciousness of abundance, confidence, and self-worth — leading to greater creativity, risk-taking, and rewards.

FOUR

Discovering Your Purpose

"This is the true joy in life, the being used for a
purpose recognized by yourself as a mighty one;
the being thoroughly worn out before you are
thrown on the scrap heap; the being a force of
nature instead of a feverish selfish little clod of
ailments and grievances complaining that the
world will not devote itself to making you happy."
— George Bernard Shaw

Live on Purpose, Not by Accident

You have a mighty purpose, a function to fulfill — a reason for
being. And it's more than just "make a living," "be a star," or
"meet hot men and women." Really, it is. You are here to make
a unique and valuable contribution, to assist (if even in a small way)
the evolution of humanity. You may not believe me, but I assure you
it's true.

Look at nature. Everything serves a purpose. Everything is connected to
a larger system that allows the whole to operate in harmony. Everything
is, in some way, an answer to a specific need. Even the chair you're
sitting on (or couch, bed, futon) came into being as an answer to a
need: a need for something to sit on, a need for a form of support.

You're no different. You came into this world (and entertainment
industry) as an answer to a prayer, a solution to a need. If there was

no need for you, you never would've shown up. The fact that you were born is the guarantee that you have a reason for being here. There's something you came to give — a gift, a talent, a message, a meaning. The world, the entertainment industry, and the global audience need you to be you.

The interesting (and sometimes scary) thing about living a purposeful life is you begin to realize that, in a very real way, your life is not your own. You're not here to just get all the good stuff for yourself — and maybe your loved ones — so you can live a happy, pleasure-filled existence. You are part of a larger organism, a larger system, and all the good that you receive, all the talent you possess, everything that you have, is not for your benefit only — but for the benefit of the whole system. And the more you surrender to this, the more the universe will pour its bounty through you so you can be a bigger giver.

Just as all the cast and crew of a movie are there to serve the film (even if they're inclined to be self-serving), so too are we all cast and crew members in a divine Play of Life. As the saying goes, "The play's the thing." That's what we serve, that's why our character exists — that's why every line of dialogue, every action, every prop is in its place — to serve the Divine Play. Sure, the "players" have a grand old time doing it, and it's full of adventure and excitement, but if it's a good play, it's also full of function. Everything serves a purpose in the overall intent of the piece.

Another useful analogy is to think of a cell in the body. Every cell has a purpose, a job to do. And every cell receives nourishment, guidance, direction, protection — everything it needs to play its part. A cell that is fulfilling its function is a happy, prosperous, successful cell. But it's that way so it can serve the body, not itself. In fact, when a cell begins to think it has a life of its own, that it needs to do things only for itself and not for the larger whole, it either dies — or becomes cancer. It begins to destroy everything around it to fulfill its insatiable needs, until it destroys its host organism and itself.

Begin opening to a greater realization and acceptance of your purposeful life. Ask how you can be of greater service to this industry, to your art or craft, and to the world at large. If you have little or no idea, try looking at the things you're good at, the things you're interested or passionate about, and the things you used to love doing as a child. These are clues to your innate talents and abilities, and thus your purpose. Ask yourself, "What would I do and be if I were guaranteed success and already had all the fame and fortune I wanted?" (This is important to ponder even if you're already successful in the business, because many successful individuals are still not answering their true calling.)

What's My Motivation?

In teaching this work, a question that frequently comes up is, "How do I know what my purpose is?" This is often followed by, "I just don't know what I'm supposed to do." "There are so many options." "I can't tell if the voice inside is my spirit/intuition talking or my ego." "What if I do the wrong thing? What if I make the wrong choice?"

First of all, you can never really make a "wrong choice" if you have the right intention. Even a wrong choice, born of a sincere intention, will lead you to learn and grow — strengthening your ability to listen to inner guidance and make better choices. Ultimately, the choices you make are not nearly as important as the *intention* behind them. We've been taught that the path to success is in doing all the "right things."

> You can never really make a "wrong choice" if you have the right intention.

But how many people have failed doing all the right things? Likewise, how many have succeeded by breaking the rules and making mistakes? There's a mystical statement that sums this up:

To she who is right in mind, she can do all the wrong things and it'll still turn out right. To she who is wrong in mind, she can do all the right things and it'll still turn out wrong.

Don't worry about doing the wrong thing. Instead — at least initially — focus on *why* you're doing what you're doing. As you tune into this dimension of your being, you not only discover the layers of false motivation — and begin to release them — but you eventually hit that soft, glowing core where the *why* turns into the *what.* In that radiant center of your being, you discover that the thing you're striving for, the thing which fuels your "why" is actually the very thing you're made of. You're already it! The word "desire" means "of the sire" or "of the father." In other words, that strong impulse to achieve something is actually the "something" already in you, seeking to come out!

Let's take some time to look at your desires and goals. All the things you want to have and achieve in the entertainment industry. Create two columns on a page. On the left side, write down your desire/goal. On the right side, write down why you want it. Be honest. Start with the things you want most and work your way down.

If the reason you want something is to get something else materially, add that new object to the desire column and write down why you want it. For instance, if you wrote, "I want to sell a million-dollar script." And in the *WHY* column you put, "to get a house." Put "Get a house" in the desire column. And put why you want the house in the opposite column. Ultimately, you should end up with non-material reasons in the right column.

Now take a look at those reasons. Why do you want what you want? Do you see a pattern? Did you put the same thing in more than one entry? Are your "whys" based on what you want from others, or are they inner qualities? For example, let's say you wrote in your goals/desires, "I want to be a star." And in your *why* column, you wrote, "So people will love and respect me." You still haven't gotten down to the real *why* at your core. This entry also belongs in the "goals/desire" column. Take the "whys" that depend on getting something from someone else — even if it's non-material — and put those in the goals/desire column. Then write down why you want those. Working with the entry, "I want people to love and respect me," you might put in the *why* column, "So that I will *feel* loved and respected" or "So that I'll love and respect *myself.*"

Ah-ha! Now *that* is a real "why."

But something else important has occurred. You started out thinking that what you wanted was to be a star, have fame and fortune, and gain others' love and respect, but discovered that what you really want is "*to feel loved and respected.*" And here's the best part: *Feeling loved and respected is an inside job!* It has nothing to do with fame, fortune, or *anything* outside of you. You, and only you, have the power to generate these feelings.

Generating these inner feelings is your real goal.

Another interesting thing begins to occur as you break your goals and desires down like this. As you start to realize your real motivations behind things, they begin to lose their luster, their irresistible pull. It's like the story of the musk deer who journeys through the forests, trudges across rivers and streams, over hills and mountains, to find the object of its desire: *musk.* Then, in utter exhaustion, the animal collapses, only to discover that the object of its search, the scent of musk, was in its very hide the whole time!

The more you realize that what you truly want is already within you, the less appeal the outer struggle has. As you begin to rest in this awareness, a sense of true joy, peace, fulfillment, and freedom emerges. When you realize that what you're really going for, in all of your pavement pounding on the Walk of Fame, is self-love and acceptance (or whatever quality you're after), and you realize you can only find this inside — your journey both ends and finally begins. And as the resistance falls away, you find that an experience of self love and acceptance wafts up from your own hide, without any effort.

> The more you realize that what you truly want is already within you, the less appeal the outer struggle has.

This doesn't mean you stop doing things in the world. Far from it. As a matter of fact, you become more productive, prolific, and prosperous — because you know from whence your good comes, and aren't blocking it by projecting it onto someone or something else. But there's something more that happens. All of the "false desires" based on "false motives" fall away. And what remains is the true path you are meant to walk. On this path, there are tasks, goals, and a grand purpose, to be sure, but they are not motivated by what you can *get* — but rather by what you are here to *give*. From this space, knowing that you already have everything you need within you, your actions unfold from a desire to share what you have and who you are. Not because you need self-expression to feel whole, but because your wholeness cannot help but express itself.

So take a look at that list again. If you've gone through the process, you should have a right-hand column filled with qualities that you want to embody within yourself. If you've done this thoroughly, however, you'll probably also discover some goals/desires that aren't attached to getting something from someone. For example, you may have written as a goal/desire, "I want to give my gifts to the world." And in the *why* column, you may have genuinely written, "So that people can benefit from them." This is an effective motivation. It's not created by your ego. It's not *created* at all. It is your very nature announcing itself — and that nature is *always* about giving, shining, sharing, pouring forth that imprisoned splendor *for no ulterior motive.*

This isn't a judgment on other types of motivation. There's a place for everything on the ladder of our evolution. But when you have a motive that doesn't seek to *get* anything, a "core desire," it won't create any new "karma." It won't perpetuate old wounds and keep you and those around you unconscious. Quite the opposite. It will have a liberating, illuminating, expanding effect on you and everyone it touches. It will also emerge free of the resistance that normally accompanies our ego's agendas.

You should now have two sets of goals/desires here. On one hand, you know the material things you're after: the record deal, the spec script sale, the financing for your film, whatever. And that's all good. But you also have a list of "inner goals." And you are (hopefully) becoming increasingly aware that what you *really* want is primarily an inner experience, a quality of being, such as self-love, confidence, security, abundance. From this perspective, the phrase "living a quality life" takes on a whole new significance. You don't need to take specific action on the outer goals yet — although you can if you're inspired. Instead, your assignment is to create an *inner exercise program* (prayer, affirmation, meditation, etc.) that helps you strengthen these spiritual muscles.

As you practice these activities on a consistent basis, making them part of your regular routine, you'll begin to embody the qualities they are eliciting in you. And what does "embody" mean? It means to ingest them, feast on them, until they literally become part of your physical, mental, emotional body — and, finally, your "body of affairs." When this happens, you have achieved your *real goal*. You are fulfilled. You feel like a success, a superstar — you feel the way you would if all of your dreams came true.

I remember a period of my life when I was working on embodying the inner feeling of success and fulfillment. Then one day, I was driving in rush-hour traffic, and all of a sudden a wave of empowerment washed over me. I suddenly felt so successful and abundant that it startled me. I started flipping through my Mental Day Runner to see what had happened to cause my inspired state. Did I just land a great gig? Did someone just tell me how wonderful I was? Did I win the frickin" lottery?! Why was I feeling so good? I became suspicious. Was this a trick of my mind? Then I remembered the inner work I had been doing, and realized I was experiencing the "fruits" of my labors.

Laying this inner foundation is not the end, however, but only the beginning. Upon this concrete base of spiritual certainty you will build a house that the tempest of this turbulent industry will not blow down. So let's move a little further above ground.

Dreams & Desires

As you began to articulate your goals and desires, you (hopefully) gained some clarity about what you want to be, do, acquire, and become in this business of show (and the world). If you followed through with the exercise, you further discovered that what you really wanted was primarily an inner essence of your own being, a part of your soul that had been locked in a prison of materialistic perception. Now that you're free from that prison — or at least out on parole — let's delve back into the solid goals of this world.

In this journaling exercise, you're going to revisit the realm of your dreams and heart's desires, and write about them passionately. If you've had a chance to practice some of the exercises from the previous section, you'll be even more fueled to articulate your vision. If you haven't, that's okay. But you might want to revisit these preceding sections as you embody more of the qualities referred to above.

You're going to do this exercise twice — once for the left brain and once for the right. To begin with the left brain there is no need to prepare. Just take pen in hand (or fingers on keyboard) and begin writing about your vision for yourself in this industry. Ideally you want to write without thinking. But since you're exercising your left hemisphere, if thinking arises, allow it to inform what you write. Try to write for at least two pages.

Great! Now take a moment and prepare yourself to write from the right brain. There are several ways to do this. You could pick some music that makes you want to dance, then dance your heart out. If you're a singer or musician, you can play your instrument or wail out a passionate song. If you're an actor, act out a monologue, without any concern of doing it well. Pick something that is pure self-expression and throw yourself into it with abandon. When you feel you're sufficiently buzzing with creative juices, sit down and start writing your vision again, this time not allowing any pauses for thought. If you feel yourself slipping into your head, put the pen in your left hand and continue (this taps the right brain). If you're adventurous, alternate between the right and left hand throughout the process, allowing more of the right-side, subconscious material to surface.

Your Greatest Passion

The things that elicit your greatest passion are clues to where your purpose and proclivities lie. It might seem like I'm overstating the obvious, but you'd be amazed at how many people believe that if they're passionate about something, it couldn't possibly be connected to their purpose. It's like a cognitive blind spot. They overlook the areas and interests that bring them the greatest fulfillment. It's not as common in the entertainment industry, where many individuals are pursuing their passions, but even here, there is a glass ceiling of possibility that many still bump their heads on.

For instance, if you're a writer, are you writing from your deepest passion? If you're an actor, are you working on the parts that turn you on and make you spring out of bed in the morning (even if only at a local theater or the privacy of your bedroom)? If you're a producer or executive, are you looking for, developing, and making films (or other media) that stir your soul and make your heart sing? I can hear some of you saying, "Get real, man. I gotta make a living. I gotta get that gig. I can't just do what I love!" Sure, there are times when you need to just pay the bills. The danger arises when you become seduced by the false sense of security a paycheck brings — and no longer spend quality and *quantity* time pursuing your deeper purpose. Spend too much time focusing on pleasing others, conforming to the industry, or just trying to "get a job," and you'll lose that precarious thread to your true passion. Like a fire, if it's not fanned, it fades. It can never die out, because it's part of your eternal being, but it can diminish to a mere flicker, a pilot light on the back burner of your heart — leaving you feeling cold and in the dark.

Turn to your trusty journal and, for the next few minutes, free-write about your greatest passion. It doesn't need to deal with the industry. If you've already thought a lot about your place in this business, it might be *better* to write about things that seem unrelated. It will break you out of the myopic vision that happens when all you think about is the "biz." The truth is, many top people in the industry get so sick of talking about it that they find it refreshing when someone comes along with a life beyond the Hollywood sign! Individuals with a broader, richer perspective bring something unique, less cliché, to their work. So exercise all of you. Let your deepest passions pour onto the page: "I want to play in the dirt!" "I want to lie on the beach and read Proust all day!" "I wanna go to New York, and do off-off-off Broadway!" "I love bugs!" Hold nothing back.

Strengths & Talents

Here's your chance to brag about yourself. For the next few minutes, write about all your strengths, talents, and skills. Not just in your art, craft, or business — but anything. If you're a good gardener, write it down. Now is not the time for humility. When you start to run out of steam, ask yourself what others would say your strengths and talents are. Don't think too hard. Trust what comes out. You may even be surprised.

If you already know (or think you know) what your strengths are, and/or you're already a working professional in the area of your talents (writer, actor, filmmaker, musician, etc.), do this exercise anyway. You may be expressing your authentic self, communicating the ideas you came here for. But I suspect, if you're reading this book, you're looking for something more, something deeper. By expanding the boundaries of what you normally contemplate and how you see yourself, you'll uncover treasures that have been buried for a long time or that you never knew existed. And as the artifacts deep in your soul are excavated, they'll have a powerful influence on what you do, how you do it, and why.

> By expanding the boundaries of what you normally contemplate and how you see yourself — you'll uncover treasures that have been buried for a long time or that you never knew existed!

For example, you may be a writer who writes action adventure. You may even be a working writer. But as you practice these processes, you may discover (remember) that what you're most passionate about is nature. Maybe deep down you just want to live in a tree! You might realize that one of your skills is hiking or camping, and that you have a deep reverence for nature and a desire to protect Her. Bam! You're suddenly struck with a story that embodies all of these elements, ignites your passion like never before and, lo and behold, *that* becomes the one that sells, gets made, or takes home the statue.

At the intersection of your passion and talent stands a sign pointing to your true power. But you must sometimes be willing to take the road less traveled to arrive there.

Triumphs & Defeats

Just as our victories give us clues to our inherent potential, there is also great meaning in our defeats. Ironically, just because we succeed at something doesn't mean we're meant to do it. And just because we fail at something doesn't mean we're not. This is often where we see the difference between "talent" and "skill." Skill is something you can learn, master, and win awards at — but it doesn't necessarily mean you should be doing it. Talent, on the other hand, is something you're born with and can cultivate, and a life lived without expressing it is a life not lived at all. (In case you're wondering if you have talent, if you have a *burning* desire to do something — not just a casual interest — that's a clue you have talent in that area. The desire is your talent talking, seeking to get out.)

There are many individuals considered great successes, held in high esteem by their colleagues, who really aren't "called" to be there — but have done so out of fear or necessity. I'm not just talking about being a lawyer when you really want to sing. I'm talking about being a game show host when what really turns you on is acting, or writing shallow teen comedies when you were really born for poignant, Woody Allen–type comedy. You may even be a successful sit-com writer but, like Paul Haggis (*Crash, Million Dollar Baby*), have a deep desire to write and direct meaningful feature films. He was willing to risk bankruptcy to follow his true passion. What are you willing to risk?

Don't let past failures determine what your future success will be. Walt Disney went bankrupt — twice — before finally gaining lasting momentum. The Beatles were rejected from numerous record labels, as was Tom Petty. Shane Black wrote over a dozen scripts before selling one. Scores of others in every area of the "biz" were (and are) regularly rejected before finally finding some success. Thomas Edison failed at creating the light bulb *ten thousand* times before getting it right! If he used failure as an indicator of his true path, you might be reading this by candlelight — and we wouldn't have movies!

Failures serve another purpose — they give us wisdom. Every time Edison failed at creating the lightbulb, he *succeeded* in eliminating one more way to *not* do it. He also learned many lessons about the nature of electricity, conductivity, and patience. Your failures are just as valuable and rich with blessings. But you must be willing to contemplate them, ask what lesson they have for you, and apply it the next time around. If you just whine, complain, bemoan your fate, and engage your failures like enemies, you'll not only fail to retrieve their valuable secrets, you'll remain a failure. Likewise, if you just ignore the failure, deny it, or look away, you'll be destined to repeat it. One definition of insanity is to do the same thing and expect different results. Take a look at your life and career. Are you doing the same things that have failed before, but expecting different results? Have you actually, without realizing it, gone insane?

> One definition of insanity is to do the same thing and expect different results.

Let's do some more writing. Write about your failures and successes, your triumphs and defeats. Write about the lessons you've learned and the wisdom you've gained (if any) in each case. Looking at a few key experiences, ask yourself these questions:

- Did this success make me happy? If so, why? If not, why not?

- Did this success move my mission forward? If so, how? If not, why?

- What clues to my talent, passion, and purpose did this success/failure reveal?

- What was the lesson in this failure? What did it try to teach me? What did I learn?

- Am I still doing the same thing that I failed at before? If so, why? If not, why not?

Keep writing until you have nothing left to say on this subject. Then write some more.

What You Value Most

What do you care about deeply? What would you dedicate your life to if you could? What would you die for? What we feel strongest about, what we tend to argue, defend, or fight for — all of these are indications of our purpose, our message, and our talent. The things that move us to our core — making us angry, sad, or elated — contain clues to what we'll find the most joy, fulfillment, and true success expressing in our work.

Take a moment to turn within and connect with something or someone you deeply value. Perhaps it's a loved one, a religious figure, a cause. Feel the power in it, the passion. When you're sufficiently connected, open your eyes and start writing about what you value most. Don't monitor it. Don't think. Just write. Fast and furious. Let whatever surfaces be okay. Let whatever emotions bubble up be okay. Let your whole being participate. If it makes you want to shout, shout it out. If it makes you want to cry, cry me a river. If it makes you want to drop to your knees in reverent prayer, rub that carpet raw.

While your talent is your tool and your passion is your fuel — your values are your core. They are the center that doesn't move, that keeps you anchored, rooted in the ground so that the fickle winds of change may bend you but never break you.

Losing Track of Time

Another strong clue to what you're meant to do can be found in the activities that cause you to lose all sense of time. When you're connected to your authentic self, you're dipping into the timeless dimension of your being. It's true that "time flies when you're having fun." But it's not the whole truth. In fact, time *ceases to exist* when you're truly connected to your joy. The clocks may still be ticking "out there," but "in here" the ravages of time have slowed to a crawl or stopped altogether. Why do you think you can go hours and hours without taking a break, being hungry, thirsty, fidgety, or needing much sleep? When you're engaged in your passion, rooted in the "now," the normal physiological effects of time-boundedness diminish or disappear altogether.

What activities cause you to lose track of time, to look up and see that hours have flown by in what seemed like minutes? If you have a hard time thinking of peak experiences — if you suffer from the opposite effect where minutes crawl by like hours — you're not alone. And it's not a lost cause. Turn the clocks back in your memory, back before you had to act "responsibly." Think back to those childhood days you didn't want to end, those mornings that couldn't come soon enough. What activities did you throw yourself into with abandon, losing yourself for hours at a time? They're there. Just keep looking.

Begin writing about these times. What were you thinking, feeling, what prompted you to engage in the activities? If you no longer participate in them, write about why. If you can't think of anything in your life that caused you to lose track of time, write about what you think *could* make you lose track of time. Imagine what you would dive into if you had a stretch of uninterrupted hours and no responsibilities. If you still can't drudge anything up, imagine a character who *does* know what their greatest joy is. Write about that character doing something that causes them to lose all sense of time.

If You Could Be Someone Else

We've all had (or still have) fantasies about being other people. Historical figures, celebrities. While it's not healthy to want to be someone else, it can be illuminating — because the things we admire in others are actually qualities lying latent in ourselves.

Take that hand of yours — by now probably suffering from writer's cramp — and begin scribbling about the person (or people) you would like to be if you could be someone else. It doesn't have to be all of one person. Maybe you would like to have the looks of Brad Pitt, the coolness of John Travolta, the smile of Tom Cruise, the vision of George Lucas, the eye of Steven Spielberg, the empire of Oprah, and the heart of Buddha! Don't think. Don't monitor. Just free-write about anything and everything it brings up.

If You Were Guaranteed Success

It's easy to rationalize our way out of following our bliss. As the pressures of daily living crowd in on us, our motives for doing what we're doing can become convoluted. When you pose this question, however, it immediately strips away the excuses:

"If you were guaranteed success, what would you do with your life?"

Another way to frame it is, "If you already had all the fame, fortune, and power you could ever want, what would you do with your life?" Can you see what these questions do? They rip the costume off our back, giving us nothing to hide behind. They immediately give our ego everything it's been fighting for, leaving it with no resistance to push back against. And very quickly we see — if we're willing to look — just how crowded our lives have become with things that really don't matter in the long run.

So start writing. Imagine you are guaranteed success. You have everything you want, everything you thought was so important. Now what? I remember an interview with Brad Pitt, where he talked about the inner crisis he faced when he realized he had all the bobbles that so many strive for. He had the fame, the fortune, the material stuff, and what he discovered was that when he finally got everything he thought would make him happy, all he was left with was *himself* — and all the unresolved issues. For some folks, that may not be good news. Many people are doing what they're doing to *avoid* being with themselves. It might be because they don't like who they are. But I think there's something else, something even scarier than low self-esteem. I think many people, even creative types, are *strangers* to themselves. For these individuals, the idea of being alone in a room is as terrifying as meeting a shadowy figure in a dark alley.

Discovering Your Hero's Journey:
A Visioning Exercise

Using the visioning process, it's time to open up to your personal role in the industry. You may be surprised, confused, or even scared by what you see. Remember the acorn? Can you imagine how it would feel if it saw it was destined to be this massive oak? Freaked out, maybe? So don't worry about what comes up – or what doesn't. Just breathe and let it be. Often the subconscious will speak in symbols, so be aware of that too.

Get comfortable. Preferably sitting up, back erect but not stiff. Feet flat on the floor, hands resting in your lap. If you need to lie down, make sure you can stay awake. Close your eyes. Take three slow deep breaths, releasing everything that has come before this moment with each exhalation. Let it all go, all your ideas of who you are, where you've been, what you think the entertainment industry is, and what you think your role is in it. Let it all fall away. Allow your breath to find its own rhythm. Don't control it. Just watch it. Flowing in and out, continuing to release and relax, becoming still and quiet inside.

The following process can last as long as you want, but at least long enough to pose the following questions, which can be repeated for a deepening effect. As insights or images emerge, you can write them down and return to meditation, or wait until afterward.

- What is my role in the entertainment industry? What does it look like, feel like?

- What are the unique talents, gifts, and abilities I bring? What does it look and feel like to be maxing out to my full potential?

- How must I change, what must I let go of or embrace, in order for this vision to manifest?

- Is there an action I must take to step out on this vision with confidence and faith?

Allow gratitude to well up, be thankful for what has been revealed.

Begin with the End

If the visioning exercise yielded a clear sense of your purpose, you can potentially skip this guided visualization. If you didn't have much come up, or if you would like to take it to another level, then read on. This process can bring surprising insights if you surrender to it fully. So make yourself comfortable, preferably sitting up, back straight but not stiff. Close your eyes. Feet firmly on the floor. Hands relaxed in your lap.

Imagine you are highly successful in your area of the entertainment industry, doing meaningful work, having a powerful, positive impact on people in the business and, ultimately, around the world. See yourself providing excellent service and impeccable quality. See the faces of your satisfied customers, clients, and audience members as they experience the benefits of your products and services. Feel the fulfillment it brings you.

Now imagine you've been invited to an entertainment conference to be honored. You walk down a busy hall, saying hello to colleagues, fans, and admirers, shaking hands, signing autographs. A host shows you into a ballroom, packed with satisfied clients, colleagues, family, friends. A large poster of your most recent movie, album, or book hangs on the wall. You're led to the stage and greet the crowd — *who rise to their feet with a standing ovation*. You're floored by the love and respect coming at you.

Then, one by one, past clients, industry colleagues, friends, and family members stand up and praise your unique qualities and talents, thanking you for how you've helped them and added great value to their lives (similar to the eulogy exercise, only now you're alive to receive the praise). Don't monitor their comments. Take a deep breath and let them flow. You might be surprised by what you hear. If you find it difficult to imagine what they'd say, contemplate the following questions to spur your heart:

- What qualities of character would you like them to have seen in you as an artist, entertainment professional — and as a human being?

- What contributions or achievements would you want to be acknowledged for?

- What impact would you want to have made on their lives and work?

Fully experience what it's like to have your talents, abilities, and contributions honored and affirmed. As each person speaks, you may open your eyes and write down what they said. Then return to the visualization until you have gone through four or five tributes.

A Deeper Look

Find a place where you won't be disturbed or distracted for a while. As you contemplate each question, let it sink in. Don't censor your answers. Trust. Take a deep breath...

- What are your personal strengths and skills, (don't be humble)?

- What strengths have others noticed in you?

- What talents do you have that no one else really knows about?

- What natural abilities do you have, that you aren't using?

- What do you most admire in others (think about specific people)?

- Who has had the greatest impact on your life and why?

- When you daydream, what do you see yourself doing?

- What things, deep down, do you feel you really *should* do?

- What are the most important goals you want to fulfill in your work/career?

- If you had to teach something, what would it be?

- Who inspires you (artists, authors, leaders, friends) and why?

Whether or not you received the answers you wanted or expected, your synapses are firing, creating new neuro-pathways, opening new windows of insight.

Personal Values

Based on all material you've written in this chapter, list what you believe are your core values. You can choose from the list, or write your own (these are just a few examples):

Love	Peace	Security	Health	Wealth
Service	Creativity	Recognition	Freedom	Spirituality
Family	Friendship	Contribution	Home	Accomplishment

Now go through your list of values and choose the top five.

Creating Your "Enlightened Entertainer" Agreement

If you don't like that title, you can use "Sacred Artist," "Conscious Media Maker," "Conscious Communicator" — or whatever term inspires you. The purpose here is to take all the work you've done so far and create a mission statement. Think of it like a compass, something against which you can judge everything you do, in order to keep you on course. Without this tool, it's difficult to know for sure what your destination is, and if the steps you're taking will lead you there. It's easy to get caught up in the daily minutiae of life, the "to-do list" mentality, only to discover when the sun goes down that you haven't accomplished anything of significance. Without this tool, you might climb the ladder of success only to discover it's leaning against the wrong wall.

To craft this powerful "call to adventure," take all the data you've collected during this chapter and follow the instructions below.

1. Choose a few VERBS that resonate, inspire, or excite you — and represent your core values. For example: to Play, to Serve, to Build, to Enlighten, to Help, etc.

2. In the context of your work, decide *who* or *what* you will be *acting upon*. Will it be "Writers," "Producers," "Directors," "Musicians," "Other Professionals," "The Entertainment Industry," or "All of the above"?

3. What is your ultimate goal for the people or groups you will be serving or helping? What is the *value, benefit,* or *end result* you create?

4. Now combine these three elements to create the skeleton of the mission statement, and use all the other work you've done to fill in the flesh.

Example

As an artist and entertainment professional, I create projects that hold up a mirror to humanity, inspiring individuals to heal their past, awaken their full potential, and fulfill their destiny — creating a world that works for everyone. By conducting business with honesty, integrity, enthusiasm, and generosity, I provide a safe and productive atmosphere for people to make mistakes, take risks, create and perform in ways that exceed their expectations, and grow in ways they never thought possible!

Your mission statement doesn't have to be long. It can be one sentence if it inspires you and sums up your purpose. Don't worry if it's not perfect either. It's not carved in stone. It's something you "try on," like a new coat. If, after wearing it a while, it makes you itch or sweat or feel like you showed up to the party overdressed — get a new one.

Creating the mission statement is a major move in manifesting your dreams. But it's only half the equation. The other half is creating a plan. If you're eager to do so, you could skip to the section, "Lights, Cameras, Take Action!" But I encourage you to be patient and go through the rest of the work. You may decide to re-do your mission statement. You don't want to create a plan that is obsolete before you put it into action. For now, just use this mission statement as a compass on this journey through the "jungles of self."

Acts of Courage: "and Action!"

The inner work is incredibly important. But it's often rendered impotent if it's not put it into some kind of action. As you've gone through this chapter, you have no doubt discovered things you want/need to act on. You may also have discovered many reasons why you *can't*. Over the next week, your assignment is to pick something that came up, something that makes you nervous, something you're afraid to attempt, *and just do it.*

> Faith without works is dead. Action, finally, is the true religion.

Faith without works is dead. Action, finally, is the true religion. By taking this bold step, regardless of outcome, you're sending yourself a message that your dream is real. You're cutting a new groove in consciousness that says you will no longer be held back by fear or perceived limitation. You're setting the law of freedom in motion, allowing it to gain momentum, until you won't be able to prevent your progress even if you tried!

Check-In

How are you doing? To further ground your work in this chapter, answer these questions (yes, they're the same questions as last chapter. That's by design):

1. How do I feel about the entertainment industry and its greater possibilities? Do I feel more inspired/empowered than before I started this? Why? Why not?

2. How do I feel about my place and purpose in show business? Do I feel more inspired/empowered than before I started this? Why? Why not?

3. What inner and outer changes must I make in order to achieve my purpose in this business? Am I willing? If so, why? If not, why not?

4. Is there something I know I'm being called to do, but am afraid to do it? Why?

This is a work-at-your-own-pace book. But if you haven't done the material from the last chapter, I encourage you to complete it on some level. Each chapter builds upon the one before. You're free to jump around as you choose, but I've found that when someone doesn't complete one aspect of this work before moving on, they're often resisting something, afraid to look at something, or on the verge of real change — all of which can cause them to get bored, tired, procrastinate, "skim through," or skip over entire sections.

If this describes you, don't beat yourself up. It's part of the process. If you haven't tried the Night Pages, give it a shot. It's a great practice to grow your consciousness of abundance — which leads to greater creativity, risk-taking, and empowerment.

And speaking of power, I'll see you in the next chapter, where we'll talk about how you can fully reclaim yours!

PART III
Character Development

FIVE ~

Reclaiming Your Power

"Knowing others is intelligence; knowing yourself
is true wisdom. Mastering others is strength;
mastering yourself is true power. "
— Lao Tzu

Don't Be a Star, Be a Light

Like most people, I have my favorite stars and I wouldn't necessarily refuse an opportunity to be one myself. Nevertheless, I believe the "star system" is a destructive aspect of the business. Not just because of the impact star salaries have on the economics of the industry, but because of the unraveling of the original purpose and power of this part of the story-weaving process. Remember, storytellers and performers (actors, writers, directors, singers, songwriters) are just the messengers. That doesn't mean they're not important. They're very important, as far as messengers go. But the most vital element is *the message*. And, by that, I don't mean something sent by Western Union. I'm talking about The Story and its Greater Purpose — the heart, the pulse, the truth that touches people. That's what everything is in service to — that's what is meant to be exalted.

In a sense, the problem with the star system is the same problem with religion. Religions go astray when "followers" build a "following" around the messengers and worship them instead of the message; when followers fail to realize that the light they see in their leaders is a reflection of the light within them. When this happens, the message gets personalized and misunderstood; systems and superstitions are built around the messenger, and the original purpose and power of the process is corrupted or obscured.

When the star system prevails, projects are not always chosen based on their real merits, but on the politics of pleasing the star elements. A film project is given the "green light" because a "bankable star" is attached, not necessarily because the story is great. Projects are rushed into production before they're ready because the star only has a small window of availability, they have a pay-or-play deal, or for some other externally-driven reason. Even before the project reaches this stage, the whole development process is often geared toward showcasing the star elements, in order to get the star attached, in order to rush it into theatres while the star is still hot. And if there is more than one star involved, the problems can multiply with geometric progression! This is, of course, an oversimplification of the process. But it's not *that* oversimplified.

And it's not just the film companies' fault. They're simply trying to supply the demand. People, for the most part, purchase tickets to movies, concerts, and other media because of the "star element." Whoever or whatever is hot, hip, trendy, or scandalous. The mighty PR machines stir this cauldron of unconscious wish-fulfillment into a bubbling brew and serve up one heaping helping after another until the target audience is stuffed to the gills with the glitz, glamour, and gossip that masquerades as real entertainment. But, like eating fast food, the feeling of fulfillment is short-lived. Because they're not being nourished, they crave more and more. The insatiable cycle continues. And the whole purpose behind entertainment is largely, in many cases completely, lost. This leads to a predominantly empty entertainment experience that leaves the audiences dull,

> The mighty PR machines stir this cauldron of unconscious wish-fulfillment into a bubbling brew and serve up one heaping helping after another until the target audience is stuffed to the gills with the glitz, glamour, and gossip that masquerades as real entertainment.

uninspired and, ultimately, in low attendance. And as the downward spiral continues, the lack of real entertainment (that which provides amusement for the senses *and* sustenance for the spirit) creates the "soul hunger" I talked about earlier — and the whole thing eventually collapses under its own "bloated nothingness," as Emerson would say.

I know this is hard for some to hear. Certain executives, producers and studio heads will reject it out of hand. They'll say that the headache, heartache, and financial cost of having a star in your project are well worth it. It's the best insurance policy money can buy. And there's definitely statistical data to back up this rationale. If you were really trying to make a case, however, there is ample data to back up the theory that truly good material, without a star, is not only much less expensive, but can also have a much higher ROI (return on investment) than traditional commercial fare. Anyone ever see those little non-star driven films, *Star Wars, E.T., The Full Monty,* or *My Big Fat Greek Wedding*? And those were just off the top of my head. Insiders try to write these off as flukes. But I think it's like the atheist who tries to write off miracles, for fear that they might discover there really is a God — and have to radically change their outlook on life, let go of their need to control everything, and surrender to the mystery. What do you think?

Despite all the posturing and rationalizing, when the "sure things" start imploding at the box office, many industry execs secretly admit that things are out of control, that William Goldman's wizened "nobody knows anything" is more of an axiomatic truth than a bitter barb. When their guard is down, many industry professionals will admit that they're sick of the whole thing; how it has compromised the business, the craft, their own desire to create better material; how things have turned so upside down and inside out that their job seems more and more about constantly compensating to balance the inherent imbalances, rather than doing what they signed up for — creating great entertainment.

Even some stars are tired of it — some even consciously work against it. Consider for a moment the significance of a movie star's salary — many of them getting $20 million or more per movie. (And that's just base pay. When all the profits are finally split, some walk away with hundreds of millions for a single film.) I won't pretend I would be above accepting such salaries if they offered. And I can't blame stars for taking them either. But it's a symptom of a dis-ease in the system. A sign of how off-center our priorities have become. (What do teachers make? Healers? Public servants?) But moral issues aside, it's simply unsustainable. And it's creating a business on the verge of a seismic shakeup that could bury many old-schoolers under the rubble of structures that simply weren't built to code (Divine Code or Da Vinci Code?). Bottom-line, the entertainment industry has become too driven by the bottom-line. A majority of the players are so terrified of failure, that they are often unable to take the kind of risk and create the kind of material that could take the business, the art, and the audience to a whole new level.

Even more important than naming the "disease," however, is searching for the cause. Things don't happen in a vacuum. The system exists because we, the people, support it on some level. If the audience didn't worship the stars, the buyers, financiers, and distributors wouldn't. So why do we make idols of these images on our big and little screens, on our concert stages and magazines? I believe it's simple, psychologically speaking: *We're projecting our own unrealized potential onto the stars.* Everything that holds great attraction or repulsion for us represents a part of our shadow. And our shadow is made up of all the things we have decided we are not — positive and negative. Show me a person who has truly embraced their innate power, talent, and genius, and I'll show you someone who isn't enamored by celebrities. They may respect and even be a fan of certain artist's work, but it lacks the obsessive *National Enquirer* mentality.

The most empowering intention we can have… is to be a light, not a star.

Our charge, as enlightened entertainers-in-training, is to not add to this already neurotic pattern. We don't want to create more "followers," we want to inspire people to be leaders. We don't want to create more groupies, we want to motivate people to express their individuality. The most empowering intention we can have — for all concerned — is to be a light, not a star. That may not gel with you right now. You might be saying, "No, actually, I want to be a star, thank you." And I understand. It's very alluring. But if you examine the motivation behind that desire, you might be in for some illuminating facts about yourself. Why do you want to be a star? So people will adore and admire you? So you'll feel confident and powerful? So you can show your junior-high drama teacher that you weren't a loser after all? What is the real motivation? When you discover it, you'll discover the limiting beliefs holding you back from embracing your true greatness.

For example, if you want to be a star because it will give you power and respect, you're harboring a belief that you *lack* power and respect. Based on the work you've already done, you know (at least intellectually) that this is false. All the power, respect, love, and admiration in the Universe are already within you. You'll never have any more power than you have right now. No position or possession can add anything to you. The "true goal" is to realize the light already in you and let it out. The "real work" is to tap into the self-respect, confidence, and fulfillment that is your essential nature — and let it shine.

Your *Star Path* is not about achieving stardom, it's about discovering the areas where you think you're lacking, where you think fortune and fame will fill you up — and filling *yourself* up. Likewise, as an audience member, your charge is to become aware of when you put celebrities on a pedestal — then reclaim and reintegrate those parts of your shadow. As you do this, you'll not only become free, you'll feel empowered, confident, and fulfilled — independent of circumstances. It won't matter how big your part is, how fast your car is, or how many people ask for your autograph. That's freedom. And from that place, you'll be able to follow your truth, create authentically, and no longer be beholden to anyone. That's when true genius emerges. That's when masterpieces are born. Those are the ones who change the course of history for the better.

What They Think of You Is None of Your Business

We're often so invested in other people's opinions about us that we actually believe they matter, that they can affect our life, prevent our good, hold us back, or hurt us. And in the entertainment industry, public opinion seems to run the town. But it's an illusion, smoke and mirrors, like everything else on the silver screen. There's nobody else out there but *you*. Your entire experience is an outpicturing of your inner experience. All the people in your life represent the personifications of your own thoughts and beliefs.

This can be so liberating, but it takes a degree of courage and willingness to get past the mirage of separation. The truth, as I've already stated, is that all the power, substance, intelligence, and law that you need to fulfill your purpose on every level is within you. It's not in someone else. What other people think about you — whether it's an agent, manager, producer, casting director, executive, studio head, critic, fan, family member, or friend — has no impact on you *unless you let it*.

The only opinion you need to be concerned about is *yours*. What *you* think about yourself — and everything else in the business — is all that has power. And as you begin thinking and believing the very best about yourself, about others, about the industry, about life, *that* is what you'll experience. Ultimately, even your own opinion isn't dependable. Finally, the only opinion you can lean on is the Spirit's within you. And what is this Higher Power thinking about you? *"You are my beloved in whom I am well pleased," "All that I have is yours, and it's my good pleasure to give it to you."* Bottom line, the Presence within thinks you're the greatest thing since sliced bread! It loves, accepts, and adores you with all the power and substance of the universe.

You are so loved, cherished, and completely taken care of by Life Itself. You are surrounded by support, abundance, and everything you need to fulfill your heart's desire. All of Life is conspiring for your good. All of life wants the best for you. This is the truth in every encounter, every relationship, every situation, every moment. This is the Truth behind every appearance, every person. That's what Life is thinking about you — the life that is moving through you and everyone else. And to the degree you accept and live by this, your life will reflect it. You'll become an unstoppable force of good, because you'll know there isn't anyone or anything "out there" who can stop you.

Let go of any concern about other people's opinions. Don't waste another moment of your precious life worrying about it. When you're tempted to buy into what someone else is saying about you — or even what you're saying about yourself — just stop, turn within and ask, "What is my Higher Self/God/Great Spirit thinking about me?" Then be quiet and listen until you hear that "still small voice" reaffirm your true value.

Stop Being a Prop in This Divine Production

Shakespeare said, "All the world's a stage, and all the men and women merely players." I believe the Bard was right. Life *is* one big show, crafted for the evolution of our soul — and we're the star of our own play, with its script, themes, obstacles, enemies, and allies. But sometimes we act like extras, mere props in our production. We're standing off stage, waiting for our cue, when we could be singing our song and shining our light!

This can come from low self-worth and a sense of inadequacy. But it also stems from a belief that "some people are meant for greatness, and some aren't." This simply isn't true. The universe doesn't play favorites. "God is no respecter of persons" (Acts 10:34), and "sendeth rain on the just and on the unjust" (Matthew 5:45). As I've already touched upon, nobody has anything more or less than anyone else. In fact, everyone has within them *the fullness* of all there is.

This doesn't mean everyone can be Tom Hanks, Madonna, or Oprah. In fact, *nobody* can be them — because they're already doing it! It also doesn't mean everyone's "greatness" will show up on the cover of *Time* or *People*. Just because a flower blooms without an audience doesn't make it any less magnificent. The key thing, however, is that all the power, substance, and genius in anyone *is in you* — according to your unique purpose. The gift has been given. It's up to you to open it. And that starts with accepting that there is greatness in you; and that you really are the star of your show.

Whatever's Missing Is What You're Not Giving

Once you've accepted this gift, you must give it away. If you had parents who forced you to give some of your birthday or Christmas gifts to charity, this might be a difficult lesson. But the truth remains: *You only keep what you give away.*

> You only keep what you give away.

The reason, as I've stated, is that everything is already in you. We didn't come to earth to *get* anything. We came to awaken our full potential and infuse this dimension with divine light. Whether it's through the flickering light of a movie projector, a performance, or our daily interactions — it's all about giving.

No matter what the situation, you're not there to *get* something (even though every cell in your body might be telling you differently). You don't go to an audition to get a job — although that might be a by-product — you go to share your talents *for the sheer joy of it.* You don't sing a song to get money or adoration; you sing to express the substance of your soul. You don't write a script to start a bidding war; you write because it's who you are. You're a writer, actor, director, singer, producer — whatever — and your job (your *dharma*), whether you're paid or not, is to give your gifts without conditions.

Don't get me wrong, I'm not saying you shouldn't charge, have contracts, and allow for an exchange of energy in whatever form. As one master put it, "Render unto Caesar what is Caesar's." In other words, while we strive to transcend the limitations of this world, we must still live in it as productive citizens — which includes paying our bills and putting food on the table. But that's not *why* you do what you do. This is not a moral concept, it's a universal principle. If you give your gifts to get something, you're programming your inner computer with the belief that you're *lacking.* And the universe, always running the software you load, will reflect it back to you as limited, conflict-ridden experience.

Wherever you find yourself, in whatever situation, be a giver, hold nothing back. Where does that hit you? Do you feel yourself constrict, tighten up? Are you thinking, "No bleeping way! People in this town don't appreciate anything. I'm not giving away my heart and soul, only to have it stomped on! I'm not gonna be a doormat! I'll give as good as I get and nothing more!" If you're feeling resistance to this idea, take a deep breath, and take note. Don't judge it, don't deny it, but don't accept that it's okay and forget it. Whatever negative feelings this brings up are a symptom of an underlying fear. When we're resistant to unconditional giving, it's usually because we've been burned, taken advantage of, or betrayed. We have a belief that there's a limited supply in the universe, that it's "us against them," that we have to protect what we have or we'll end up broke, homeless, wandering Hollywood Boulevard mumbling the pitch to our latest project.

The call to be a giver is especially needed in situations where you experience limitation. If you walk onto a set and feel a lack of love or camaraderie, guess what? *You* are there to bring it, to fill that space with it. Don't look around and say, "Who are all these selfish jerks?" Instead say, "Okay, all the love, power, and abundance of the universe are in me, how can I silently spread it? How can I be a beneficial presence?" If you walk into an audition or meeting and feel like people aren't respecting you or recognizing your talent, don't blame and attack them (or yourself) in your mind. Instead, *give* yourself the qualities that appear to be missing; fill yourself up with the feelings you're trying to get from others. Then let that light spill over and illuminate the room.

When I've practiced this, I've watched the entire energy of a room shift within moments. And in instances when the outer picture remained the same, my inner life changed — and I felt better. Remember, you're an indogenous being. You have the power to generate whatever inner-weather conditions you desire. You're never at the whim of anyone or anything outside of you. But let me offer a word of warning. Don't do this to manipulate or change people or circumstances. If you do, you'll likely exacerbate the problem, increasing your expectations and the frustration that will come when the "others" fail to fulfill your needs. Instead, practice this to open the inner channel of your being and allow the flow of life to pour through. That's all the fulfillment you'll ever need.

Another area to apply this principle is in "giving away" to others what you want to achieve yourself. This is especially important in a business where the inertia of "group-think" tends toward competition and lack mentality. In fact, what I'm about to say will probably sound counterintuitive to some people — even downright crazy! But here it is:

If you want to be a success, you need to help others in this business become successful.

More than just helping them, you need to begin sincerely *wanting* the best for them — particularly your so-called competition. When you walk into that audition, your spiritual practice is to genuinely desire and affirm total success for everyone there — even if it means you don't get the part! Where did that hit you? Did your body relax and go, "Ahhh, yes, that's the truth." Or did it tense up and go, "What are you smoking, man?! I don't want them to get the job, *I* want it! It's mine, mine, mine!" Or maybe you even felt a sense of resignation, like "Oh, well, I guess I can do it. I doubt I'll get the job anyway."

By now you know those responses aren't the truth talking. They're limited beliefs, ghosts of your shadow rattling their chains. And no wonder. We're taught that there isn't enough out there; there's a limited pie and you better get your piece or you'll go hungry; if someone else gets a chair at the banquet table, that's one less chair for you. In truth, there's an abundance of everything, a place for everyone to experience fulfillment. The more we live and give like this, the more it opens up the way for others to do the same.

There's a reason why one master teacher said, "Love your enemies." He wasn't preaching some touchy-feely mumbo jumbo. He was talking about a cosmic law. He knew there was only One of us here. That means that anything you withhold from another you're withholding from yourself. But it also means that anything you give to another, you're giving to yourself. This is the attitude we must take. On a regular basis, as part of our enlightened entertainer practice, we need to bless all the so-called competition, all the so-called enemies, and sincerely want for them all that we could ever want for ourselves.

I know it's a radical departure from "business as usual." Anything that causes real progress usually is. But think of how much energy and resources are wasted through competition, greed, gossip, and scarcity thinking. Imagine how much more we could create, and how much more powerful those creations could be, if we weren't siphoning off our precious energy in these limiting ways of thinking and acting.

Blessing the Competition

To practice this principle, we're going to do a process around the people in the business that you're jealous, envious, or resentful of. What I'd like you to do is make a list of the top ten people you have any of these feelings for — whether you know them personally or not. Then take the one you feel strongest about, and write a page-long prayer or affirmative statement, declaring their highest good, describing (in present-tense) a life where all their needs are met — career, money, relationships, spirituality, health.

As you do this, be aware of how you're feeling. On the left side of your journal, write the affirmation or prayer, and on the right side, write down what comes up for you: "They don't deserve this," "What about me?," "There won't be enough left over," "It's not fair."

Now look at the self-talk that came up. What do you see? Any patterns? Any *habitual* thoughts? Do these thoughts describe your current life experience? In other words, if you've written things like "There won't be enough," do you experience "not enough" in your own life? Even if you have a lot of material things, is your inner experience one of "not having enough"? If you harbor limited thoughts about anyone, that means you believe in lack on some level, and must therefore reap the fruits of that belief.

Go down the list and see if any of the other limited beliefs reflect some condition in your own life. The beliefs that prevent us from giving unconditionally to others are also beliefs holding the good back from ourselves. As we heal these thoughts of withholding about others, we're also healing them about ourselves. As we become a channel of good for others, that very same channel brings our good to us. Cool, huh?

Now take those limited beliefs and craft some affirmations to counter these false ideas. For example, if you wrote "They don't deserve this," the affirmation could be, *"Everyone is a perfect expression of God/The Universe, therefore all of the good there is is within them now. They deserve it. They have it. They are it."* Or if you wrote, "There won't be enough left over," you might affirm, *"There is unlimited, inexhaustible abundance at every point in the Universe. Therefore it must be right where I am and right where (their name) is. The more we express and give away, the more we have!"*

Don't Make a Mountain Out of a Mogul

It's important to recognize that whatever came up for you in the written exercise was about *you*, not the person you were writing about. In other words, if you felt like they didn't deserve the good life, on some level you don't believe *you* deserve it (perhaps to a lesser extent after the exercise). If you perceived them as the "bad guy," there's a part of yourself you are (or were) in conflict with. All of life is a mirror, reflecting back to us who *we* are, not who *they* are. There's nobody out there but us — fragmented and projected onto the screen of our experience. Whatever we feel about someone else, we are really feeling about a corresponding, and disowned, part of ourselves.

> There's nobody out there but us — fragmented and projected onto the screen of our experience.

When you are born, you start with a pile of everything (this is an oversimplification if you believe in karma, but it still makes the point). As you grow, and are impacted by the values and beliefs of family and society, you form judgments about what is good and bad, and separate this pile of everything into *"I am"* and *"I am not."* The *"I am"* pile becomes your ego, the dominant paradigm through which you experience life, while the *"I am not"* pile becomes your shadow, and is filled with the so-called negative *and* positive qualities you have disowned. But it's still a part of you. And because energy is never destroyed, but takes on different forms, you project these shadow-qualities onto other people — people that "repel" *and* "attract" you. When you feel a strong charge on something or someone, whether disgust or envy, obsessive love or hate, idolization or demonization — you're just seeing one of those disowned parts of yourself.

This is what happens in a good story at an archetypal level. The characters orbiting the protagonist are aspects of her. As they push and pull in different ways, they force her to connect with her shadow, discover latent aspects of herself, and reintegrate them in order to fulfill her mission. These "shadow characters" populate our own creative works as we try to contact, understand, and reconcile their energies. This is a useful diagnostic and development tool for actors, writers, and all people involved in any storytelling process. When done consciously, our creative endeavors help integrate our shadow. I believe that's why we (and the global audience) are drawn to certain films, TV shows, and characters. They represent, in short form, our soul's process of becoming whole and, when done right, can facilitate it.

So when you see an artist or professional and admire (or envy) their talent, beauty, and success, this is not a sign of neurosis, it's your "Call to Adventure," an opportunity to reclaim these lost parts of yourself, and become whole (as it is for an audience member when they see their own light reflected in the stars of stage and screen). In truth, *you* are the talented, beautiful, successful individual; you just haven't realized or accepted it. You couldn't *see* it in someone else if it wasn't already in you. The pain you feel is caused by your resistance, based on a limited self-concept, to the power trying to flow through you. Likewise, when you're bothered or repelled by someone — that's *you* too. Not in the absolute sense, but it is part of your shadow. Not to worry though. A quality that irritates you in someone is actually a blessing in disguise, a sheep in wolf's clothing.

For example, if you're put off by "controlling people," there's a controlling part of you that has been disowned. Why have you disowned it? Because on some level, you've judged it as bad, and determined that you would be unworthy if you possessed such a trait. And why would you want to reintegrate it? Because these so-called negative qualities contain a positive charge that is being drained from you instead of adding to your creative/spiritual wattage. To use the analogy of a good story again, these shadow characters are part of your inner cast that you (the hero/protagonist) must confront and reconcile in order to actualize your full potential and fulfill your destiny.

For example, let's say you hate some studio head or producer because you think he's power-hungry. It doesn't matter if you're right in your human assessment. What's important is that *you* feel that way about him — which means there is a power-hungry character lurking inside of you. Take a breath. I know that's a hard one to swallow. But it's a psychological fact. If it wasn't in you, it wouldn't "push your buttons." There would be no vibratory match. But, remember, this means there's a positive charge seeking to express in you. And what might be a positive aspect of this power-hungry energy? It could be an authentic sense of power that you disowned out of low self-esteem (or because a family member acted out a destructive version of it).

Another example could be the quality of "greed," or its positive side, "wealth." Many artists in show business embrace "show," but are repelled by the "business." There is judgment on "bottom-line thinking," and most business people are viewed as money-hungry, uncreative — they just don't "get it." In many cases, these artists grew up with a business-minded or pragmatic parent who suggested that they get a "real job" and warned them that most artists live below the poverty level. Because of this, some artists have developed a negative association with "business" and "making money," and rejected that part of themselves — often unconsciously. And what has been the result? Many artists living a self-fulfilled prophecy by "living below the poverty level," or unable to manage the money they make. It doesn't have to be this way. There's no law in the Universe that says "creative types" have to be broke and bad at managing their affairs.

Once you pay attention to these so-called negative qualities, honor them, and give their positive aspect a voice, they no longer need to act like monsters, throwing temper tantrums and projecting themselves onto others to get your attention. Then you're not only free from judgment against these types of people, you're free from the unconscious buttons they once pushed. You are empowered and made whole in the process. What's more, the people who pushed your buttons will often stop presenting those negative qualities around you — they'll literally change as a result of *you* changing.

Take a moment and imagine that you possess the same qualities that repel you in others. Where does that hit you? It's like the moment in *Star Wars* when Darth Vader tells Luke he's his father, and Luke realizes he's the offspring of the most evil man in the Universe. Remember his reaction? He didn't take it too well. He wasn't ready to embrace his Dark Side. You see this moment in movies all the time, where the protagonist and antagonist face off, and the antagonist says "You're just like me." This is an archetypal/mythical moment. It has become a cliché, but that's because it's based on truth. Our worst enemy *is* within. As it states in ancient scripture, "The enemy is within your own household."

So how can we work with this inner cast of characters to reintegrate them into our heroic self, receive their benefit, and gain greater facility with them in our creative endeavors? First we must admit these qualities are in us. Otherwise we'll remain in resistance to them — which further fuels their force in our life. It's not the *truth* about us, but it may be a *fact*. Truth is eternal, facts can be changed. Once we acknowledge we have a little Darth Vader in us, we can begin a conversation with him. We can ask what he's trying to tell us about ourselves, and what his positive charge will be when he's reintegrated into our life and work. We can complete our character arc, like Luke, and finally unmask the Dark Lord to see that underneath he's not such a bad guy after all.

Do you believe the Force is with you? Then let's jump into a little Jedi training!

Shadow Integration Meditation #1

Find a comfortable place to sit upright, eyes closed. Take a few deep breaths and allow your body to let go, your mind to become still. You might be aware of various points of tension or clusters of thoughts swirling around. Just watch it all like clouds floating before your mind's eye. You're not the clouds, you're the clear sky, the silent witness to the ever-changing content of your consciousness. As you witness instead of engaging, you enter a gap. This is the stillpoint in the midst of the storm of creation.

See yourself stepping into a beautiful glass elevator. Inside, there is a button marked "Sanctuary." Press it. As the elevator ascends, you feel all the weight of the world falling away, your awareness expanding. The world disappears below, as you rise higher, up through the clouds. You feel weightless, free, the light around you growing brighter and brighter. The elevator comes to a gentle stop, the doors open, and spread out before you is a beautiful, lush garden with a path. You step out of the elevator and follow the path into a quiet, tranquil meadow beside a bubbling brook. This is your sanctuary. Allow it to materialize in whatever way brings you the greatest sense of peace and security.

To your left, you notice another path. Follow it through the dense foliage, until you come to a clearing. A hundred feet away is the house where your *negative shadow characters* live. Notice how it looks. Is it big, small, rundown? Call out to the house, inviting one of the qualities you wrote down to come visit with you in the garden. For example, you might invite *Greed* out. Notice what it looks like, how it makes you feel. As Debbie Ford suggests in her classic book, *The Dark Side of the Light Chasers*, ask its name or assign it one, *Greedy Gary, Bitchy Barbara, Selfish Sam*. Then ask these questions:

- How do you feel?

- Why are you a part of me?

- Why am I projecting you on so-and-so (use a real person's name here)?

- What gift do you have to offer, in both my life and work?

- What is your positive aspect?

- What purpose have you served in my life so far?

- How can you serve me now, in both my life and work?

Promise to honor them in you from now on, so they don't need to act up or project onto others to get your attention. Thank them for their time and send them on their way.

(Do this for as many as you desire. Working with three is usually a good number.)

Walk inside the house where they live. Be aware of the characters there; how they look, act, feel, smell, and how they make you feel. Walk from room to room. How do they live? What are they doing? Hang out with them, see which ones attract you and engage them in conversation. (You can do these exercises with characters you're writing about, singing about, directing, or performing, to discover what part of you they represent, and what their core positive charge is, giving them more depth and resonance.)

Bid them farewell. Head back down the path to the elevator, get inside, and press the "return" button. As the elevator descends back to earth, you feel the weight of your body returning, but it feels lighter, less burdened. The elevator stops, the doors open, and you open your eyes, returning to the room. Journal any insights or questions that arose.

Affirmation Integration Exercise #1

Take the positive quality of each of these negative shadow characters, and create your own affirmation, declaring that you now fully own, embody, and express this quality in an effective and appropriate way in your life. If you feel sufficiently energized, you may proceed with part two of this process. Otherwise, take a break. Go for a walk. Take a bath. Get a good night's sleep. Then return to the second half refreshed.

Shadow Integration Meditation #2

As before, get into a meditative posture, and make the journey into your inner sanctuary. (Follow the directions above, or use your own process.) Once you arrive, follow the path beside the bubbling brook, until you notice another path diverging from the first. Follow it through the dense foliage, until you come to a clearing.

A hundred feet away is the house where your *positive shadow characters* live. Notice how it looks. Is it big, small, rundown? How is it different from your negative characters" house? Call out, inviting one of the qualities you wrote down to visit you. For example, let's say *Wealth* comes out. Notice what it looks like, how it make you feel. Ask its name or assign one. *Wealthy Wendy, Successful Steve.* Then ask the following questions:

- How do you feel?

- Why are you a part of me?

- Why am I projecting you on so-and-so?

- What gift do you have to offer, in my life and work?

- What purpose have you served in my life so far?

- How can you serve me now, in my life and work?

- Why don't you show up in my life (or work) very often or at all?

- What are you teaching me by showing up in others?

- What must I release, embrace, or do to reintegrate/manifest you in my life/work?

- If I follow this advice, will you become a conscious part of my life?

- If not, what else must I do or change to allow you to fully express through me?

Promise to honor them in you from now on so they don't need to project onto others to get your attention. Thank them for their time and send them on their way.

(You can do this for up to three qualities, depending on your time or willingness.)

Walk inside the house where they live. Be aware of the characters there, how they look, act, feel, smell, and how they make you feel.

Walk from room to room. How do they live? What are they doing? (You may notice some of them using talents you have disowned, pushed away, or aren't even conscious of. Pay particular attention to this.) Hang out with them, see which ones attract you and engage them in conversation.

Bid them farewell, head back down the path to the elevator, get inside, and press the "return" button. As the elevator descends back to earth, you feel the weight of your body returning, but it still feels lighter, less burdened. The elevator stops, the doors open, and you open your eyes, returning to the room. Journal any insights or issues that arose.

Affirmation Integration Exercise #2

Take each of these positive shadow characters and create affirmation, declaring that you now fully own, embody, and express these qualities in an effective way in your life. Then to wrap up, do a final check-in with yourself. What came up for you? What surprised you? Scared you? How do you feel now? Journal about any residual thoughts or feelings.

You Are the Only One You Need to Convince

This could also be titled, "You only prove yourself when you have nothing left to prove." We waste so much energy defending our seeming shortcomings, trying to convince others in this business (and our life) of our worth. And here's the rub. No matter how hard you try to change someone's opinion about you, you'll never succeed — until you change your opinion about yourself. Even if you do manage, by

> You only prove yourself when you have nothing left to prove.

sheer force, to change their mind, it won't help. Because you'll still feel the same about yourself and end up interpreting everything they do through that filter — ultimately causing them to think badly of you again! When you focus instead on improving your own self-opinion, you'll find that most people mirror it back. But even if they don't, it won't affect you any more.

For many years, I struggled with a need to convince my father that I was worthy and that my ambitions as an actor-writer were valid. But despite my deep desire and approval-seeking tactics, the Holy Grail of fatherly acceptance eluded me. He wasn't overtly abusive, he just regularly warned me of the statistics — that most artists live below the poverty level, and that I "needed something to fall back on." Whenever I talked about my creative endeavors, he would encourage me to "get a real job." My artist heart and his business mind were like two ships passing in the dark night of my soul. I thought the S&P 500 was a car race, and he thought Pearl Jam was something you put on toast.

Then at some point, around the time my own son was born, I began having greater insight into who dad was and why he thought the way he did. Instead of resentment, compassion emerged in me. Instead of wanting to get something from him, I realized I had never *given* him much. So I reversed the flow. I began embracing him and his ways — at least in my heart and mind. And as I did that, I felt better about myself. As I felt better about myself, I became more interested in the world of business and finances, and put myself through a three-year crash course. I let go of the resistance and reintegrated that part of myself — my shadow — that he represented. I recognized that the fears and limited thinking he was projecting on me were beliefs I secretly harbored. He was mirroring my blind spots. He wasn't my enemy after all — he was my teacher. What a revelation!

As I healed these fragmented parts of myself, I felt much more empowered and began to generate more success. And somewhere along the line, I realized I wasn't looking for his approval any more. I was in touch with "the father within" and was filling myself up. From this place, I could love and appreciate him without conditions. Before long, he was calling me, asking how my work was going, acknowledging my success, and expressing real acceptance. Gone were the fear-based conversations. Gone were his suggestions that I "get a real job" or have something to "fall back on." In fact, he began sharing his own story ideas and talking about entertainment-related projects we could partner on. I knew things had really turned a corner when I found myself sitting in my dad's office, creating a TV show with him! That's something I never could have imagined several years before.

Acts of Courage: "Annihilate the Competition!"

No, I'm not suggesting you go out and destroy the other players, I'm talking about annihilating the *belief* and *behavior* of competition. The first step to doing that is in *supporting* your seeming opponent. Pick someone you're jealous of, harbor resentment towards, or consider your competition — and send them an anonymous gift. Something that celebrates their greatness — a symbol of support. It could be a card, flowers, or cash! If you're really brave, choose more than one person. Journal about how you feel before, during, and after. Then pay attention for any shifts or "miracles" that occur as a result.

Check-In

How are you feeling? If you've been doing the work, you may be experiencing a sense of bliss or inner chaos. "Afterglow" or "Aftergrow," as Dr. Michael Beckwith calls it. If your "stuff" is up, it's totally normal, acceptable — and temporary.

If you're in overwhelm, take a day off. Go to the beach, the mountains, a movie. Nurture yourself in some meaningful way. But don't distract or anesthetize yourself from what's coming to the surface. You've worked hard to stir things up. Now, more than ever, you need to be mindful so the unconscious material can be processed instead of repressed.

The universe tends toward greater and greater complexity. It does this by building to a point of chaos, breaking down, then reorganizing at a higher level. If you just distract or numb yourself with drugs, alcohol, sex, mindless media, or whatever your fix of choice is, you will thwart this growth process and have to let the pressure build up all over again.

Here are some questions you can ask to process this chapter:

1. How do I feel about the entertainment industry and its greater possibilities? Do I feel more inspired/empowered than before I started this? Why? Why not?

2. How do I feel about my place and purpose in show business? Do I feel more inspired/empowered than before I started this? Why? Why not?

3. What inner and outer changes must I make in order to achieve my purpose in this business? Am I willing? If so, why? If not, why not?

4. Is there something I know I'm being called to do, but am afraid to do it? Why?

No, you're not going crazy. Those are the same questions again! Notice any difference in your answers? Are they deeper, more revealing? There are no wrong answers here. It's about becoming conscious and developing a practice, which is where we're going next.

SIX ~

Developing a Practice

"Practice means to perform, over and over again
in the face of all obstacles, some act of vision, of
faith, of desire. Practice is a means of inviting the
perfection desired."
— Martha Graham

Go Within, or You'll Go Without

By now, you know that meditation, prayer, affirmations, and other inner exercises are vital to developing the enlightened entertainer consciousness (or an enlightened anything). What I want to impress upon you, if I haven't already, is that your "inner work" is as important — if not more so — than any other work you do. Not just for your creative and show-business success, but for the fulfillment of your life and purpose.

Cultivating an intimate relationship with your inner life is the greatest gift you can give yourself, the entertainment community, the global audience, and everyone else on the planet. Within you all the power and substance of life resides. In the stillness at the center of your being is the fountain of pure genius, the source of every masterpiece, the answer to every question, the solution to every problem, and the fulfillment of every dream. But you must daily practice the art of making inner contact in order to actualize this truth.

All of Life Is a Rorschach Test

I've touched upon this concept. But I'd like to expand a bit more. What is a Rorschach test? A series of ink blots that look like butterflies, landscapes, visions of heaven and hell, your dominating mother, your scowling father. I remember taking this test as a kid, sure that the "right answers" were on the back of each card. I struggled to figure out what they were, looking at the therapist's face to determine if I was "hot" or "cold," trying to coax the answers out of her. Of course, there were no "right" answers. What we see in the cards is merely a description of what's inside *us* — the content of our own consciousness.

Life (and entertainment) is much the same. It's one big Rorschach test. What we see is based not so much on the pictures outside, but the pictures *inside*. Nothing has any inherent meaning, except the one we give it. The meaning we give something determines our experience. What we experience feeds our beliefs and perceptions, which further fuel our meaning, which we project back onto the screen of experience, in a continuous loop.

> The meaning we give something determines our experience.

For many of us, this feedback loop plays itself out with monotonous regularity through our lives. We curse our fate, blame our parents, the government, studio heads, script readers, producers, casting directors, executives — all those bad inkblots doing us wrong! But it's just a trick of perception. We're not seeing what life is, we're seeing what *we are*.

The Great Therapist in the sky is flipping up the giant inkblot cards and we're either seeing fields of flowers and cotton-candy clouds or dancing demons and fire-breathing dragons. Then we act as if it's real, perpetuating our problems until we die or suffer a fate worse than death (our show is canceled, our record flops, our agent drops us, our manager embezzles our money, we become part of the over-thirty club!), and the pain causes us to finally wake up. Life becomes a screen upon which we project our inner script, acted out by our inner characters — the entire movie playing out in our minds.

To create the life and career you want, you must become a co-creator with your inner stories so you don't unconsciously project and perpetuate them. This requires a regular spiritual practice to remain conscious. And part of that includes recognizing the meanings you've assigned these "inkblots" called life experience. You must ask yourself if your reactions to people and circumstances are based on what really exists or on your interpretation of events. This will require a major paradigm shift. As you question everything you experience in the entertainment industry and your role in it, you'll begin to realize how much you're projecting your fears, doubts, resentments, and limited beliefs. And as you see that it's your own inner script being played out, you'll be empowered to rewrite it according to a higher vision.

Uncovering the "Inner Author's" Intent

As you develop a spiritual practice to recognize and rewrite your inner scripts (and ultimately transcend them), you must make contact with The Great Author within to discover the true intention of your Life Story and avoid becoming hypnotized by the daily drama of your ego's inner movie. Communicating with this Inner Author isn't always easy. But even when you're not feeling completely connected, you can still discover what the Author's intent is by investigating the individual "scenes" of your life.

Just as every part of a hologram contains the whole image, every "scene" of your life contains the Big Picture of your life's premise and purpose. And every "action" you take illuminates your core beliefs or running theme. This doesn't mean that these scenes and actions necessarily illustrate your highest potential or the truth of your being, but they do illuminate what you "believe" to be true. And underneath this drama are the insights you need to achieve the primary objective in this hero's journey called your life story. It takes a degree of investigation, however, to uncover these clues.

To understand this practice, we can look at the process of deconstructing a play for production (whether a screenplay, teleplay, or stage play). If you're an actor or director, when you get a script you break it down to understand the characters' deeper motivations, emotional currents, and themes of their lives so you can more fully integrate and illustrate them. Sometimes the core issues, themes, and ideas embodied in a character are obvious. Other times you have to be a Dramatic Detective. You have to look closer, pay attention to the words the characters use, the way they talk, the way they move, the kinds of things they own, the kind of job they work at, until a bigger picture of who they are and what motivates them emerges. You may have the luxury of talking directly with the author and getting some of her insights. But some authors don't even know why their characters do what they do — or why they even wrote the story in the first place!

In this divine play called your life and career, you can investigate the character you're playing in much the same way. By looking at isolated areas of your life and how you do things, you can have insights into the deeper issues and beliefs moving you forward, keeping you stuck, or pulling you backwards. One of the biggest revelations you'll have is that "*how you do anything is how you do everything.*" For instance, if you're the kind of person who waits until the 11th hour to finish the big project, meet a writing deadline, or memorize your script — that gives you a clue to how you're living your *whole life.*

Because you're part of a holistic system, the core issues, patterns, and beliefs creating one event or behavior also drive the rest of your life to some extent. If you can't figure out why you aren't booking those auditions or selling those scripts, you could look at a less charged area of your life for a clue. You may feel in the dark as to why things aren't working, but by applying the principle that "how you do anything is how you do everything," you'll be able to uncover clues that can lead to a healing.

For example, you may need to look at your relationships to figure out why your production company is failing, or look at how you manage money to understand why you're not realizing your creative potential. By doing this, you begin to see that everything is connected, and the whole is contained in every part — like the hologram. You start appreciating all areas of your life, not just one or two. You see that making a change or having a healing in one area can greatly impact other areas as well. And as this awareness really takes hold in your heart, your whole life becomes your work of art.

Picking Up Your Cues: Intuition

Most people have some idea what intuition is, and have had some experience following it — or not following it — and reaping the consequences. The notion is that when you follow your intuition, you're guided to do and say the right things, in the right place, at the right time. Right? But what is this "inner guidance" really? And why do you hear it only sometimes? Some have described it as the "still small voice" of Spirit. Others view it as heavenly angels winging to your defense, causing you to hit the brakes and avoid a collision — or prompting you to audition for a part you don't think you're right for, only to have it become a career-maker. Still others believe it's the "hand of God" that intervenes and prevents something bad — or gives you the seven-figure spec script idea.

I think it's all that and more. Intuition — wherever we think it comes from — is always guiding us if we'll pay attention to it. And I believe the "It" is the divine pattern of our life speaking to us. It's like the Oak Tree speaking to the Acorn, telling it how to grow into its Oak Self. There is a majestic being in you — a genius, master artist, entertainment leader, and healer — just waiting to emerge. And this pattern of perfection has everything encoded within it: the who, what, why, and how of your existence. This isn't a predetermined fate; it's a pattern of potential, just as the oak is potential in the acorn. It's like having some Sacred Script Girl giving you cues from your Divine Script. If you follow it, you'll not only fulfill your Life Play — you'll play the role of a lifetime.

As you become adept at listening to these inner cues — this "script of your soul" — there will come a time when you're initiated into a higher way of living, when your "character" is called to evolve in order for the "play" to progress forward. This can be a difficult transition. It's tempting to try and deny it, hoping you can avoid this part of your "character arc." But you can't. Not permanently. And as long as you resist it, your "life story" will cease to unfold to the next act. It'll become a cycle of repetitive beats, the same scene happening over and over, just with different set dressing, the same players entering and exiting, just with different costumes. Your life will become a broken record, forever playing the same old song. You'll be living your own *Groundhog Day*.

And what is this *next level* that a regular practice can take you to? It's nothing less than full reliance on your Spirit, the Muse, the Inner Author. In biblical terms, it's called living by "every word that proceedeth out of the mouth of God." We've been trained to take our cues from the external world, to be "outer-directed" instead of "inner-directed." We've been taught to listen to the experts and gurus, to study the charts, the analyses, diagnoses, prognoses — then use all that external data to make our daily choices. Studio execs often do this when they try to determine what movies, music, and other media to produce. The results are often old ideas rehashed, refried, and regurgitated into something that barely resembles anything edible, budgets and star salaries spiraling out of control, pros living in fear of getting a pink slip, and crushing pressure on the bottom line.

It's a system that isn't sustainable. Nothing that depends on the outer world is. It's like a branch trying to survive cut off from the tree. "He that sows to the flesh shall of the flesh reap corruption, but he that sows to the Spirit shall reap *life* everlasting." Replace the word "life" with "creativity," "wealth," "peace," or any positive quality and you'll get a clearer picture of the promise this principle holds. Another powerful ancient statement is: "Be ye not conformed to the world, but be ye transformed by the renewing of your mind." Can you picture an entertainment industry filled with people living a spiritual practice like this? We'd be turning out Shakespeares, Da Vincis, Fellinis, Spielbergs, Pacinos, Streeps, Oprahs, and Beatles on a regular basis. We'd experience another Renaissance. Not just once. But over and over. And lest you think this is just fantasy, take a cue from another dreamer and "Imagine" it's possible, and the way will be shown.

You are here to reveal something that has never happened before, because *you* have never happened before. You are a trailblazer, a leader — not a follower. To actualize this, you must live by "insight" more than "eyesight." When you develop a daily practice — a way of life — that allows you to follow the "inner cues" and act on them, you are guided by the divine script, you evolve into a character of literary stature, and your Life Story becomes a masterpiece to be read, listened to, watched, and used as a source of inspiration long after the final curtain falls.

The Divine Actor: Playing the Part

Most people believe they're merely a human being having an occasional spiritual experience. That's like an actor believing he's the role he's playing — occasionally having the experience of being an actor.

Sounds insane, but then so does much of what we believe as humans (at least, from your Spirit's point of view. From the ego's perspective, everything in this book sounds insane!). The truth is you're a divine hyphenate, the Cosmic Writer-Actor-Director playing this human part, co-creating this play called human experi-

> The truth is you're a divine hyphenate, the Cosmic Writer-Actor-Director playing this human part, co-creating this play called human experience.

ence. You can fully invest in it, fill your role out completely, but when you walk off stage, you'll realize it was all just a "play of consciousness." Nothing was ultimately lost or gained — except for a greater awareness of who you are.

This is an important realization for the practice of an enlightened entertainer — especially if you plan on being an evolutionary force in the industry and on the planet. As long as you think you're merely a human here to do a bunch of stuff, you'll only be rearranging what's already been done — just pushing old junk into different shaped piles and calling it something fresh and original (sound familiar?). And you'll be doing it all from a consciousness of separation, fear, and impotence — because on some level you'll believe that someone or something out there has power over you. How creative does that make you feel? How courageous, bold, and visionary can you be from that state of mind?

When you realize you're the Cosmic Co-Creator of the Greatest Show on Earth, the rules change in your favor. From this perspective you know you're connected with everyone and everything; that the spirit within you *is you* and is the source of all creation; and that no person, place, or thing can have any power over you — unless you grant it. From the perspective of being the co-creator and divine actor, you're free, unencumbered, and guided to express through grace and inspiration, not struggle and desperation; you're an instrument of something new, something the world has never seen before, something that adds value to everyone it touches. It's like waking up in your dream (lucid dreaming), where you realize the "real you" is not of this world, and that the whole experience is being created in your mind. From that awareness, you lose all fear and can achieve anything you can conceive. When you realize you are the divine actor/co-creator of this play called life, your whole world becomes increasingly like a "waking dream."

Play the Part Until You Get the Part

Once you realize you're just a character in this divine drama, you need to start *playing your part* — like your whole life depends on it. Everything you need to master your craft, become a success, and fulfill your purpose in this business is within you. I think we've established that idea fairly well. If there's any part of you waiting for something to change "out there," you're being untrue to yourself. What's worse, you're setting the law of creation in motion with the affirmation "I'm not there yet." The universe, only being able to say "yes," reflects more of that energy back to you. And you find yourself always waiting to get somewhere, to get something, to become someone.

Your challenge is to begin acting like you already have what you seek, like you already are what you wish to become. If your desire is to be a successful filmmaker, creating powerful projects that reach millions — then you must begin thinking, feeling, and acting like that character *now*. I'm not telling you to go out and buy a new Mercedes and start telling everyone at parties that you're an A-list writer or director. Instead, ponder the question, "What would I be thinking, feeling, and doing if I was the person I want to be?" Then find ways to begin stepping out on that vision, even if only symbolically.

For example, if you were a million-dollar writer, you probably wouldn't be worrying about money (although it's all relative, since many people spend more than they make no matter how much they earn — and worry in equal measure — making them broke at a higher level). Look at your thoughts and the words you speak, and notice how often they express lack. "I can't afford that," "I don't have enough," "I'm broke." Maybe it shows up in your actions, where you don't leave a good tip, don't give to charity, withhold supportive words from a fellow artist, or generally horde your goodies (money, love, creativity, wisdom). These are not the thoughts and actions of a wealthy writer (or a wealthy anything). *"I wouldn't be that way if I was more successful,"* you might say. But it doesn't work that way. Thought and action precede form.

If you're not expressing at the level you desire, take a look at how you talk and act as an artist or entertainment professional. How do you speak about your projects, the business, and other colleagues? Look at your conversations around these topics? Do they sound like the words of a successful person? Or are your conversations filled with complaints, self-criticism, doubt, and fear? You can always tell when a person isn't on purpose, when they're not "playing their part," because they constantly complain about what's wrong, what they want, what they don't have, and all the reasons why things can't get better.

In contrast, someone who *is* living their vision is usually too inspired and creative to waste much time or energy on such unproductive nonsense. They're too busy thinking about, talking about, and work-ing on their art, craft, or business — and they're psyched about it. There's a high-energy, possibility-thinking quality to them that tends to attract more opportunity and success. Sure, they have bad days. But they don't wallow in them. Their problems are opportunities for greater self-actualization and creative expression. They don't just see the cup half-full, they see it completely full — half air, half water!

I'm not saying you should walk around preaching like Pollyanna. I'm not saying you can't be authentic in all your humanness. I'm not even saying you can't have a deep, dark well of pain from which you quench your artistic thirst. But ask yourself, "Are my thoughts, words, and actions generally those of an inspired artist or entertainment profes-sional?" If they're not, that's a clue to your struggles. It's not a reason to beat yourself up, just a piece of the puzzle; a chance to see you're not a victim of anything, but are, in fact, creating your experience. And now that you see *how* you're creating it, you have the power to change it. Imagine that every word you speak is a seed of a future experience. Then ask yourself before — and during — your conversation, "Do I want this to become my next experience?" If the answer is no, it's time for a little dialogue polish!

A crucial part of "playing the part" is obviously the actions you take. This doesn't mean you should waltz into Spielberg's office and demand a meeting because you're playing the part of an A-list filmmaker — although I'm not telling you *not* to try outlandish things. Spielberg is a perfect example of this principle. His beginnings are legend now. When he first started out, he snuck onto the Universal lot, found an empty office, put his name on the door, and began hanging out like he owned the place. He was "playing the part" in a big way. And he's done pretty well since. What I'm suggesting doesn't require such chutzpah. It's more about the little things you do — or don't do — although they may not feel like little things if you're stuck in resistance, denial, or doubt.

For example, if you call yourself a singer, and you're not out there singing your heart out as often as humanly possible — because you're waiting for your big break — you're not a singer. You're a "*person waiting to be a singer.*" And that is where you will likely remain for a long time. The same is true of actors. I've met many actors who spend a lot of time "thinking about acting," "talking about acting," and "complaining about the business of acting," but not much time actually *acting*. I can't help but wonder if they really like to act at all.

Some of the worst offenders are writers. I've met so many "writers" who don't write. Or they've written the first 25 pages of a few different scripts, but never finished one. Or they've written one script they've been peddling for ten years! Can you imagine Jack Nicholson not acting, Ron Bass not writing, Spielberg not making movies, Madonna not singing? It's in their blood and bones. It's who they are. It's something they would find a way to do even if they weren't paid. If you really love something and want to succeed — do it every chance you get. Be like a child who's into something. They spend every spare minute — and every spare dime — indulging in their passion.

So look at your actions. Are they the actions of a successful writer, actor, director — whatever? Are they the actions of someone living their passion and purpose, or someone waiting for something to change, waiting for someone to "discover them"? If you're a writer, write! Every day if possible. But at least several days a week — like any professional. If you're an actor, act! When I was studying to be an actor, I didn't just go to class a couple times a week and wait for auditions, I rehearsed and worked on scenes every single day — many hours a day — like an athlete training for the Olympics. And when the auditions came, I was able to bring something unique — and get a good deal of work. It couldn't have happened any other way in my mind. I was an actor. I lived and breathed it. I inhabited the reality of it inside. That's what you must work toward as well.

Spend the next week paying close attention to your thoughts, words, and actions (especially those on a loop in your head or conversations). Make note of them. Write them down. Ask yourself if this is the way a successful "you" would be. Then adjust until your thoughts, words, and actions are aligned with your vision. If you play the part — really invest in it — you'll get the part! Through this daily practice you are literally building the inner structure of your dreams. If you build it, they will come. As that invisible reality becomes more real to you than anything, it will show up. As the mystical axiom says, "When you believe more in what you don't see than what you do see, what you do see you won't see and what you don't see, you will." Say that five times fast!

> "When you believe more in what you don't see than what you do see, what you do see you won't see and what you don't see, you will."

Failing Forward

Part of going for it, really "playing your part," includes being willing to make mistakes, even fall on your face. Any great comedian knows they have to get through a lot of bad jokes to find the good ones. The best actors tend to take the most risks. Most good writers have to carve their words into a forest of wood before they find any pages worth keeping. I remember one writer telling me his ratio was about 15 to 1. For every fifteen pages he wrote, he only kept one. That's a lot of "failing." My favorite is Thomas Edison, who reportedly tried about 10,000 times to create the electric light bulb before hitting upon the right way. How many of us are willing to fail ten thousand times without giving up?

The good news is that if your failures are in the process of moving toward your vision, they're propelling you forward. It's like the act of walking. Every time you take a step, you're actually falling forward. When you were a child and hadn't yet developed this skill, you actually fell on the ground. Eventually, you mastered your ability to balance (at least in your more sober moments) and learned to walk, then run. But even now, every time you take a step toward something, you're "falling forward." And this will be so for the rest of your walking days. The only thing is you'll (hopefully) catch yourself each time. The key is that you must be willing to "fall" in order to move forward. If you're not "playing your part" or moving fully in the direction of your dreams because you're afraid of falling, you're not moving forward at all. And if you're not moving forward, you're actually moving backwards — because life is forever progressing.

As a writer, I love the saying, "Don't get it right, just get it written." This is a good practice for whatever area you work in. Don't worry about getting it right, just go for it. Take risks. Be willing to fail, to make mistakes. Then embrace the "falls" that inevitably come, dust yourself off, and ask how it's making you a little stronger, able to stand a little taller, and walk a little farther than you otherwise ever would.

Infinite Patience Equals Instant Results

In the West, we tend to be impatient people. And in an industry that always seems to be in a race against time, our impatience is often magnified. The problem is that impatience is a strong force of resistance. When you're impatient, you're basically saying you don't have what you want, that your life isn't okay, that something is missing and you don't entirely trust that it will show up. This is an affirmation of limitation. And the universe, always obeying what you're affirming, will act upon that belief and multiply it in your experience. The result: you'll be more anxious, experience more delays and obstacles, and if you manage to force things into manifestation you'll never feel satisfied or fulfilled — because on some level you'll be waiting for the bottom to fall out.

When you practice cultivating a consciousness of "infinite patience," however, you'll begin to feel peaceful and content *now* — despite outer appearances. You'll start appreciating what you *do* have, what you *are* doing, who you *are* being. You'll relax and begin to trust life. Heck, you'll even be happy — and for no particular reason at all! Joy will bubble up within you and you'll find yourself looking around wondering what "good thing" happened that caused it — and discover that nothing "out there" is causing it at all. The joy is just here. What a novel concept. "You mean I can be joyful, peaceful, and content regardless of what's going on in my life, or what's on my resume?"

YES!

That's your true nature. And here's the kicker. Because all the struggling to "make something happen" is actually the resistance you have against the good trying to move through you, when you let go and rest in patience, you become an open channel for the Infinite Good to flow out of. When you "take your bloated nothingness out of the path of the divine circuits," the abundance, creativity, and fulfillment that is expressing everywhere all the time, gets to express as you! It's like trying to think of a word, straining to grab it, then finally surrendering with, "Oh, I'll remember it later" — and it immediately shows up. The fulfillment of your desires are the same. When you're willing to proceed patiently, without any attachment to outcome, they show up — often right on time!

Don't Just Do Something, Sit There: A Meditation

This is a powerful process I've used many times. We've been hypnotized by a belief that nothing happens unless we do it. This is especially true in the Western world, where the message is "do more, do better, do faster, or do without!" I'm not saying you shouldn't do things. Obviously I had to do something to write this book. It takes a lot of people doing a lot of things to keep the entertainment industry pumping out products. But often we're doing from a sense of fear and limitation. We're a ball of reactions, running around trying to prevent bad stuff and trying to get all the good stuff that will make us complete.

This sets the law of creation in motion to multiply our fears and limitations, making us hamsters on a treadmill, going round and round until we drop. But when we stop, get still, and mind-fast from the mind-chatter, we create inner weather conditions more conducive to the unfolding of our seed of potential. When I find myself trying to "make things happen" in the industry, trying to figure out what's selling, twisting myself into what I think they're buying, I do this meditation to reconnect with the *stillpoint* within.

This is a simple closed-eye meditation. You can follow your breath or focus on a spiritual quality. The challenge is to *not* act on your normal patterns of behavior. If you find yourself frazzled, frantic, and working overtime to make something happen in your life, it would be ideal to take several hours or even an entire day off and meditate. I don't expect everyone to be willing to do this. But my experience has shown this to be one of the most healing, empowering things you can do. Every time I've practiced it, new opportunities and insights have flooded my life. Recall the story I told earlier, where I didn't have rent money. Instead of freaking out, I turned within, and a few weeks later I booked a commercial that made me tens of thousands of dollars — all without any struggle.

To practice this, commit to a space of time where you won't do anything, unless it comes from a place of peace and inspiration, versus fear and desperation. During this period, simply meditate and become aware of what's moving through your mind without engaging or reacting to it. Just watch it pass before your inner eye, then put your attention back on your breath or mantra. If inner guidance arises, take that *one* action — make a call, write an idea down — then go back into meditation. *And don't do it to get a reaction from the world or make something happen.* You're just "following inner orders" like a humble servant. As you do this, you'll become aware of a lot of other impulses and ideas that are really just mind chatter or the ego's fearful machinations. Try not to engage these. Over time, you'll get better at discerning the difference. If you practice this *mind-fasting* with sincerity, willing to let go of the "doer," you'll detoxify your mind and emotions and create a clearer space for your authentic self to emerge.

I remember when I first started practicing this, so much chaos would erupt in my mind and emotions when I disengaged my ego's tactics and got still. My ego would go crazy, kicking and screaming, throwing tantrums: "You're going to fail, go broke, become homeless, and end up roaming Hollywood Boulevard! You're such a loser — nobody will ever hire you again!" This would often be accompanied by intense emotions. But as I just witnessed these demons trying to "scare the heaven out of me" — without engaging them — they lost their power and faded away. And in their place came a sense of peace, and sometimes life-changing insights.

There's a saying, "To he who can most perfectly practice inaction, all things are possible." Your real power lies at your center, in that stillpoint; that silent, invisible, ground of being. When you turn away from the turbulence of the world, and tap into this "eye of the storm," you allow the good you are striving for to flow easily into your life, in greater ways than you could have accomplished with your own human might and power.

> "To he who can most perfectly practice inaction, all things are possible."

No Muse Is Good Muse: Dark Night of the Creative Soul

In spring, trees burst forth with flowers and fruit. In winter they become barren again. The tide comes in, the tide goes out. In order to breathe, you must exhale. In other words, for everything there's a season. There will be times when things aren't "manifesting" the way you'd like them to, when you're not working as much as you think you should — when the well just seems dry. This isn't necessarily a sign that you're doing anything wrong, that you need to start "visualizing" more, or that the business is failing. Instead, it may be a sign that it's time to dive deeper — and take things to the next level.

When winter comes and the land appears stark and lifeless, it's actually anything but. Deep beneath the frozen landscape, in the dark, new life is being born and nurtured. If you mistakenly believe that something is wrong and plow up the snowy soil, you'll destroy the fragile life trying to take root. Likewise, if you try to force growth during these times of winter in your own life, career, or a particular creative project, you'll disrupt or destroy the new life preparing to burst forth in its rightful season. This can be a painful part of an enlightened entertainer's practice, but it's absolutely essential. It's like the previous meditation extended out over a longer period of time.

Remember the bamboo tree? For four years it barely grows at all, revealing only a bulb and tiny shoots. But in its fifth year, it grows eighty feet! If you judged its value and potential by this four-year performance, you might pull it up by its roots, plant another one, or abandon it all together. *And you'd be making a huge mistake.* How many times have you seen people give up after a few failures, or even a few years? How many times have you wanted to give up after getting another rejection notice? Maybe you've dug up the roots, trying to see what's wrong — only to sabotage your growth and have to start all over again. Maybe you're at that crossroads now. Maybe you're staring at that tiny little shoot called your entertainment career and thinking "why won't you grow, damnit?!"

If you're doing the inner and outer work, during your "low points," when not much seems to be going on, there are powerful potentialities growing in you. For the branches of your life to reach their highest heights, your roots must dig deeper into the dark soil of your soul. The "darkness" is the light in potential, just as the soil is life in potential. Embrace these periods. Know that your greater good is going to break through the surface. Nurture yourself, the way a mother nurtures a child in her womb. She knows that everything she puts into her body, mind, and emotions is the substance creating this new life. She knows she must rest and take better care of herself to give this new creation all the energy it needs to develop. For a mother, it's easier to have faith since she can see and feel this child. It's more difficult when the "child" is a new idea, a new identity, a new career path, or a new level of being. But for you to progress to the next stage of your creative vision and career, you must practice being still during these periods.

Your Disappointment Is a "Divine Appointment"

From a human, ego-driven place, we don't really know what we need. Even if we were neurosis-free, our vision of what's right would still be limited by the "known," by past experience and current possibilities — instead of the infinite, unbounded realm where all things are possible. When we make decisions and plan our life merely from our human mind, we set in motion a law of limitation — and set ourselves up for disappointment.

The good news is that your disappointment is an appointment with your higher self. When all hell breaks loose, it makes space for Heaven to emerge. When you're disillusioned, your *illusions* are shattered — allowing you to see more clearly. It doesn't always feel

> When all hell breaks loose, it makes space for Heaven to emerge.

like a good thing (okay, it never does). When you find out there's no

Tooth Fairy, it's painful — especially because you won't be getting five bucks a tooth any more! (What's with that anyway? I got like a quarter when I was a kid.) But in its place is a greater world of possibility and responsibility. Now your parents can treat you like a "big kid" and you can enjoy more of the perks that go with that newly attained title.

The same is true when your illusions are taken away as an artist and entertainment professional. You may have been living in a fantasy that someone out there was going to rescue you, "discover" you; that if you were a good little boy or girl you'd wake up one day to find all your dreams delivered in a waiting limo parked at the curb! Then you realize everyone is looking out for themselves and no jolly man in a red suit, bunny suit, or winged leotard is going to be paying you a visit anytime soon. This can be devastating. But as you move through this transition, the universe can now treat you like a "big kid." You're initiated into a world of bigger opportunities befitting this next stage of evolution.

But I must offer a word of warning: When you are disappointed, *don't miss your divine appointment.* Your soul does not like to be kept waiting. It wants to express its potential and fulfill its purpose — and it *will* have its way, one way or another. The choice is not between fulfilling your full potential or not — that's inevitable — it's whether you choose to grow willingly or be dragged, kicking and screaming into your destiny.

Living on a Prayer

When you find yourself experiencing painful disappointments, doing more "falling forward" than moving forward, and you feel like you're "living on a prayer" — that might be exactly what you need to be living on. Prayer (or prayerful affirmation) is a powerful — and practical — tool. Not just to move your soul, but to move mountains. The power of prayer is being proven more and more every day, through scientific experiments in major universities, hospitals, government studies, and other publicly funded organizations. Dr. Larry Dossey is a pioneer in this field, as is Deepak Chopra. I highly encourage you to read their books. They will inspire and bolster your faith.

Spend some time in your inner laboratory, where you can be a scientist of the mind, an anthropologist of the heart, an archeologist of the soul. Create a prayer for yourself. At this stage in the journey, you've probably had a lot come up. Hopefully some of the issues have been resolved through this work, but there are likely to be some painful areas still nagging you. If you already have a strong prayer/meditation practice, you might be processing these issues on a regular basis. If you don't, there's a danger that they'll build up until they cause burnout, blowout, or become suppressed and turn into more negative unconscious beliefs. Just as it's a good idea to keep your office clean so you can see what's really there, it's a good idea to keep your consciousness (and conscience) clean, so you can see who you really are. Prayer is a great way to accomplish this.

Take out a clean piece of paper, or open your Enlightened Entertainer Journal, and begin writing down the areas that you are still struggling with. List them on the left side of the page. Then on the right side, write down their affirmative opposites. For example, if you're struggling with abundance issues and it sounds like "I don't have enough money to pay the rent once again," then on the right side you might write, "I have an infinite source of abundance within me that always meets my every need with ease." Use whatever words of truth you can muster up. It's okay if they're not perfect or poetic. The key is to work with your highest idea of truth and put it into regular practice. As you do this, you'll discover deeper realms of truth to align with. But you must start right where you are, *using* what you know, or you won't be given any more. "Faith without works is dead."

Once you fill a page — or two — take all the affirmative words you've written and write them out in one long monologue, as if you're "spiritually gossiping" about yourself. Allow your creativity to fill in the gaps and create a cohesive piece. This is not an intellectual exercise. It's not in your head, but your heart. Take a moment to get centered before writing. When you've completed it, take a moment to become still, then read it aloud with all the power and passion you can manage. Another way to get you connected is to pick a song and sing or dance along until you're completely out of your head. Then write and speak — or sing — the prayer from that place. Don't worry if you don't entirely believe it. Just play the part. "Fake it till you make it." You'll be surprised at how much you begin to feel what you're saying by simply saying it with feeling.

When you're finished, put it away. You've planted the seed. Let it grow. If the issues surface again, do the prayer again, and let it go again. Each time it is complete in and of itself. Each time say the prayer as if that's all it takes to fulfill it. Each time affirm as if it's the first time. As you get more familiar with this process, you'll begin to pray and affirm spontaneously. You'll no longer need to write them out. But for now it's a good practice. Do it as often — and about as many issues — as you feel moved. This is called "prayer without ceasing." And it's the state where Grace happens.

Acts of Courage: "Practice, Practice, Practice!"

If you're studying to be a master in your field, you know you have to create a disciplined structure to get the work done. Likewise, when you decide to embark on a course of Self-Mastery, you need to apply the same rigorous principle of planning. I'm not suggesting you meditate six hours a day, sleep on a bed of nails, and go begging for rice in the streets of Hollywood. But I am calling on you to take your practice of personal growth to the next level — by making it part of your everyday schedule.

If you already have a consistent practice, this is a call to crank it up a notch. You may not know what that looks like, but if you take a moment to reflect you'll probably begin to see areas where you've wanted to stretch, but have avoided. If you don't have a practice, don't try to create one that rivals the Dalai Lama's. It's not a contest. It's not a race. It's not about "how big your altar is," but how willing your heart is. In fact, you may want to start with just one exercise that you can commit to doing each day, no matter what — like blessing everyone at auditions or studio meetings, consciously affirming the greatest good for all of your competition (breathe). As you strengthen this muscle, you can add another and another, until your whole life is a practice of the Presence.

A good place to start is meditation. A good time to start is first thing when you wake up. It's not about the quantity of time, but the quality of your attention and the sincerity of your *intention*. What you do is not as important as *why* you do it. Before you begin, dedicate your meditation to realizing your oneness with Spirit/God/Higher Self. Feel your connection to that inner light. Take a few deep breaths and release. Then just listen within and pay attention to what shows up. Sit for five minutes if that's all you have time for — or is all you can stand without joining the Mad Hatter's tea party. When you're done, bless your day (and anyone else on your mind — like, uh, the "competition").

You can also complement this morning meditation with the Night Pages, which becomes a meditation of its own. You might even choose to stop at some point during the day to reconnect to your intention for being alive, for being in this business of show. The key is developing a regular practice of mindful contemplation and prayerful affirmation. As you do it over and over, day after day, a new groove will be cut in your subjective mind — until it becomes second nature. I remember a time when I was first practicing gratitude, giving thanks for everything in my life. The moment I knew I had embodied it to a degree was while standing in the checkout line at a grocery store. The clerk rang me up, handed me my change, and I blurted out "Thank you God!" Needless to say, she was taken aback by this rather high estimation of her. But for a moment, as we hung in the incongruence of the exchange, we connected. She smiled. I grabbed my Newman's Own and strolled out.

So grab your daily planner and schedule your practice. Write it down like any appointment you intend to keep. 7 a.m.: meditation; 12 noon: affirmations; 10 p.m., Night Pages, whatever structure feels right. Keep it simple. Keep it real.

Then keep your appointment with yourself!

Check-In

We're about a third of the way through this work — so you should be about one-third transformed by now. How are you doing? (I'm joking about the one-third transformed part.) Are you in *aftergrow* or *afterglow?* Are you feeling rooted in your purpose and passion, overwhelmed by chaos and confusion, or just comfortably numb?

There's no right or wrong state, but you want to be aware of the state in which you're currently taking up residence. Your simple mindful attention will allow the body-mind-spirit's natural unfolding process to flow more smoothly. If you haven't already done so, take a few minutes to journal about this chapter's work, to summarize what you've learned, what insights you've had, what's coming up for you.

Here are some questions you can ask yourself:

1. How do I feel about the entertainment industry and its greater possibilities? Do I feel more inspired/empowered than before I started this? Why? Why not?

2. How do I feel about my place and purpose in show business? Do I feel more inspired/empowered than before I started this? Why? Why not?

3. What inner and outer changes must I make in order to achieve my purpose in this business? Am I willing? If so, why? If not, why not?

4. Is there something I know I'm being called to do, but am afraid to do it? Why?

Aren't you glad to finally have some new questions? They actually *are* new, because the person asking them is not the same person who asked them before!

PART IV
The Artist's Path

SEVEN

Finding Your Voice

"To be nobody but yourself — in a world which
is doing its best, night and day, to make you
somebody else — means to fight the hardest
battle which any human being can fight; and
never stop fighting."
— E. E. Cummings

Stand for Something or You'll Fall for Anything

I once heard about a social experiment done at a college: In it, a group of students would run up to a stranger and start accusing them of doing something. If they did it long enough, other students would join in the "stone throwing", even though they didn't know anything about the incident in question. The experiment proved that human beings have a tendency to blindly follow the prevailing thought, to get caught up in the contagion of popular belief — in other words, to become sheep.

In the entertainment industry (and throughout society) there are herds of "sheep" — well-intentioned though they may be — blindly following fear-based beliefs right into the slaughterhouse. Not just promising careers, but creative geniuses and potentially brilliant concepts, are being butchered, processed, and packaged for quick delivery to the hungry masses. But this can't happen to someone who is rooted in a vision, someone who knows who they really are, what their true source is, and what they stand for. This kind of person will

> Not just promising careers, but creative geniuses and potentially brilliant concepts, are being butchered, processed, and packaged for quick delivery to the hungry masses.

not go silently into the night, but will rage, rage against the dying of the (green) light.

In the entertainment industry there are a lot of prevailing beliefs of what's possible, what's commercial, who's important, and who you have to know (or sleep with) to make it. If you've done the earlier work in this book, you've uncovered some of these limited ideas and fabricated rules. They aren't based on truth principles and therefore can't stand in the face of someone standing in the truth of their being. If you get nothing else from this book, get this: *All the apparent limitations in the entertainment industry are illusions with no real power, substance, or universal law backing them.* But if you aren't anchored in a vision of truth bigger than the *Daily Variety*, you'll likely succumb to these lies. What's worse, if you "go along with the crowd," you'll be like those college students hurting innocent bystanders (audience members and colleagues) without knowing why. You'll just be another you-know-what heading you-know-where.

If you haven't already done so, I encourage you to complete the work in the chapters on throwing out the old scripts and writing a new one. Uncover the false beliefs you're living under. Question everything the industry (and the world) tells you is true: the rules, "the way it's done." Ask yourself if it's Truth talking or just someone's opinion? Affirm the highest vision of your being — then take a stand for it. That's how you take back your life and co-create a conscious path of empowered expression and true fulfillment.

If You Act Like Someone Else, You're Unnecessary

How often do casting breakdowns say "we're looking for a (insert flavor of the month) — type?" How often do actors try to change their taste into whatever that flavor is? When a movie is a hit, studios scramble to fill the pipeline with similar films. Screenwriters are just as guilty. When a genre comes back into favor after a hit, production companies are flooded with knock-offs. *Die Hard* has been rewritten in every possible location on the planet — and outer space. So have *Speed*, *Lethal Weapon*, and *The Matrix*. When *Scream* reinvented the genre, everyone was a horror writer. When *Pulp Fiction* blew its brains across worldwide screens, suddenly everyone wrote like Quentin Tarantino.

There's a strong inertia to do the same thing over and over and disguise it as something new. They say they're looking for a "fresh voice," but if you close your eyes everything starts sounding the same. It's bizarre that with all of the creative genius of the universe in us — we get *The Dukes of Hazzard* movie. (I actually enjoyed the series as a child. But then I also enjoyed watching my friends light their flatulence on fire!) Have we really run out of creative steam? Are there truly no new ideas under the sun? Of course not. This is an infinite universe, teeming with unbounded creative potential. Many of us have lived such rich, meaningful lives, and we live in such mind-blowing times. Each of us is a walking library of living masterpieces. There's no reason to regurgitate stale leftovers!

If you're trying to do what someone else is doing or be what someone else is being, you are unnecessary, irrelevant. If you're not living on the edge, you're taking up too much space! You're like one of those leftover parts in a box from IKEA. Or a duplicate CD people get as gifts. What happens to those? They get traded in for something else.

> If you're not living on the edge, you're taking up too much space!

The universe doesn't make spare parts. Everything has its place, everything fits. When everyone is being authentic, fulfilling their unique function, things run like a well-tuned engine. When people try to be like someone else — what Hollywood, family, or society tells them to be — problems ensue. Imagine a play with two actors performing the same part. If you're a storyteller, you know that every character fulfills a specific function. If two characters do the same thing, they're combined into one — and someone gets the ax! This divine drama called life is just as efficient. If you're trying to be like someone else, you're playing *their* part, and you are destined to fail — or at least be fairly unhappy.

The good news is you've been given a role that is uniquely yours. Life didn't make any extras in this play. Everyone is the star of their own show. But you won't experience your true potential if you're trying to perform someone else's part. You are an unrepeatable idea in the mind of God/Universal Intelligence. You have never happened before and will never happen again. The special gifts, talents, and perspectives you bring complete this sacred story called life. We need you to be *you*, so that the grand idea, the Great Theme of this human drama, can be illuminated. When you start being your authentic self, the universe backs you up. A host of Guardian Agents — uh, angels — wing to your aid.

Permission to Be Great

Part of playing the role you came here for involves your willingness to shine. You really are the star of your own show. A star exudes "star quality" (not to be confused with the "star system"). This has something to do with confidence, charisma, mystery, power, authentic expression, and ownership of their part. Whether you're in front of an audience or behind the scenes, these qualities are a part of your character, waiting to be embraced.

Regardless of what religious dogma or family dysfunction has led you to believe, you are not a "worthless clod of dust." You are a totally original composite of every quality in the universe, every divine idea in the Mind of God. This is not hype, hyperbole, or airy-fairy New Age gobbledygook. Whether you believe it, feel it, see the evidence of it, or find a casting director, producer, A&R person, or studio exec to corroborate it — this is *who you are.* You might believe it's arrogant to think this way, that it's your ego talking. In fact, it's the opposite. It's arrogant and egotistical to think anything *less.* You were "*made in the image and likeness of God.*" To think less than holy thoughts about yourself — to think you are anything other than a magnificent expression of life — is the greatest sin you can commit. (By the way, the word "sin" has its roots in an archery term that means "to miss the mark.")

This concept isn't mutually exclusive from the idea of humility either. You can be both supremely confident *and* deeply humble. Remember, your ego is the one telling you you're a worthless pile of you-know-what — or worse, the fly buzzing around that warm mound. It scares the hell — or the Heaven — out of the ego to consider itself in the light of its infinite nature, because it knows that to identify with this eternal spirit will lead to its ultimate destruction (or at least to its appropriate placement in the divine pecking order). In other words, keeping you small is a matter of life and death to the ego.

"What about arrogant people who think they're all that?" you might ask. "Isn't that the ego puffing itself up?" Yes. But "puffing itself up" is not the same as identifying with your awesome, empowered nature. Again, it's just the opposite. The reason someone needs to "puff themselves up" is because subconsciously they believe they're small and insignificant. Peel away the onion skin on an arrogant person, and you'll find a scared child cowering in the corner of their consciousness. If you're involved in the creation of stories, you know this is the truth beneath the characters that play these parts. When these frightened, cocky characters finally have their facade broken down, and discover how worthy they really are, they don't become arrogant — they become humble. When you catch a glimpse of your real nature — the nature of the Universe — it brings you to your knees in awe and gratitude. And the impulse becomes to share, shine, and serve.

It's time to let go of any voices in your head (parents, teachers, priests) that tell you to hide your light under a bushel, to not rock the boat, to not outshine others (which is impossible since we're all the same Light). You can't add to the peace of the world by living in chaos. You can't eradicate poverty by being poor. You can't help others achieve their dreams by living in a nightmare. And playing small doesn't help anyone accomplish anything! In fact, it perpetuates an environment of smallness, an atmosphere of limitation and fear. But when you play big, when you give yourself permission to shine your light instead of hitting the dimmer, you give a silent, sacred approval for those around you to do the same. When you accept your greatness and achieve your dreams, you take nothing away from anyone — you become a generative being, adding to the good of all.

Be excellent. Be beautiful. Shine your light so bright people have to wear frickin' sunglasses around you! But do it all in honor of the living spirit within all of us, not merely for self-serving reasons. Know that the more you express the awesome power, presence, and genius within you, the more you become an example of what is possible for everyone. The greatest spiritual teachers, creative geniuses, business leaders, and other major figures throughout history were not the Great Exceptions to the rule — they were the Great Examples. The Way-Showers. Nobody has ever been granted a special dispensation from the Almighty. I don't care what any race, religion, philosophy, college, country, or academy of the arts says! The Great Spirit bestows Its gift of divinity equally within every individual. That's what every master has tried to teach.

Next time you find yourself feeling envious or small and insignificant compared to someone "great" or more "successful," take a moment to say this silent prayer/affirmation:

> There is only one Life. One Mind. One Creator. One Actor/Writer/Musician/Storyteller. And that One Life is expressing as everyone equally. God is no respecter of persons. The Universe has bestowed Its Gift equally on all. In fact, because this Infinite Intelligence is omnipresent (everywhere present), it must be right where I am in exactly the same measure as it is where they are. Therefore whatever I admire in this person, must also be in me. I accept that I am (beautiful, talented, successful, a great actor, writer, etc.). I claim it. I own it. I breathe it in. I relax in it. I am it now. For this, and so much more, I am grateful. Thank you Life (God, Spirit). It is done. And so it is. Amen.

The flip side of this is that *everyone else* — even your worst enemy — is equally great in their unique way. You can't claim your own inherent worth and believe something less about someone else. If you do, you put yourself back under the law of duality and will experience the limited beliefs of that level of consciousness. *Everyone* is a magnificent expression of the Great Spirit. Your mission — should you choose to accept it — is to affirm, celebrate, and support the success of *everyone*, as if it were your own. As you dissolve the boundaries of "me" and "them" you'll discover that what you affirm for that part of you called "*them*" also begins coming true for that part of you called "*me.*"

How do you feel when I encourage you to want the best for your "competition?" Be aware of any part of you that doesn't want this for everyone — or someone in particular. Remember, you only keep what you are willing to give away, what you are willing to accept for others. Why? *Because there's only one of us here.* One omnipresent life appearing as the "many." It's like a tree. If the branches could compete and "cut each other down," they would destroy the tree from which they spring. As the Ojibwa Indian saying goes, "*No tree has branches so foolish as to fight amongst themselves.*"

Connecting to Your Joy

In developing your mission statement, you delved into your deepest passions. If you threw yourself into it, you may have discovered passion's close partner, joy. You've probably heard, "follow your bliss." Simple enough. Except most people don't know what their "bliss" is. They knew once, as a child maybe. But it became buried by burden, responsibility, parental fantasy, societal pressures, and a need to be practical, logical, and just "get by." Perhaps that's you. Or maybe you're someone who started out knowing your bliss — and following it — only to let it be covered up by "bottom line" thinking.

Joy is independent of circumstances. Nothing "out there" causes you to feel it. Joy simply is. It's a quality of your being, like wetness is to water. Water doesn't have to do, get, or achieve anything to have wetness. Likewise, you don't have to twist yourself up in a pretzel to have joy. It's what you're made of. I know that sounds abstract, maybe even silly. But it's the truth. The same goes for Love, Peace, Beauty, and all the other "positive" qualities. They are the "ingredients" that have been mixed together to create you. The reason some circumstances or actions give you the experience of joy is not because they are the source, but because the meaning you assigned them ("good" versus "bad') allows you to become aware of the joy imprisoned within you.

Because joy is your essential nature, whenever you are living from your authentic self, joy is there. It can't be otherwise. When water is "watering," it's wet. When you are being you, you're *in* joy (en-joying) — you're literally the substance of joy expressing. Following your bliss or joy is about recognizing when this quality is (or was) present and using that information as a "clue" to who you really are and how you're meant to be expressing. It's also about being aware of when this quality isn't present, and using that as a signal that you might be off track, not expressing your authentic voice.

Take a moment to contemplate your life. What activities bring you joy? What things can you indulge in for hours, losing all track of time? Don't judge anything. Maybe you love bird watching, babysitting, bungee jumping, or maybe it's the Discovery Channel that fills up your TiVo. Write it down in your journal. These are clues to your voice and vocation. Who knows, maybe you're supposed to write a script about the extinction of animals, become a producer for the animal planet, or incorporate "animal behavior" into your next role. Every piece of joy is part of the puzzle. Take nothing for granted.

If you can't find anything you love now, go back a few years. Then a few more, until you find something that brought you great joy, something you lost yourself in. Maybe you have to go all the way back to childhood, back before you imposed all the "shoulds" and "shouldn'ts" that covered up your authentic voice. Take a look at life through your childhood eyes. What things did you like to do? What things interested you? What could you get lost in for hours without getting hungry or tired or thinking about anything else?

I used to love drawing characters and strange worlds, creating animated stories on my computer, making animated flip pads. No pad of paper was safe from my creative scribblings! I could literally sit for hours on end, lost in the worlds I was creating, until my body was stiff and aching. The same was true with making home movies. Whole summers were lived through the lens of my 8mm Sears movie camera. Then it became about going to the movies. I would walk miles, through washes and onion fields to get to the theatre and watch flicks back to back. Then girls entered the scene and, well, let's just say I got distracted from these endeavors for a whole — and holy — different kind of joy.

Another clue I found in my early years was that I loved to compliment people, pointing out their talents and strong points. (One of my friends called it the "love bomb.") Then as I went through high school, I became really interested in religion and the brain. I was even going to become a brain surgeon. Ultimately, however, my search for higher meaning outweighed my interest in the physical organ of the brain and became more about the mystical dimension of the Mind. In looking at these childhood circumstances, it's no surprise I ended up where I am. The clues were there. Even the style and tone of work I was meant to do were there to some degree — being a student of truth teachings, a lover of storytelling, and an advocate for seeing the best in others.

Your experiences may not have been as obvious, but the clues were there — and still are. In addition to the activities you get lost in, or did as a child, pay attention to the themes and ideas that interested you. In your current life or years gone by, what topics have attracted, inspired, and impassioned you most? When you were a child, what was the quality of your friendships? Were you adventurous, mysterious, loving, kind? The things you love to talk about, read about, the movies you like to watch, and the quality of your childhood interactions — all give clues to your "life theme." This is where you begin to discover your *voice*. So put on your pith helmet and start digging into your childhood (and adulthood), until you discover the hidden jewels of your real joy.

It's All About the "Play"

Although Life appears to be a serious endeavor, it's really all about play. Look at nature, the crazy styles, shapes, and sizes. Look at a platypus! Are you telling me a Serious Being created that? The Bard said, "All the world's a stage, and all the men and women merely players." This is a meaningful metaphor for life. More than a metaphor, a model. Life *is* a divine play. When we realize this, we are liberated. We can "play" serious and tragic, but the Divine Actor inside knows it's just a play — and is free to enjoy the part!

When you're in the spirit of play, you're in your authentic self and, consequently, tapping your true voice. When you're taking life and yourself too seriously, you're coming from the ego, from a ball of entrenched reactions, from your conditioned, time-blinded self. This is not real creativity. You may create something. It may even sell, get made, and make a lot of money. But it won't be likely to advance your soul or the soul of society, because it won't have much — if any — transformative value in it. It might elevate mediocrity to an art form, but it will do little more than maintain the status quo. It'll be a rehash of what's already out there and will probably be forgotten quickly. What's worse, the lasting residue will not be happiness or fulfillment, but a greater soul-hunger.

Many of us are stuck, to some degree, in the "starving artist" syndrome, in the idea that creativity comes out of chaos — that we must suffer for our art. That's nonsense. I'm not saying pain isn't valuable, or that our wounds don't carry a creative wisdom. But our authentic self doesn't *need* to suffer to create. The creative impulse is inspiration — the "breath of God" — a desire to give meaning, light, and truth to the raw material of life. And it's fun. Even if it hurts a little. Look at the great masterpieces throughout history and see if you can find that spark of playfulness in them. Read the bios of these creators, particularly their experiences in the moment of creation. Van Gogh may have cut his ear off in misery, but when he painted "Starry Night," that cat was blissing out!

Look back on your life, or your current circumstances, and see where there is/was the greatest sense of play. That's a sign of where your treasure — and your voice — lies. Nurture that part of yourself. Find ways to bring more playfulness into your creative endeavors — into everything you do. Picasso's goal was to get back to the innocent quality of a child while maintaining the wisdom and raw life experience of an adult. Look at his work. That guy was doing some serious playing! There's a reason the word "play" is the common denominator in "stage play," "screenplay," and "teleplay."

It's all about the play!

You *Are* God's Gift to the World

One of the most powerful ways to get in touch with your authentic voice, and coax it into expression, is through total and complete self-acceptance. Some of the so-called experts out there say our children are suffering from "too much self-esteem." I shake my head when I hear this. It's a dangerous and ignorant statement. They have misdiagnosed narcissism for self-worth. Narcissism comes out of fear, insecurity, and a *lack* of self-worth. But this kind of thinking permeates our society, creating false humility, resistance, and even contempt for those who confidently accept and express their inherent value.

While show business *seems* to be different, welcoming confident, charismatic people, the dark side of this industry actually feeds on the failures of others. On one hand, we want each other to succeed and be great — *as long as it benefits us in some way.* But get too big for your britches and we secretly hope you take a big fall. It's practically a spectator sport in Hollywood. You can almost hear the glee in some people's voices as they watch careers crash and burn that were once on the fast track. It's a strange irony to want — to literally need — the very best talent, and at the same time to derive a sadistic satisfaction in that talent's destruction.

Ask yourself — and answer honestly — have you ever taken some degree of guilty pleasure in the failures of your fellow peers? To the extent that you participate in this kind of thought, you will also hold yourself back. Why? Because on some level, you know that if you truly take

> It's a strange irony to want — to literally need — the very best talent, and at the same time to derive a sadistic satisfaction in that talent's destruction.

your place center stage, others are standing in the wings sawing away at the ropes, waiting for the set to come crashing down on you.

When you were a kid, if you walked confidently, poised and self-assured, you were probably attacked by others, slinging such statements as: "Who do you think you are, God's gift to the world?" And you probably responded with something like, "No, of course not!" and quickly dimmed your light. The correct answer to that bully would have been, "As a matter of fact, yes, I am God's gift to the world. What else should I be, God's curse?! So put that in your peace pipe and smoke it, pal!" Okay, I wouldn't recommend that last bit. In fact, I wouldn't advocate any kid going around saying this out loud — or they might end up with a bloody nose and their lunch money stolen. But I am suggesting that we think it, believe it, and teach our children to know it about themselves.

Every single individual is a gift to this world — although many don't recognize and express it. Can you imagine an all-loving, all-powerful, all-giving God sending a bunch of junk to the world? What is God, a used-car salesman?! Just look at it from a human perspective. When you're giving a helping hand or a hand-out to someone you care about, do you give them shoddy quality, bad service, and garbage — or do you try to give them the very best you have to offer? The answer is obvious (at least I hope it is). Well, that's just a small version, a micro-example, of how the Universe is giving to us all the time. Life doesn't send us second-hand people, lacking in talent, to clog up the system, use up the resources, and die! The Great Spirit cares enough to send the very best. Whether or not we unwrap the gift of our life and share it is up to us.

Your authentic voice, and how you express it in your area of expertise, *is* God's gift to the world. I believe it's not just a choice whether to give this gift, it's an obligation. Who are we to withhold God's gifts? It's not egotistical to claim that you're a gift to the world, it's egotistical *not to*. Not to mention selfish. You have no idea the impact your life and work could have on people. It could awaken them to their greatness, inspire major change, and help create a world that works for everyone. Don't be stingy with it!

I know how difficult it is to follow this guidance. There's such a subjective resistance to letting our light shine that it has become an archetype. Throughout history, we've seen the result of people willing to go for it. Jesus, Gandhi, Martin Luther King, Jr., Kennedy, John Lennon. All cut down. Their lights (seemingly) snuffed out. And because of this tradition of "shooting our messengers," there's a deep fear in many of us that if we "come out from amongst them," they'll shoot us down too — if not literally, then on the cover of the *Enquirer*, or in our families and social circles. I coined a term to describe this: *"The Crucifixion Complex."* I think a lot of us suffer from it.

You can see this playing out in our movies. Whenever a character becomes "enlightened," "awakened," or carries a message of higher truth, they usually die, get killed, go back to their planet, or escape into seclusion. Look at *Phenomenon*, *E.T.*, *Starman*, *Powder*, or *The Green Mile*, to name a few. It's like we can't conceive of what it would be like to actualize our divinity (not to be confused with celebrity), to open our gift, then stick around to share it. But it can be done. How? I think we have to start by exorcising this "crucifixion complex." Then we need to recognize the gift we've been given, and give it — to as many people as possible. We can't control our destiny, but we can determine whether or not we live it. And to be completely honest, if we're not living an authentic life, we're just the walking dead anyway. So what do you have to lose?!

> Because of this tradition of "shooting our messengers," there's a deep fear in many of us that if we "come out from amongst them," they'll shoot us down too.

Acts of Courage — "To Thine Own Self Be True"

Over the next week, identify someone or someplace where you know you're "hiding your light under a bushel," or "conforming to this world." Maybe it's at your parents' house, on the studio lot, or at the office. Maybe it's when you hang out with your friends, in acting class, or your writers group. Locate a place or person where you aren't able to truly be yourself — and commit to taking that lamp shade off and letting your light shine.

When I first began this practice, years ago, I was working as a waiter. There was a lot of gossip amongst the servers. They would criticize the customers, the boss, each other (behind their backs, of course). I didn't like it. I wanted to live at a higher level. But I didn't want them to dislike or reject me. Finally, the pain of living the lie began to outweigh the fear of living the truth. So I made a decision. I stopped participating in gossip or complaining. I didn't act self-righteous, I just excused myself and went on with my work. I also began to give the best possible service, stopped watching the clock, and stopped holding anything back because "they weren't paying me enough." It felt exhilarating. I looked forward to work. I felt more connected to everyone and, most importantly, to my spirit. I became more creative and productive. Customer compliments started rolling in, tips piled up. Life was good!

And the other servers hated me for it.

They stopped gossiping and criticizing around me, and didn't let me "join in any reindeer games." But that's what I wanted, right? So why was I so miserable? It was the old tapes, the scared ego fighting for its life. And it had good reason to fear. It *was* dying. It was the death of a lesser identity to allow something better to be born. It still didn't feel good. But I persevered, kept my profile low, head held high, back straight. Victory was at hand.

And then they fired me — three times!

I kid you not. I was fired three times. Every time, they discovered that it was a mistake, that I was being made the "scapegoat." But rather than feeling crushed by it, each time I was fired and rehired, I felt a renewed commitment to my practice. After the third time, however, I decided the universe was sending a message. There was something more for me. And in a very short time, I was hired as an actor in a troupe that traveled the country — first class all the way. It was an amazing, adventurous experience. I made good money, good friends, and grew in so many ways. And as I made this principle a regular part of my practice, my life has continued to evolve in an ever-widening upward spiral.

Wherever you are, whatever situation you're in, it is uniquely crafted for your next stage of growth.

Wherever you are, whatever situation you're in, it is uniquely crafted for your next stage of growth. There's a *vibratory match* between you and your circumstances. As you put more of your potential into practice — despite the seeming resistance — you raise your vibratory level. When this occurs, one of two things happen — your conditions and relationships will evolve to match your higher vibration, or the universe will take you out of that situation and put you somewhere that *is* vibrating at your level.

But it takes courage to confront the "Threshold Guardians," those forces that stand at the border between who you *were* and who you're *becoming*. Their job is to test you: "Are you really strong enough to handle more?" "Do you really have what it takes?" This "crossing of the threshold" can be pretty scary. The temptation is strong to answer, "Uh… maybe I'll just… go back to where I was sitting and, uh, try again later — like in another life, thanks." But if you're willing to be strong in the face of these seemingly-powerful forces (I say "seemingly" because the power they have is really your own), they will retreat and let you cross over into the new territory, where your greater potential lies.

Check-In

How are you doing? Is this experience exhausting or invigorating? We're almost to the midpoint, and at this juncture in the journey it's not uncommon to hit another wall. You might feel anxious, because on some level you know that when you pass the midpoint, there's no turning back. Whatever's going on is okay. In fact, if you're feeling stirred up, that's a good sign. It means there's movement. Change is afoot!

As you journal about this chapter, here are a few questions (they're actually new ones):

1. If you had six months to live and were given one last chance to play a part, sing a song, make a movie — whatever your expression is — what would it be? Why?

2. If you *had* to be someone else, who would it be? Why?

3. Imagine you're a child. Really get back into your childhood body and mind. And then answer the above two questions again.

Treat yourself to something special. Order the more expensive meal. Take a longer bath. Get a massage. Do something that says, "I honor and appreciate myself."

See you in the next chapter.

EIGHT ~

Opening Your Art

"Each word before leaving my lips seemed to
have passed through all the warmth of my blood.
There was no fibre in me which did not give
forth an harmonious sound. Ah, grace! The state
of grace! Each time it is given me to touch the
summit of my art, I recover that unspeakable
abandonment."

— Eleonora Duse, describing a performance

The "War of Art"

As sacred artists and enlightened entertainers, we have to fight
a never-ending battle for our art. Or so it seems. Our imple-
ments of war are not guns and bombs, but awareness and
attention. And the only enemy we ever truly have to face is "the enemy
within our own household." (Mystically speaking, this refers to our
consciousness.) Finally, the greatest "act of war" we can take is to "be
still and know," to "take our bloated nothingness out of the path of the
divine circuits," as Emerson would say.

Still, we fight skirmishes almost daily. Mapping out the terrain we want
to conquer. "Humping it" through the jungles of our mind, where
voices echo from behind every tree. Trudging through the thicket of
our heart, where a firefight of unresolved emotions threatens to cut us
down at every turn. Slugging through the swampland of our soul, where
strange and terrifying creatures stir just beneath the murky depths.

And this is just to get out of bed!

Resistance. Procrastination. Competition. Fear. Doubt. Worry. Desire. Ben & Jerry's New York Super Fudge Chunk! These are just some of the combatants we confront as we sneak behind enemy lines, secure the bridge, and try to claim that frickin' hill! But claim it we must. Whatever that hill is to you: your daily script pages, writing a song, rehearsing a scene, researching a character, having a production meeting. The path to our creative potential seems riddled with land mines. But there is a strategy to winning this war. Ironically, however, it begins with giving up the fight. In fact, the first step to claiming any kind of victory begins with one simple act.

Surrender.

Heal Your "Broken Art"

Whether or not you consider yourself an artist, you are a creative being by nature. Yes, even if you are a studio executive. We were all created out of the same Creator (or Creative Intelligence), which has endowed us with Its creative capacity. As the ancient teaching states, "Ye are gods." This could have just as easily said, "Ye are creators."

That being said, many of us — even the "artists" — have experienced so much criticism and negative conditioning around creativity that we suffer from a "broken art." And what does that feel like? Much like a broken heart, only the core of the wound is around our artistic endeavors — although it ultimately permeates every area of our lives and sense of self. Approaching the object of our artistic affection brings up emotions akin to a jilted lover. We feel anxious, unsure, self-doubting, angry, sad, depressed. We procrastinate making a connection to the object of our "art." We are bipolar in our relationship to it — an "approach-avoidance" pattern — feeling both an aching to be in its warm embrace, and a fear of getting burned by it. We're not ourselves. We get involved in addictive, self-destructive habits, like eating or drinking too much, compulsively cleaning our office, mindlessly surfing the Internet, and watching infomercials all the way through!

We think there's something wrong with us: We're lazy, stubborn, chemically imbalanced, creatively impaired, karmically challenged —

just plain retarded! Maybe we're not meant to do this after all, maybe we've been lying to ourselves all along, maybe this whole "creative thing" is just a pipe dream — maybe our dad was right and we should get a "real job"! In fact, a career in the food services industry is sounding really good about now...

That's not the problem. You have a broken art. Your art is aching. It has Coronary Artistry Disease! It hasn't been given the kind of love, attention, and recognition it needs to feel nurtured — initially in your childhood, then later by you. Your broken art feels abandoned, betrayed, wounded, stepped on, walked all over, treated like a doormat, cheated on. And there's only one way to reverse this hardening of the art-eries (I couldn't resist). Take off the protective armor, open your art, and risk breaking it all over again.

Everything in this book is geared, in one way or another, to giving you back to yourself, to reconnecting you with your heart and your art. By doing the work in these pages, you are taking a big step on the road to recovery. But you'll need to do some very specific things to really heal your art. The rest of this chapter is dedicated to that. If you don't already own *The Artist's Way* by Julia Cameron, I encourage you to get it. Ms. Cameron understands this path and brilliantly guides her readers along it.

Feed the "Starving Artist"

I've already talked about the destructive effects of Starving Artist Syndrome. If you believe you have to be starving in some hovel to create great art, you'll set up a personal law — through the power of your belief — that manifests as either living in a shack while you slave away at your craft, living abundantly but too guilty to create at all, or giving up altogether in favor of a career that affords you something other than mac 'n' cheese.

The problem with this thinking, besides being a false concept of the creative process, is that it sets up an "either-or" mindset. Damned if you do and... well, you know. But that's not how life operates. There is no lack in this infinitely abundant universe. The key is to think in terms of "this AND that," versus "this *or* that." You can choose to be rich AND brilliant. Pacino, Streep, and Hanks are all pretty good actors AND have made a few bucks. Spielberg, Fincher, Eastwood, and Howard are powerful directors AND their bank accounts are doing okay. Ron Bass, Akiva Goldsman, and Steve Zallian are Academy Award–winning screenwriters AND million-dollar ones. At the height of Picasso's career, he could doodle on a napkin and pay for anything. That's artistic success, baby!

But feeding the starving artist in you goes beyond merely the monetary aspects. If you harbor a withholding consciousness toward yourself in this area, you're likely to be depriving yourself in other ways as well. It's like the idea of spiritual ascetics, who think the way to God is by starving themselves, isolating themselves, and sleeping on a bed of nails. While I understand their reasons, and bless their path, I don't believe you need to torture yourself to reach enlightenment. And I don't believe you need to chew glass or contort yourself into bone-numbing postures to achieve artistic Nirvana either. You don't need to be in painful, insane relationships that end in bloody betrayal and heartbreak in order to write deep, passionate love stories or love songs — even if Tom Petty supposedly did just that to rip songs out of his soul. And you don't need to be a neurotic mess to be a great writer or actor — although I knew an actress who refused to get therapy for fear that if she "healed" she wouldn't be able to act any more!

I'm not passing judgment. Every artist has a right to put themselves through hell to create something heavenly. But I am challenging the idea that you *have* to suffer for your art. Suffering is not a requirement, it's a choice. In every moment. In every project. The point is, it's not an either-or issue. You can have great art AND happiness. You can create great work AND be a functional person. You can get your act together AND still have enough material to write that second act! If you're living in the world of normal human beings, I guarantee you've got a warehouse full of painful experiences to draw on — more than you could use in a lifetime. And if that's not good enough, look around. The world is full of suffering. Millions of people have already done the heavy lifting — and continue to. Just be empathetic, compassionate, and perceptive, and you'll have a palette full of all the emotional pain you'll ever need to cover the canvas of your creative life.

So how do you "starve" your artistic self? Like I've touched on, if you're harboring a belief that good art comes out of pain or suffering, on some level you'll create painful circumstances; you'll sabotage relationships that could've otherwise thrived; you'll blow opportunities that could've fulfilled your creative and practical needs; you'll send a message to the universe that says, "I'm not worthy," "I can't have all of my needs met," "I don't deserve to be happy," "I'm afraid if I'm fulfilled, I'll become artistically empty."

> If you're harboring a belief that good art comes out of pain or suffering, on some level you'll create painful circumstances.

There's a reason many artists are unhappy, broke, in dysfunctional relationships, and on an emotional rollercoaster — and it's not because that's the *nature* of artists. It's also not because people with emotional or mental problems are more likely to become artists than healthy people. It's because of the ego's long-running war to rid the world of art and its inherent power to set us free. The dimension that art arises from is a mystery with the capacity to transform the soul. That's a big threat to the ego's reign. And over the centuries it has sought to scare us away from this realm — or at least render us relatively impotent in it — by deriding, judging, and spreading a smear campaign about it.

This has conspired to create a limited belief system around the creative endeavor, a belief system powered by our fear, a belief system that becomes our experience when we accept it. Many creative people have consciously or unconsciously signed this contract and bought into its litany of lies. And because "a lie acts as law until it is neutralized" many artists continue to starve themselves, believing there is a famine — when in fact they are surrounded by fields "white unto the harvest" and "cattle on a thousand hills."

So how do you release these lies and reap this bountiful harvest? First, you become conscious of the false contracts you signed under duress — and tear them up. Next, you create a new contract in consciousness by affirming the truth of your divine birthright:

> I am a thriving artist!
> I am rich AND artistically fulfilled
> I am happy AND dynamically creative
> I have a totally abundant life AND I'm a prolific creative genius!

And then you begin *acting* as if it's so.

This might mean "getting therapy" and becoming a healthy, functional person again. (If you're reading this book, I imagine you're willing to do this.) It might also mean being willing to have a healthy romantic relationship that lasts longer than a few months, trusting that you can still write great love stories or songs without all the drama and theatrics in your real life. It might mean that you become willing to "adopt a life of luxury," as Deepak Chopra says. This will look different for different people. But essentially it looks like having enough of what you need — more than enough — an abundance of everything. You might be thinking, "Well, of course I want this, what do you think I am, a masochist?" No, not consciously. But the mind always moves toward its definition of pleasure. So if you're experiencing lack, limitation, pain, or suffering in any chronic way, you're getting a psychological or emotional "payoff" from it.

Feeding the starving artist also means nourishing your creative self by living a life of variety and adventure. It means breaking out of habits and routines; taking a different route home, eating at a different place and eating something you never thought you would, shopping at a different store, traveling to a different vacation spot, hanging out with different people, reading books and magazines you wouldn't otherwise look at. *Feeding the starving artist within you means being open and available to the infinite creative input and possibilities that exist in every moment.*

Rather than living in lack and suffering to generate creative expression, a sacred artist binges on a banquet of abundance, variety, sensual, soulful, and spiritual ecstasy. Can you imagine what you could create out of that alchemy? Life really is a cornucopia of delights. Let your inner artist feast on it until it is fat and jolly with fulfillment. Then watch it burst forth with a level of creative strength and stamina heretofore unimagined.

Romance the Muse

What is the Muse? Where does it come from? Why does it appear to serve some people while "reserving the right to refuse service" to others? Whatever your definition of this seemingly mysterious force, you probably believe that it's unpredictable at best — and downright infuriating at worst. Well, it doesn't have to be that way. The Muse, by whatever definition you give it, does not act on a whim. It is that creative source within you, the fountain of inspiration. *And it never runs dry.* Creativity is a *quality* of life — like love, peace, and joy. It's infinite and inexhaustible. And, like these qualities, the more you express it, the more of it you have; the more you appreciate it, the more it *appreciates* (grows and expands within you) until it is spilling out all over the place!

To "romance the muse" you must have an intimate relationship with that creative being within. Pay attention to it. Talk to it. *Listen to it.* Acknowledge and reward it. Tell it how much you love and appreciate it, how you'll always be here for it, how you'll never leave or forsake it. Take it out on frequent "artist dates," as Julia Cameron says in *The Artist's Way.* In other words, treat it like any partner you'd want to make happy. A happy partner is a productive and peaceful one — eager to serve you in return. An unhappy partner is harder to trust and more inclined to do things to sabotage your efforts.

I believe I'm always connected to my creative source, that my Muse is always ready and willing to spring forth with fresh inspiration and creative ideas to meet every need. And I haven't had a case of "writer's block" for years! Sure, I've had days when I didn't feel like writing, when the words weren't flowing like I wanted them to. But the problem wasn't a block, the ideas were still gestating and I needed to take a break. I needed to take my Muse to a movie and nice meal (I never said she was a cheap date!). When I romance and respect my creative partner that way, I always get "lucky" when I get home.

Here are a few ideas to keep things between you and your Muse hot and steamy:

- **When an idea comes, no matter how small or silly, record it** (on tape or on paper). When you honor the creativity coming through — no matter how seemingly trivial or inconvenient — it feels welcome and continues to flow in an ever-increasing manner.

- **Schedule time with your Muse, where you do nothing but express your creativity — and keep your appointment!** When you establish a pattern of creative expression, you build a subjective belief and trust in your creative capacity. And because "it is done unto you as you believe," that capacity continues to grow.

- **Pay yourself first — creatively speaking.** This is based on the financial concept of investing a portion of every dollar you make in your savings and retirement — otherwise the pressure of everyday expenses will rob you of your financial freedom. The same is true creatively. If you work a "regular job," or are a "hired gun" as a writer, actor, director, etc., you need to make sure you're investing time and energy in authentic creative expression. Every day if possible. Every week at the very least. When I'm doing a "work for hire," I try to schedule time every day to work on my passion projects *before* the other stuff — unless, of course, they're one and the same!

- **The Artist Date.** This is from Julia Cameron's *The Artist's Way*. It's essential for a healthy relationship with your muse. Like any long-term love affair, you have to "keep dating." Whether it's going to a matinee, browsing the bookstore, checking out a museum exhibit, or having coffee at a cool café with a friend, this practice always refills and refuels me. It heals my broken art and romances the pants off my Muse. After one of these dates, me and "my old muse" can't wait to get back to my office and "play around." In fact, sometimes we're so worked up, I have to pull over to the side of the road, whip out my pen and... well, you get the picture.

- **Study something you normally wouldn't.** Watch a program or read a book on a subject outside of your field of work or interest. Talk to people you wouldn't normally converse with. Throw a dinner party and invite friends you wouldn't normally bring together. I remember one friend who committed to reading the entire works of Shakespeare in a year, and another guy who committed to reading the entire Encyclopedia Britannica! I never heard from either of them again. As an actor, my thing was to go out and role-play different characters in public.

There are unlimited ways to romance the muse. With a willingness to break out of the ruts, and a bit of imagination, this practice should spice things up between you and that "old flame" of creativity, no matter how familiar you've become to each other.

Check Out of the ICU
(Intensive Criticism Unit)

One of the most destructive forces to your creativity is criticism. Not just from others but from yourself. Others can fire you, ruin your project, slander you, betray you, blacklist you, do all manner of things to your body and body of work — but nobody can stick it to you like you can. You know I'm right. You can point fingers at all the "bad people" you think are to blame for your "creative blocks" or lack of self-confidence, but the truth is *nobody knows how to hurt you and your creative core better than you.* You know where your weak spots are. You know just where to push, and how hard, to sabotage your creative process, cut your confidence off at the knee caps, and beat yourself to a pulp.

> Nobody knows how to hurt you and your creative core better than you.

If that imagery makes you cringe, there's still a creative pulse beating inside. If it doesn't faze you, maybe you *should* be afraid — because lurking within is a beast hell bent on snuffing out your creative spark and ultimately destroying you. This "beast" is not a thing per se, but a series of fear-based thoughts that have clumped together and gained psychic weight. Don't underestimate this beast's power, however. It's more dangerous than any external antagonist. *It knows how to disguise itself to look and sound just like you,* allowing it to gain access to the innermost chambers of your heart and mind if you let it. My intention is not to scare you, but to make you mindful and encourage you to do what you must to capture, tame, or eliminate the antagonistic forces within you (which really means to release those self-loathing thoughts and create new, empowering ones).

We've talked extensively about how beliefs are created, but you might still be asking, "Where do these self-loathing habits come from?" I'm not part of the blame-your-parents-first crowd — but the way we "parent" ourselves is primarily a product of how we were parented. Of course, our parents were doing the same thing, based on their parenting. They were doing the best they could. But that doesn't change the fact that you were probably taught how to parent yourself in a less than totally loving, compassionate, and understanding way. Your parents may not have even outright criticized you. If they had, your natural defense mechanisms probably would've fought to the death to maintain a strong sense of self. On the contrary, it's the subtle, "well-meaning" comments like:

- "Do you really want to be an actor?"

- "Actors are selfish, flaky people." (Okay, maybe not so subtle...)

- "Writers are suicidal drunks — look at Hemingway!" (...or well-meaning.)

- "Musicians are drug-addicts and derelicts."

- "The entertainment industry is morally bankrupt and corrupt."

- "Do you know how many artists live below the poverty level?"

Or it might have been more subtle, like:

- Praising your academic prowess, but ignoring your creative endeavors

- Funding and supporting your desire to pursue academics, but withholding support and/or money for your creative aspirations

- Responding to your early creative efforts with a patronizing, "That's nice, honey."

These are just a few examples of the ways you may have been trained to parent yourself. But there's an even more problematic thing that happened to many of us: We were turned into narcissists. Before you start slinging expletives at me for saying that, let me explain. Many of us had parents who were not "at their best." If this describes your childhood, then at some point you most likely made a decision that your parents weren't qualified to take care of you. With this came a general distrust and disrespect of "adults," or "authority figures," a belief that they were stupid, incapable, whatever.

This defense mechanism can show up in many ways. But one of the most destructive ways is the "boomerang effect." That child who made this decision is still alive in you. You know the one, the proverbial "inner child" ("inner brat" is often more like it). It views *you* as its parent now. And guess what it thinks about you? Sure, it loves you. It *wants* to trust and respect you. But it *can't*. Instead, it demands perfection. It demands that you shape up, get with the program, and don't you dare stumble. In fact, it's waiting for you to screw up so it can spew all its pent-up pissosity. It also shows up as a superiority complex, either pitying others or holding them in contempt. The inner child thinks it's pretty smart. And if anyone disagrees, they're a "total fool," a "complete idiot" — especially all the producers, execs, and development people who don't "get" you.

Any of this ringing a bell? Or is it just me?

But that's not the worst part about this defense mechanism. There really is only One of us here. So you are judged by the same judgment you mete out to others. Or as the Inner Brat puts it, "I'm rubber, you're glue, what you say bounces off me and sticks on you!" There's also the old standard, "What goes around, comes around." This is a powerful mystical statement. Bottom line, if you pass judgment on others in their human dysfunction, when *you* stumble and fall, you'll judge the hell — or Heaven — out of yourself. It can't be any other way. It's the Law of Oneness. But it's not too late to tame the Inner Tyke. You can break out of this vicious cycle of judgment and criticism. You just need to begin parenting the inner child the way it was meant to be parented — loving but firm, caring and competent. As you do this, you'll regain its trust, respect — and your authority — allowing you to access an untapped reservoir of power and creativity.

Here are a few specific ways to create an "inner home" environment so the inner child and you can be one big happy creative and prosperous family again:

1. **Listen.** This is the first, and most important, thing you can do. Listen to what that part of you is saying — or shouting. And do it without judgment, control, or manipulation. That rug-rat raging inside you has already been judged, controlled, and manipulated enough. It will only rebel if you try those tricks again. When you feel it flaring up, just sit down and witness it. Become aware of the emotions bubbling up — or boiling over. Doing just this much will begin to release the old, repressed feelings. Being still and allowing this inner voice to finally have a voice — without any resistance — will begin the transformational process that turns the pain of past wounds into the potential of future fulfillment.

2. **Be aware when you're acting superior or critical of others**. When you realize you're doing this, consciously stop — mid-sentence or mid-thought if you need to — and witness what's going on inside. You might experience a lot of resistance. The Inner Brat might put up quite a fight and rationalize (rational-lies) its position. Don't panic. Just listen. It'll quiet down. It'll get easier. I promise. Embrace humility. Admit it, there have been instances when you were sure the executives, producers, actors, writers — whoever — were totally wrong and had their heads stuck up that place where only proctologists should dare tread — only to discover that *you* were the one hanging out where the sun don't shine! I know I've spent my fair share living there. How many times have we sabotaged ourselves by criticizing, blaming, and defending — when if we had listened and learned, our lives and careers might've taken a turn for the better?

3. **Keep your word.** One of the biggest emotional deposits you can make is to always keep your word with yourself. If you say you're going to do something, do it — no excuses. This builds trustworthiness. It shows the inner child you can be trusted; that you're a mature, disciplined "parent." The result is that the inner child begins to relax and play more. Remember how important "play" is?

4. **Honor your truth.** When you honor yourself by honoring your truth — especially when you're afraid of losing something — you show the inner child you'll never forsake him/her, no matter what. It allows this dimension of your being to have greater respect for you, to relax, trust life, and just let go.

5. **Follow your heart.** This one is pretty obvious. When you do what you truly love, you and your inner child become one. The pure and unconditioned creativity that is your natural birthright gets to come out and play like never before.

6. **Let the Inner Victim vent.** When all else fails and the inner critic starts beating you up, go ahead and let it spew — for a limited time. Then parent it the way a strong parent would. Be compassionate but clear, gentle but firm. In other words, don't take any crap! Sometimes you just have to look in the mirror and say to yourself — "I will not have that in my house! I will listen to your pain, but I will not let you criticize, condemn, or judge me any more! If you don't like it, there's the door, bucko!" This is called tough love, folks. And sometimes that's what the Inner Little Shit needs. Yes, it can have a voice. Yes, you will hear it, witness it, and love it. But in the end, *you* are the boss.

Got it? Good. So let's check out of the ICU (Intensive Criticism Unit). The food here really sucks!

Check In to a SPA (Self-Praise Attitude)

Now that you've begun quieting the inner critic, it's time to lavish yourself with praise. Where does the idea of praising yourself hit you? Does it make you cringe, feel stupid, goofy? Does it seem arrogant, pointless, a waste of time? If you haven't done this kind of work, it probably makes you feel uncomfortable. That's normal. But don't stop there.

Here's the thing: The vibration of sincere praise is very high. It's love in action. The vibration of criticism, not so high. It's a lack attack. When a low vibration is confronted with a high vibration, it pushes the low vibration into chaos. This chaos doesn't feel so good. And, depending on your unique make-up, the energetic turbulence could be interpreted by the ego with thoughts like, "This is stupid," "You're an idiot," "I can't do this," and feelings of being "uncomfortable," "ashamed," "guilty," "angry," "critical," and so on. That's how the ego tricks you into staying the same, staying small — because to the ego, this higher vibe portends real change, and change equals death. The thing to keep in mind is that once you start pouring in the higher-octane energy, it will cause the negative, lower-octane crud to surface and begin fighting for its life. Don't be fooled!

On the other hand, as this powerful praise enters your field of aware-ness, your system could accept it. When this happens, you feel "inspired," "energized," "uplifted," "blissful." Whatever your experience is, it's okay. In fact, when it feels chaotic — that's good news! It means you're on the verge of change. Keep pouring the positive *prana* in, surrender to the process, and the old structures will be rebuilt at a higher level. That's how systems grow. They take in energy until they reach critical mass, hit a wall, and begin to break down. If no new energy is fed into the system, it eventually ceases to exist. But if new, higher energy is poured in, it reforms at a more complex level. Like the caterpillar liquefying in the chrysalis before becoming a butterfly. That's evolution!

Okay, back to praising yourself. (Thought you got off the hook, didn't you?). Again, it goes back to how you were parented and how you parent yourself. If you were praised, cherished, acknowledged, rewarded, and validated as a child — besides being one of the lucky few — you will have a tendency to think that way about yourself now. Your inner "self-talk" will reflect a certain level of self-love, self-accep-tance, and confidence. If this is authentically embodied, it doesn't lead to arrogance but to true humility and an ability to easily validate others. When you are lacking in this positive inner programming, however, you create defense mechanisms of arrogance or inadequacy to overcompensate. And because you feel lacking, even cheated, in this area, you are usually much less willing to give or receive uncondi-tional praise — especially from yourself.

We've discussed affirmations and prayer considerably, but I'm going to add an exercise to this list. It's simple, but not always easy. In fact, it will show you rather quickly what dark thoughts are lurking in your consciousness. Are you ready? Are you sure?

"Mirror, Mirror, on the Wall"

Stand in front of a mirror. Look into your eyes. And say: "I love you (your name)." Groan. Cringe. Sigh. I can imagine some people will recoil in horror, saying there's no way they'll do this exercise. While it is certainly your right to refuse, contemplate this: How can you expect others to love and appreciate you and your work in public, if you can't give these things to yourself in private? If you can't sincerely praise yourself, you'll attract people in this business (and elsewhere) who will give you false love and approval — or no love at all! If you feel resistance, ask yourself these questions:

> If you can't sincerely praise yourself, you'll attract people in this business (and elsewhere) who will give you false love and approval — or no love at all!

- "Why do I think it's a stupid waste of time to tell myself 'I love you?'"

- "Why do I have such resistance to intimately, actively loving myself?"

- "What am I afraid of?"

Listen to your answers. Write them down. You might be surprised, saddened, even angered by what is revealed. But here's the blessing: Whatever comes up is what's standing between you and total self-love and acceptance. And this feeling-tone of self-worth is the foundation upon which everything else you want is built. Without it, you're building your house on shifting sands. Without it, you're building a house of cards. Without it, you could have all the riches in the world — and you wouldn't have a thing!

As you stare at yourself in the mirror, repeat the phrase, "I love you (your name)" slowly, and listen to how your inner voice responds. It might say things like, "No you don't." "Shut up!" "Go to hell!" "Nobody loves me," "Why would you love me?" Be aware of this inner script. Write it down. These are the limited beliefs standing between where you are and where you want to be. This can be a cathartic, cleansing experience — like pouring water down a pipe to flush out the blockages (a Roto-Rooter of the soul). Don't panic if a bunch of black gunk comes out. As time goes by, this negative self-talk will get quieter, or disappear altogether. And one day, in the not-too-distant future, it will actually start agreeing with you. You'll say, "I love you," and the inner voice will respond, "I know," "I love you, too," or just "Thanks." That's when you know you're beginning to embody the truth. That's when you know you have laid a solid foundation.

As you progress, you can begin adding other work-specific affirmations like "You are a great artist," "You are a success," "You are incredibly talented," etc. You can also shift the point of view of your affirmations to fill in the full perceptual picture — what I call the "3D Affirmation." Our self-perception models are not flat, but multi-dimensional. They've been created not just by what we've said about ourselves, but by first-, second-, and third-person perspectives. To more effectively and efficiently rebuild this 3D model of self, we can utilize all points of view. For instance, I could say, "I love myself," "I love you, Derek," and "People love Derek." This last perspective is called "spiritual gossip," where you talk about yourself behind your back — saying all the good things! For example, I could say, *"Derek is a hard-working, talented guy. I really appreciate and respect him. And did you get a load of his biceps? That guy's got some serious guns!"*

As you praise yourself from all of these angles, you not only re-program your subjective awareness in terms of how you feel about yourself, you also change the way you feel *in relation to others*. For example, you can have a subjective belief that people love you, then walk into a room where most of them don't like you at all, or just don't care — and yet *feel* as if they're giving you a standing ovation. Sounds crazy, but it's true. Can you grasp the significance of this? Do you realize the power this gives you? No matter how people think about you, you can walk into any situation and feel totally loved, respected, recognized, rewarded, and on top of the world. When you're in that state of mind, you're free to express your true genius, your true voice. And when you begin living from there — look out! E. F. Hutton won't have nothin' on you, baby! When you talk, people will not only listen, they'll hear the call in their own souls — and be transformed by it.

Don't Get It Right, Just Get It Written

This is about procrastination and perfectionism (another form of procrastination). And it is one of the worst culprits to fulfilling our full potential. As mentioned before, I know writers who have written the same 25 pages of a script for five years. Or actors who have studied acting for a decade and barely made an effort to audition! Scratch the surface of these actions — or inaction — and you'll find fear and low self-esteem. It's the inner critic, the inner judge — the whole inner dysfunctional family — all saying "You're not good enough," "What if they reject you?" or "This is your one shot, don't blow it!"

If you follow these inner voices, they'll lead you, your creativity, and your career right into a ditch. If this describes you at all, I'm sure you have many good excuses to rationalize (rational-lies) your actions. But here's the thing: if you argue for your limitations, you'll own them. Instead, try making excuses and rationalizations for why you *will* complete what you're working on — then go for it no matter what!

There are many ways to get out of the rut of perfectionism or procrastination. Becoming aware of your thoughts is one way. If you're willing to sit and witness them, they'll loosen their grip on you. But beware! Meditation and contemplation can become another way to avoid doing what it takes to move forward. If you suspect you might be stuck in this pattern, one of the quickest ways to break it is to follow Nike and "just do it"!

If you're a writer, let go of all the reasons why you can't start that project — or finish what you started. Just write. Write badly. Tap those keys until your fingers bleed! You can always revise. If you monitor yourself as you go, you'll never succeed. If you're an actor, sitting in class week after week, year after year, waiting to be good enough to audition and be a working actor — stop it! Do whatever you have to do *now* to find out where you can audition for student films, plays, commercials,

movies. If you're a singer/ songwriter, finish those songs and start singing — or sing cover tunes! Do it in coffee houses, open mics, churches,
synagogues, street corners — wherever people will listen. If you're a
producer, produce! Find scripts, plays, books, true stories and start
putting packages together. If you're a director, start shouting "action!"
and "cut!" until people start listening! This goes for anyone in this business, from aspiring craft service chefs to dancing Foley artists. Don't let
the fear of sucking suck the life out of your dreams!

I'm not saying you shouldn't study, train, and learn your craft. I'm
not saying you shouldn't do your homework and create a plan. I'm
simply trying to lead you to a place in consciousness where you stop
putting your life on the layaway plan. The cosmic truth is that all the
art, music, stories, and movies you'll ever create are already within
you. If you were a completely clear channel, you could actually sit
down and write a script from FADE IN to FADE OUT without stopping to think about it. You could sit down and write a complete song,
then sing it fully realized, without a single rehearsal. Mozart created
this way. Many masters have had the experience of being channels for
the Great Creator, creating works so complete they never had to make
corrections. This possibility exists in you. I don't know if you'll actualize it, but I know that as long as you're waiting to be "good enough,"
or for circumstances to be "just right," you'll be waiting forever.

One of the fundamental errors that causes us to struggle is that we
think *we're doing the work*. We think it's by our own might, mental
capacity, and personal talent that we're creating this stuff, instead of
recognizing that there is a greater Intelligence using us. It's like the
branch of a tree thinking it's creating the fruit. The fruit come *through*
the branch, but not *from* it. If the branch could think independently of
the tree, it would hinder the flow of life appearing as fruit. If it continued to exert its will, it would cut itself off from the tree's life force, lose
the ability to produce fruit, wither and die. As one spiritual master put
it, "The Father that dwelleth in me, He doeth the works." Masters in
every field have articulated this, calling it "Providence," "the Muse,"
"Higher Power," "The Force." To quote Emerson again, we must "take
our bloated nothingness out of the path of the divine circuits." I think
that's a pretty accurate picture of the process.

When you release your ego from the burden of creating, and surrender the process to the "Force" within, the genius that has lain dormant in your subconscious (soul) can spring forth unencumbered. There is such power, such immense talent and masterful creations waiting to express from the depths of your being. Let your true Creative Self come out of the dark caves of your consciousness, and stand fully in the light of day. It will surprise and delight you, I guarantee it. In fact, one sure sign that your latent talent is beginning to emerge is that what comes out shocks you. When you find yourself saying, "Wow, I didn't expect that," "I didn't know *that* was in me," "I can't believe *that* came out of me," you know you're striking oil. If you don't have a little "shock and awe," you're probably working from your head, rehashing old material and just trying to put a new face on it.

Writing the Wrong: Exercise

Here's a quick exercise to get you out of your head, off your butt, and into the creative game. If you're a writer, take out a piece of paper (open your word processor), or turn to a project you've been procrastinating on. Set a timer for twenty minutes. And just start writing. Do not think. Do not pass go. Free fall into the mystery. Write the worst garbage you've ever written. Make no sense. Spell badly. Free-associate. At some point, you're probably going to run out of things to write. Excellent! That's just the beginning. Keep writing, dear scribe. Write until your head feels like it will surely explode! But whatever you do — don't stop until the clock ticks off twenty minutes. Got it? Good. Go!

If you're an actor, pick a monologue you've been working on (or resisting working on), grab one from a book, or make one up. For twenty minutes, do that piece. Over and over. In different voices. Different accents. In pig Latin! As one of our greatest teachers would say, "Do it with a limp and with a lisp, on your head and in your bed. Do it while you jog, do it in a bog, dance it naked, even fake it! Do not judge, do not stall, just act, dear thesps, act your all!" Like our fellow scribblers, you'll probably reach a point where you're exhausted, nothing left to give. Brilliant! Now the real acting can begin. Push past the pain. Let the words fall trippingly over the tongue — or trip and fall over the tongue!

If you're a singer or dancer, the same goes for you. Pick a song and cut loose, baby! Reach for those impossible notes. Stumble through those unreachable moves. And barring war, a hole in the floor, or a natural disaster — don't stop for twenty full minutes!

For those of you in less outwardly active disciplines, write about your work, a project you're stuck on. Pick a task related to your craft and dive in! Twenty minutes. No less. Make mistakes. Take risks. Come up with the stupidest, craziest, most impossible ideas imaginable — then take it even farther! You will not be the same when you're done. A mind stretched never retains its original shape. So go ahead — streeeeeeetch!

Listen to What the Masters Listened To

You are a master. You may not believe it. You may not be actualizing it. But the same power, intelligence, and genius that expresses through the greatest masters is also potential in you. How is that possible? Because "God is no respecter of persons." In Universal Mind, there are no "people" per se, just spiritual ideas, unique composites of everything Infinite Intelligence is. In other words, there's only One Master, and you and I and everyone are individual expressions of it. You can't make this mastery happen, but you can make it welcome. And the first step is accepting that it's the truth about you.

> The same power, intelligence, and genius that express through the greatest masters are also potential in you.

The key to actualizing this mastery lies in your willingness to let go of the "specialness" attributed to the experts, masters, and superstars. Instead of listening to them and trying to emulate their actions — *listen to what they listened to* — and let it express through you. You may never compose like Mozart, but you can listen to the same "music of the spheres" he listened to, and allow it to interpret itself through your instrument, according to your unique design. You may never write like Shakespeare, but you can listen to the Great Author that he listened to, and let it fashion its words according to your unique voice. It's all in you. All the talent, wisdom, genius, and ability possible anywhere are potential within you now. Turn within. Listen to it. Trust it.

Finding a Mentor, Being a Mentor

While some are born with an innate ability to tap into their unique genius, most of us need it to be coaxed out through time and training. Throughout history, many of the greatest artists, athletes, and innovators had masters to apprentice under and coaches to guide them. Indigenous cultures still understand the value of mentoring. And in the more functional families, parents take on this role or choose an appropriate mentor for their child's development. For the most part, however, mentors are sorely missing in society. And in the entertainment industry, finding a true mentor (someone who's been where you want to go, and can show you how to get there) can sometimes feels like a daunting task.

Taking the place of true mentoring are groups — writers groups, actors groups, networking groups, master-mind groups. These are valuable. But they can't replace the face-to-face, in your face, experience of working with an expert on a regular basis, someone who will gently guide and aggressively push you down the path of your purpose. One popular trend is the emergence of Life Coaches. This is a powerful approach to self-mastery, and you might want to consider adding a personal coach to your team. A great coach can help you clarify your mission, craft a plan, and execute it. But they're not necessarily specialists in your field, and might not be able to help you overcome some of the unique obstacles you're likely to face in this business of show.

That's where working with a professional in your chosen field can make a difference. They can steer you away from the pitfalls, shorten your learning curve, recognize your unique gifts, and help you actualize them in a concrete, results-oriented fashion. But finding a professional who can spare the time is another story. Many of them are busy working on their own projects, or they don't seem accessible. But they're out there. And many of them will offer help or advice in some form. You just have to be on the lookout.

So where can you make these mentoring connections? You can start with classes and conferences. If you find a professional or teacher you "click" with, that's someone you should stick with. Keep studying with them — until you know as much as they do. When I started out as a writer, I worked with a script consultant on every script I wrote. I really worked these sessions, asking questions, arguing points, rewriting until my finger bones ached! One day, he looked at me and said he could no longer charge me — because I knew as much as he did. Then he asked me to read *his* scripts and give him feedback.

There are many professionals who speak at these events or sit on panels. And many are available to answer additional questions afterwards. You'd be amazed how much you can learn by huddling in the crowd gathered around the speaker post-event. Sometimes there are even opportunities to assist them at these events. This can be a great way to watch them in action, get their ear, and pick their brain. If you're willing to make a bigger commitment, you may even be able to snag a full- or part-time assistant job.

Many pro writers, actors, and producers have assistants, sometimes more than one. These jobs are usually coveted. But for the lesser-known TV staff writer or the occasional show runner, there can be opportunities to get in on the ground floor. This is a powerful way to build long-term relationships in the business. Find people who are on their way up, but haven't "popped," then find a way to serve their needs. In other words, don't think about "What's in it for me," instead ask, "What can I offer to make their lives easier?"

You could also try writing letters to industry professionals you admire. Make a list of everyone you'd like to know, work with, and be mentored by. Then begin firing off short, sincere letters expressing why you admire and appreciate their work, how it's impacted your life, and how you hope your work can add something of value to the entertainment industry and worldwide audiences. I wouldn't necessarily suggest asking them for any advice or assistance — unless you have something very specific that you think would have a particular meaning to them. For instance, if you know they are serious animal-rights activists and you've just written a script about that subject. Remember that most people's radio station is tuned to WIIFM — *What's In It For Me.* So always try to keep in mind the "What's in it for *them?*" element. If your letter is an act of genuine respect and appreciation, you may get a response, even a chance to talk or correspond with them.

Finally, there's always reading books, listening to tapes, and soaking up everything that a person has created in their career. This isn't usually as powerful as a real-life connection but it's still a potent form of mentoring energy that can fill in some of the gaps of your developmental process. In other words, get it however you can. This is a people business. That's not a statement of limitation. Of course, you can achieve a lot on your own. But it's difficult to grow and progress in a vacuum. We all need feedback, assistance, mirroring. We all have blind spots, areas we're not doing all we're capable of, areas where we're caught in inertia and need to be pulled out of a sinkhole by someone who's walked that street before. (If you're interested in a powerful mentoring program, check out *Star Paths* at *www.EnlightenedEntertainer.com.*)

As we begin to achieve our goals, however small they may seem at times, we also have an opportunity to give back. No matter where you are, there is always someone who's a few steps behind you. Maybe it's a friend, a peer, a family member. And this is where you have a chance to *be a mentor.* I'm not suggesting you try to tell someone how to sell a script if you've never even finished one — and believe me, there are plenty of people who do this! But I am suggesting you be generous with whatever knowledge and wisdom you've gained. Share it openly and unconditionally. The more you give away the wisdom within you, the more you'll have. If you hoard it and are stingy with your gifts, you'll stagnate — like a swamp without an outlet — and have less and less. The quickest and most joyful path to success is by helping as many others as you can achieve success too.

Making Meaningful Material

Finally, this is what it's all about for the sacred artist or enlightened entertainer. You can't achieve true mastery by scraping the surface, treading water, or digging shallow wells. I'm not saying mastery and meaningfulness can't be light and fun. As I've already touched on, "play" is the essence of mastery. However, I believe in the final analysis our work must serve a purpose that *adds* to life. There are many ways to do that, paths through the darkness and the light, through pain, suffering, and joyful celebration. Your creative DNA will determine the way you bring meaning to your work and the world.

One thing that is essential to becoming not only a fully realized creator, but a fully realized human being, is living life fully. My acting teacher, Robert Carnegie, used to tell me that, no matter how hard I worked at my craft, when I got up on that stage I would always bring myself with me. No more, no less. That made an indelible imprint on me. I believe that's why, despite the pyrotechnics and fancy techniques, a person's work won't resonate beyond who they are. You just can't fake depth or meaning. If you live life on the surface, that's what will show up in your work. If you play it safe off stage, your work on stage will be more predictable, formulaic, and shallow. If you avoid intimacy in relationships, your characters will struggle with the same issues — without much conscious awareness or illuminating insights around the subject. If you fail to find the humor in life, you'll have a hard time finding it in your story, song, or acting role.

If you want to make meaningful material, don't obsess about discovering the latest technique for "creating more depth" and "adding more dimension," just live life more deeply. Challenge yourself. Let your heart feel so much it breaks open. It'll mend itself again, I promise. But the new version will be able to lift heavier feelings, like a muscle that's been worked out. Let yourself lose control. Be adventurous. Look for the humor in everything — even tragedy. Laugh until you cry. Cry until you're empty. Then plumb the depths of that emptiness until you find fulfillment. Live your life like a great literary character, like the person you always wanted to be. Live as if everything was supporting you. Let go of the old ideas, the conformist human conventions, the facades, the fake smile, the knee-jerk defensiveness. Surrender it all! Be willing to completely fall apart, to liquefy like the caterpillar in the chrysalis, and be reborn again, and again, and again…

I know this might sound crazy. Impractical. Even pointless. And in a way, it is. Only when you can release your rigid "point" can you become one with the creative force whose "center is everywhere and circumference nowhere." Only when you can go "out of your mind" can you go into your heart and soul. And when you live and create from there, your work will have a universal resonance — because you'll be creating from a place where we all live, where we're all connected, where we are literally the same being. And that oneness, that connectedness is, finally, the "meaning" we're all seeking.

Spiritual Interpretation of Story

Another powerful way to strengthen your ability to create meaningful material is through the practice of *spiritual interpretation of story*. For me, this is the ability to "read" the deeper meaning and spiritual messages in the "stories" of our everyday life. As you begin to look closer, look deeper, and open wider, you start seeing the "fabric of meaning," the very meaning-creating mechanism of our lives and our life stories. You see that nobody comes into our lives by accident, and nothing happens on a whim. You see that truly "All the world's a stage, and all the men and women merely players." You understand the greater themes of this Play of Life — and the different parts people play.

You also start reading stories, watching movies, interpreting music — whatever the medium — on a whole new level. What before might have seemed like merely an entertaining distraction suddenly pulsates with mystical meaning. A line of dialogue that might have previously gone by as an interesting moment now triggers a string of connections that brings rich insight. The whole gestalt of a piece of material becomes more than just a cool chorus, a clever pitch, or a powerful one-sheet, and instead becomes a metaphor for a profound spiritual principle.

As this shift in awareness occurs, you cannot help but weave it into the stories you write, the characters you play, the songs you sing, and the movies you make. You cannot help but see the vast network of connections between the world "out there," the world "in here," and the world of your creation. Indeed, you begin to see that it's all just One World, One Song, One Story — being reflected on various levels. You find yourself on an amazing adventure, where your work becomes more than just what you *do*, it becomes an expression of who you *are*, a process where you excavate the deeper layers of your self, being transformed as your work transforms others. When you study the works of masters, you discover that, for the most part, they were just documenting their own growth. By shining a light on *your* journey, you become a light on the path of others.

From Performer to Trans-former

As this process refines itself, you'll discover a greater call to let go of your ego's grip. You'll be summoned by the spirit within to release attachment to outcome, attachment to other people's opinions, and even all desire for personal gain. This can be scary. It can feel like you're losing something, like you're making yourself too vulnerable — especially in the entertainment industry, which can seem like it's filled with people *only* interested in outcomes, opinions, and personal gain! Remember, the trick of the ego is to make you think *you're the one doing the work.* So if you let go of that self-control, it seems like everything will fall apart, like nothing will get done. This couldn't be further from the truth. In fact, the more you get your small self out of the way, the more life can work through you, making you a channel of its wisdom, genius, and transforming power.

It is no more noble or courageous for a warrior to risk his life on the physical battlefield than for an artist to risk her very identity charging into the fray of the "inner front line." The path of an artist, an enlightened entertainer, can feel as frightening as a combat zone. If a creator is doing the alchemical work of turning the dust and grit of his journey into the gold of true creation, he is risking his heart and soul in creative battle on a regular basis. As Marlon Brando said, "Acting is the art of self-betrayal." In some ways, the warrior, with his armor and

> It is no more noble or courageous for a warrior to risk his life on the physical battlefield than for an artist to risk her very identity charging into the fray of the "inner front line."

weapons, is more protected than the artist, who must stand naked, without shield or sword if she is to create something of real power.

A mere performer just "plays" the part. A "transformer" lives it. They "hold up a mirror," as Shakespeare's Hamlet indicated, showing us the deepest, darkest, noblest parts of our being. They dare to enter the "jungles of self" and confront the monsters that dwell there. They're willing to descend into Hades and stare Death in the eyes — even scarier, to stare themselves in the eyes! They're selfless enough to rise into heaven, where there's only room for One, and let their personal identity be sacrificed on the altar of Truth.

Are you game? It's not too late to turn back, to be just a performer, a writer, a filmmaker. There's nothing wrong with that. It's a viable role to play. But what I'm talking about is something more. What I'm talking about is being initiated back into the sacred covenant of conscious communicators; the origin of story, myth, parable; the place where true entertainment was born, not as a tool of distraction but an instrument of awakening; a tribe that has included the great prophets, philosophers, master teachers, gurus, shamans, high priests, priestesses, and creative geniuses. That's one heck of a mastermind network!

Maybe you think this is "pie in the sky" talk, that they just don't make 'em like they used to. Remember, "God is no respecter of persons." There is no reason why we can't be living in a time of rich culture, of prolific genius, of true renaissance. Everything in the universe is supporting us. Nothing is against us. Or maybe you think that creative genius and commerciality are incompatible. Think again. There have been many successful geniuses. Even in our current times. We must let go of the idea that these great artists and their commercially successful masterpieces are aberrations, exceptions to the rule. Life doesn't operate on a whim. As Einstein said, "God does not play dice with the universe."

There are no accidents. Genius and mastery are not arbitrary occurrences. This is a universe of love, but it's also a universe of law. And those laws that allow for a genius to appear, masterpieces to be created, and abundant success to follow — are in operation all the time. They are as reliable as the laws of gravity, aerodynamics, and electricity. There was a time when we thought electricity was magical, when we thought flight was impossible, when we thought the world was flat. And now we apply these principles and reap their benefits as a matter of course. Likewise, there will be a time when we apply this same faith and practical rigor to the principles of spiritual-artistic excellence and find ourselves in an entertainment industry — and world — filled with masters!

Can you imagine an industry run by artists and other professionals who are living and creating at the level of the great geniuses throughout history? If you can't, that's part of the problem. But if you can embrace this possibility, you're part of the solution.

Beginner's Mind

Ironically, one key principle to becoming a master is by remaining a student. Sure, there will come a time when you have a degree of mastery over your craft. But that's only the start. Sanford Meisner, the renowned acting teacher, said it took twenty years to become an actor. He said this, in part, because he believed an actor needed significant life experience in order to bring real depth to a role. I don't entirely agree with this premise since we all have access to the One Mind (what Jung called the Collective Unconscious) and thus have the ability to tap into any experience. Nevertheless, it's no accident many of the greatest works have been created by artists in their later years. Hollywood's obsession with youth is one reason we don't see much of this seasoned work in the marketplace. (As our consciousness around age shifts, and we no longer buy into this limitation, more of these "seasoned" pros will find their place in the mainstream.)

Regardless of where you are in your training or professional experience, the most potent place to create from is a Beginner's Mind. In that pure, unadulterated state, you are open to the constant inflow of fresh, unpredictable, and unprecedented insight. Picasso said he wanted to be able to hold on to a child-like openness and perception, while maintaining his adult wisdom. He was talking about Beginner's Mind. He was talking about getting back to the unconditioned awareness of a child who has yet to cloud his worldview with all the cultural and societal values, all the rules — all the "shoulds" and "shouldn'ts."

There's a story of a spiritual teacher who finally got the chance to visit the leader of his particular discipline. This was the meeting of a lifetime, a chance to sit at the feet of the master. When the visiting teacher sat down, however, he launched into a passionate proclamation of all the wisdom he had realized in his studies, hardly stopping to breathe, oblivious to anything else in the room. The master just listened, nodded humbly, and poured them both a cup of tea. The teacher continued to talk, spouting off every lesson he had learned, every truth he had discovered, while the master continued to pour him tea — until it spilled over into the teacher's lap, shocking him out of his lengthy lecture. When the teacher asked why the master had done that, the wise man explained that the teacher's cup was so full there was no room left in it. Needless to say, the teacher left this potentially profound encounter without ever truly benefiting from his master's wisdom.

The Master Teacher/Artist within you is always ready to dispense new insights, new ideas, and profound truths. But It can't do this as long as "your cup is full." And there's a reason we're stubborn about keeping our cup full. It's a defense mechanism. We tend to seek out and learn the things we think we *need to know*. Whether it's to get a job, impress a colleague, or achieve our dreams — our knowledge ultimately becomes equal to our survival.

To the ego, it's not really "what you know," it's "what you *are*." Your stored knowledge becomes your identity. So letting it go can feel like a vital part of *you* is being lost, falling apart, being made vulnerable. But this isn't the case. This identity isn't *you*, it's the internal map or script you've created. The script is not the play. The map is not the territory. *You* are not what you've done or what you know. Our inner maps are blueprints or diagrams to help us take our vast life experience and "chunk it down." If we are to evolve as artists, professionals — as human beings — we must continuously let go of the old maps and scripts and be willing to rest in the emptiness, the gap, the "desert experience," so that a new, more complex, more refined map or script can be revealed.

When you think you've "arrived," that you "know it all," that you're an "expert" — when you become too attached to the content of your cup — you become blocked. You become a closed system. Closed systems eventually wear down and die. To put it in industry parlance, you become "irrelevant," "outdated," "so yesterday." The phone stops ringing. The offers stop coming, or never even start. And you find yourself booking a seat on the *Hollywood Squares* — or sitting in the audience! On the flip side, if you manage to become "open at the top", willing to have a beginners mind, new opportunities and ideas flow in and, as the ancient promise says, "Behold I make all things new!" The next unfoldment of your evolution is able to come into manifestation. Then, of course, everyone proclaims that you have "reinvented yourself"!

The practice of reinventing is an ever-evolving, never-ending process. Every day, every moment, we must be willing to let go of what came before — all of our great ideas, creative works, former abilities, personal identities, past successes — and be open to the unconditioned substance of the spirit within us. We must eat of "fresh manna." That's why the Lord's Prayer says, "Give us this day our daily bread." It doesn't say, "Give us this week our daily bread," or "Give us enough bread to last through pilot season!" Universal Intelligence doesn't work that way. It can't. It doesn't know time. Your long-term plans, your entire future, are all part of God's now. Now is the only time there is, ever has been, or ever will be. Dying and being reborn/reinvented daily is all about living fully in the present.

You have never happened before. What you're here to express has never happened before. You are an unrepeatable event in the Universe (which is another reason to feel some obligation to be yourself fully).

You, your life, and your work are, quite literally, unprecedented. You can't lean on past examples or present conditions to determine who you are or what you're meant to be and do.

> What you're here to express has never happened before.

What you see "out there" are *effects*. They have no substance, no power. They're images projected on the screen of material, mental, emotional experience. If you look to the past (what was successful before) and try to repeat it, or look to the world (what is successful now) and try to conform to it, you're not just rehashing old, outworn ideas — you're dancing with the dead.

Walking this path requires great courage. It's living on the razor's edge, holding on to nothing but the invisible hand of Truth within. This is where the enlightened entertainer, the artist-mystic, is called to live. This is where masters are most comfortable. Mastery is not a static thing. It's a state of mind that knows there is an infinite idea trying to express through a finite instrument in a finite realm. One of the first steps to mastery is to relax and know you'll never "arrive." It's the old saw that the journey is more important than the destination. In fact, the journey is *all* there is. You'll never reach the end of the road. Like the horizon, no matter how fast you run toward it, it recedes into the distance.

Forget yesterday's insights. Forget what worked before. Enjoy what you're doing and creating now, be nourished by the ideas and insights flowing through you now. Then let it all go and step into the next NOW naked, empty, ready to be reborn again — catapulted through the birth canal of consciousness into a whole new world of possibilities. Every moment, the Big Bang explodes anew. Every moment is Genesis. This is not a metaphor. It's what's happening. When you get still enough, quiet enough, you can see with insight that this entire universe is being re-created, reincarnated in every instance. It's flashing on and off so fast, the senses can't perceive it. In every "on" moment, the collective consciousness of the race — which includes your individual consciousness — is manifested. And in every "off" moment, the entire universe disappears back into the void.

In that gap lies the power to "begin again."

Your Life Is God's Masterpiece

We're all creative beings, artists at heart — whether or not we create literal art for a living or a hobby. It could be no other way. We are the offspring of the Great Creative Force of the universe. And as we open more to this identity, we find that our "art" is only one small aspect of the greater creative project — our life. In the final analysis, our entire life is the canvas upon which we paint our picture, the screen upon which we project our inner movie, the instrument through which we play our music.

When you live this way, you don't wait for an opportunity to express your creativity in the entertainment industry, you pour it into everything you do. Every relationship, every circumstance — every moment — becomes a part of the portrait you're painting, the script you're writing, the song you're singing. It unleashes the great creative power within you — a power that has the ability to find a solution to any problem. It makes you a more perceptive, fully alive human being able to create from a deeper, richer place. But there's an even greater payoff. When you know you are not only the artist of your own life, but the instrument through which the Divine Artist is creating Its Masterpiece — you become free from the victimhood that grips so many people (in this business and elsewhere). You truly realize that nothing is by accident. Every brush stroke, every scene, every resounding note is a part of your co-creative experience with the Infinite.

Another benefit of realizing that your life is a work of art is that you don't take this business too seriously. It's so easy, especially in the entertainment industry, to become all-consumed. I've met aspiring and working artists and entertainment professionals who were so obsessed with "the biz" they couldn't talk or think about anything else! All work and no play doesn't just make Jack a dull boy, it makes his work dull as well. And that will soon make Jack an unemployed boy. It's great to be passionately committed to your work. Just remember it's only one part of the picture you're making.

Acts of Courage: "Going Out of Your Mind"

One of the paths to Mastery is to transcend your rigid, rational thinking mind, enter into the gap of the stillpoint, and express from there. This can be consciously cultivated through meditation and mindfulness techniques. Below are two exercises to get out of your familiar frame of reference and experience a deeper dimension of being:

1. **Scaring the hell out of you.** What is something you would do if you were crazy enough, something you might've done when you were "young and foolish" — something that scares the hell out of you? I'm not talking about risking your physical life (although doing scary but relatively safe things, like skydiving, could work). What I'm referring to are things like public speaking, open mic night, going to a nude beach, telling someone what you really think, making intimate contact with someone that terrifies you. It's interesting to note that scaring the "hell" out of us is what we want. "Hell" represents where we *don't* want to live, what we *don't* want to be. So why are we so scared to scare that hell out of us? What are we afraid we'll find when we've scared all the hell out? What will be left? Heaven? It's worth investigating.

2. **Tapping the Mind of a Master.** This exercise not only gets you out of your head, it gets you into someone else's. In this process, the point is to see your life — or a project — through the mind of a master (alive or passed on, in your field or another). For example, maybe you're stuck on a song and can't crack the chorus. And let's say you have a deep admiration for John Lennon. In this meditation, you could call the consciousness of John into your mind, feel the connection, then begin writing.

Get in a comfortable position (like previous mediation exercises), close your eyes, and watch your breath. Don't force it. Let it flow, in and out, at its own pace. As you become still and quiet, bring to mind the master of your choosing. See them with your inner eye, doing the thing they mastered. See their passion, their energy. It's contagious, like an aura that draws you closer, until you're right beside them. Feel the electricity arc off their skin. Take a deep breath and relax — as you let them step *into* your body. Feel the jolt of energy as their spirit infuses yours. Be aware of how you feel and what you're thinking.

When you're ready, open your eyes, take a pen in your left hand (to tap your unconscious), and start free-writing about whatever project you're working on, feeling stuck on, or preparing to begin. It could even be general ideas about your life and work. Whatever the subject is, write about it without thinking — *as if you are possessed by this person.* If your hand gets tired, switch. After a few moments, switch back. If you start to lose the connection, go back into meditation. To add a twist, this time see yourself stepping into *them,* so that you are literally in their body. Write for at least ten minutes. When you're done, look at what you've written.

Any surprises, breakthroughs? There is only One Mind. When you accessed that master's mind, you were simply tapping into a part of the One Mind, which is *your* mind. What it means, in substance, is that what is known anywhere, at any time, is known *everywhere now* — just waiting for you to plug in.

Check-In

If you've diligently done the work thus far, there have probably been significant shifts — at least in your perceptions. And it's only the beginning. This is planting seeds that will, in due time, sprout fresh insights, ideas, and even healings.

So how are you? If you haven't done so, now might be a good time to go back through your journal and reflect on what you've written.

See any patterns? Changes? Do you feel differently about the industry, your role in it, your art, craft, or job? How? Why?

Take a moment to "catch your breath," because we're about to take things up a notch.

PART V
The Business of Show

NINE

Doing the "Real" Deal

"Ethical existence is the highest manifestation of spirituality."

— Albert Schweitzer

From Your Artist's Heart to Your Business Head

We've spent a lot of time on your inner life. This is essential to become an enlightened entertainer. But it's only half the equation. It's true that to be spiritually empowered, you must disengage from the limited beliefs of society and be *not of this world*. But to be spiritually effective in this material dimension, you must also be *in this world*. Buddha called it the "Middle Path." And a big part of being "in this world" is building a business sense, cultivating your ability to "render unto Caesar what is Caesar's."

As an enlightened entertainer, in whatever capacity, you have three primary tasks:

- Spiritual/personal growth (mastery of mind, body, spirit, relationships, etc.)
- Mastering/expressing your gifts, talents, and abilities at the highest level
- Marketing your gifts, talents, abilities — and the resulting "products'

The last one, "marketing," encompasses everything from building a network, exposing yourself and your work to more people, and creating a system and structure to sustain continual growth and expansion in your professional career. It stands for the "business" part of "show." And it's the area that usually trips up us "creative types." We want to create our art, but we don't want to market it. In fact, the word "marketing" is a four-letter word to some "arteests." But that's just a misunderstanding of what it is.

Put simply, marketing is the process of articulating your work's features and benefits (whether it's a script, song, film, acting ability, etc.) in a way that compels others to buy it. I'm not only referring to the actual sale of the product. I'm talking about every level of its journey — from conception to exhibition. You're always selling or marketing. And people are always "buying" or "rejecting" what you're selling. Every time you speak to someone is a *marketing moment*, even if you're not talking about any project in particular, because you're always marketing your most valuable asset — YOU.

The idea of marketing yourself may go against everything you believe. Calling your art a "product" might provoke a desire to set fire to it — or yourself — before you'll let it be violated in the stench-ridden troughs of those capitalist pigs! But marketing and artistic excellence are not mutually exclusive. Picasso, the Beatles, and Elvis were great marketers. Spielberg, Madonna, Brian Grazer, and M. Night Shyamalan understand the fine art of the pitch. Van Gogh: brilliant painter, lousy marketer. He sold one painting his entire life — to his brother. This was not an indication of his talent, but of his ability to expose that talent in a way that was accessible.

I know this will upset some who say he was "ahead of his time." "People just didn't *get him*" is the common refrain. Besides, it doesn't matter if your work finds an audience — all that matters is you created it. Give me a break! It's the tragic tale of unrealized genius. A powerfully motivating story to *tell*. Not a great one to live. It's true you must create for the joy of it. It's also true that whether or not you sell anything, if you commit your life to expressing your creative heart, you have added great value to the consciousness of humanity. But I'm assuming you want to get paid for your work. This requires you to engage the world head-on.

If you want to live life toiling at your craft in obscurity, that's your prerogative. But I don't believe a universe as elegant and intelligent as this creates parts that don't fit NOW. It's like a master watchmaker creating a beautiful piece for a watch — and not creating a watch to put it in! Would you do that? And if *you* wouldn't, don't you think the Infinite Intelligence that created the cosmos — including you — would be at least as smart? Seriously, if you had everything in the universe at your disposal, would you create something that wouldn't have any real use or application *until long after you were dead?!* As you can see, I'm a bit passionate about this subject? I don't want you to "hide your light under a bushel." I want you to throw that damn lampshade off, and shine your light for all the world to see! (Even if your "world" is simply your city, community, or church).

Look at nature. Everything has a specific place. The unique talents and abilities of everything are put to use now, not in the future. The fruit that falls from the trees is eaten or used as fertilizer. The tree doesn't create a fruit that won't be utilized until after the tree is decomposing in the dirt! Many people — especially creative people — walk around with the thought that maybe their work will never be put to good use — and, hey, that's just the life of an artist. *Wrong.* That's not a life, that's a lie. The fruit that we produce is meant to be eaten, to be savored, and to nourish others. Not only after we die. Not in our next life. Not after we burn away all our bad karma. But today. Tomorrow. And for the rest of our lives on this blue jewel hurtling through space.

The universe that Infinite Love created can only produce fulfillment. Everything has its place to come to fruition. I'm not casting judgment on van Gogh, or anyone who experiences similar struggles. I don't know what his soul's path was, but I believe it was exactly what he needed for his evolution. My issue is with the *idea* of the artist-martyr as some supreme expression of real artistry. It perpetuates the lie that if you create something worthy, you'll be unrecognized, unsuccessful, broke, depressed, alcoholic, insane, and suicidal! This isn't about good or bad, right or wrong, even true or false — it's about effective or ineffective. We have to ask ourselves if the choices we're making *work*. Are they bringing us closer or taking us further away from the life we want to live?

Many artists romanticize
this starving, suffering,
tormented artist life...
then complain that they're
not able to pay rent and
blame it on the business!

I know I'm hitting this pretty hard; it may even seem like a tangent. It's not. The problem is many artists romanticize this starving, suffering, tormented artist life and have a lot of judgment about the business side of things — then complain that they're not able to pay rent and blame it on the business! For some it's a badge of honor they wear and proclaim every chance they get. For others it's largely unconscious. They're trying hard to succeed but the brass ring — or even that plastic decoder ring in Cracker Jacks — eludes them. Perhaps you don't think you fit this group. Perhaps you're right. Just look at your life and see if you're actualizing your true potential. If not, chances are you're harboring limited or judgmental ideas about business, money, and success. This can be a painful, oppressive way to live. What's more, you're not only withholding from yourself, you're withholding from the world — a world that needs what you have to offer.

Perhaps you or those in your circle think it's not "spiritual" to market yourself. If that's true, it was a blasphemous act that brought this book to you. If it wasn't for some form of marketing — even word of mouth — you never would've known about it. What about the most inspiring, life changing spiritual book or class you ever had? How did you find it? Unless you were "divinely guided" with your eyes and ears closed, odds are some form of marketing paved the way. If the individual who created it didn't "market" it, you never would've received the blessings it brought you. One of the best-selling holy books of all time — the Bible — is also one of the most mass-marketed!

Jesus and Buddha were marketing giants. They didn't just sit in a cave and contemplate the cosmos. They pounded the pavement (dirt and sand), went from town to town, speaking, performing miracles — which, by the way, were the perfect marketing hook. If Jesus

Jesus and Buddha were
marketing giants.

was alive today, he'd probably promote his path as The Good News Tour! Now before you start sending me hate mail, hear me out. JC didn't *need* to perform miracles — he already passed that temptation in the desert — he used them to *sell* his message. He knew the people needed proof that he was credible, that what he had to offer was of real and immediate value to them — so they'd accept it. Both JC and Buddha packaged their spiritual principles so the people would "buy" them. And it worked brilliantly. The fact that they were enlightened masters also didn't hurt. If you're waiting for a lightning bolt to strike, don't worry. This isn't sacrilegious. It's practical. And I'm confident that JC and the Big "B" would, at the very least, get a good chuckle out of it. The greatest masters understand the need to be spiritual, artistic, *and* practical.

The bottom line is that you want — even need — to get your goods into the hands of those who can benefit from them. You want your movies, music, and any other media you create to impact as many people as possible. If you had something you knew could truly help a lot of people, something that could add real value to their lives, wouldn't you want to do everything you could to get it to them? That, in essence, is what business and marketing is all about. Contrary to what many "business people" will say, a business's primary function is not merely to make a profit. A business's primary function is to provide valuable services or goods. Profit is the by-product of a job well done. In other words, true business and marketing are all about "service."

Sometimes simply putting it out there is enough, especially if what you're doing is truly innovative — or can turn water into wine and raise people from the dead. But more often, just "putting it out there" doesn't get the job done. There's too much competition. People are too skeptical. They've been burned too many times, wasted too much money on junk. And they are, quite literally, on information overload. So in order to truly stand out from the pack and connect in a meaningful way with your prospective audience, you need to creatively promote yourself and your work. And you need to do it in a way that calms the buyers' fears, overcomes their doubts, and convinces them that they really need what you're offering. This sounds like manipulation, but it really isn't. Remember, you have something that can add real value to people's lives. Your job is to help them see that.

Going back to the master spiritual teachers, they knew they had something that could help people. But they also knew that people were
caught in various forms of lack, limitation, fear, and doubt. They didn't
just spew out a bunch of spiritual ideas and leave it at that. That wouldn't
have been "effective marketing" — and they knew that. Instead, they
framed their ideas and teachings in a way that the "audience" could (a)
understand and relate to in their current cultural context; (b) see the
value and significance of these teachings in their own lives; and (c) be
convinced that they needed what was being "sold." That's the aim of
marketing. The rest of business is just delivering the goods.

How Can You Be a Light If You Can't Pay Your Light Bill?

Many on a spiritual path believe that money and spirituality are mutually exclusive. They have, consciously or unconsciously, taken a vow of
poverty. They think money is the root of all evil and will corrupt their
soul. They believe the pie is finite, and if they have a lot, others will
have a lot less — or the other way around. They not only withhold the
good from themselves, but resent the good others have (believing that
it's taking away from the "little people"). This is a false belief, based
on a limited perception of an abundant universe. It not only hurts the
one believing it, but perpetuates a lack consciousness.

Many artists (pronounced "arteests") share this belief system. Like
marketing and business, they believe art and *commerciality* are mutually
exclusive. They believe money will corrupt their art — that it's the root
of all mediocrity. As I've already discussed, this breed of starving artists
believe good work comes out of pain and suffering. They not only
withhold joy and fulfillment from themselves, but regard successful
artists with contempt. While their work may be evocative, its negative
energy perpetuates the starving artist syndrome and slows the evolution of the creative community. Bottom line, the work they produce is
probably not worth the price we all pay.

What you believe and how you live impact the entire artistic/entertain-
ment community and beyond — for better or worse. Your playing small

doesn't benefit anyone — it perpetuates the fear and limitation that is holding others hostage. When you let your light truly shine, however, you light the path for others. As you are lifted up in consciousness and in the world, you pull others up with you. As you embrace an abundant perspective about your craft and career, you create a new paradigm of possibility that creates a space for others to expand into. As you accept, articulate, and act on a greater vision for this industry and yourself, you create an environment where it can come into fruition for the good of all. In other words, it's not just your right to be an abundant artist and entertainment professional — it's your spiritual obligation as an enlightened entertainer.

Selling Yourself Without Selling Your Soul

As we've been discussing, to succeed in show *business*, you'll need to do a degree of self-promotion and marketing. No matter what your position or profession, you have to sell yourself and your products or services. The challenge for the enlightened entertainer is to do this in integrity with your deeper values and creative vision. You want to market your wares without losing your awareness, sell yourself without selling your soul. This requires that you be rooted deeply in who and what you really are, and know where your good truly comes from. (Hint: it's not from Hollywood.)

This might also mean you "wash some dishes" in the beginning, doing work that doesn't feel like your destiny but pays the bills and puts you in a position to make more contacts and develop your skills. At other times, the inner call may prompt you to sacrifice "good" work for the "best" work. You might have to say "no" to an immediate reward, to be available for a bigger "yes" in the future. There have been several times where I risked failure and poverty (or so I fantasized) to work on a script, book, or business that wasn't bringing immediate benefits — only to have it pay big dividends down the road.

I'd rather live under a bridge doing *my* work than live in a mansion doing someone else's. There may be times when you're tempted to stray from your integrity in a business deal or take advantage of

> I'd rather live under a bridge doing "my work" than live in a mansion doing "someone else's" work.

someone else's weaker position, times where you'll need to take a stand and reject a deal to honor yourself, and times when you'll need to accept "less than your worth" to gain greater humility and a recognition that your employer is not your source. (The Spirit within is.) All these stages are about growing in consciousness — not just creating a successful career or artistic creation. They test your faith, uncover blind spots, and force you to expand beyond your known self.

Beyond Your Business Card

In the entertainment industry, as in other fields, we gain a great deal of identity from our professional status. When we meet at parties, it's usually "So what do you do?" or "What are you working on?" These aren't innocuous throw-away lines. These questions — and their answers — *matter*, at least at this level of the game. Watch how the light in the greeter's eyes changes based on the answers. "Oh, I'm a producer, putting together Mel's next picture." Even if the greeter plays it cool, their eyes will twinkle and their rate of respiration will increase. However, if the answer is "I'm an actor, looking for an agent," not only will the light in their eyes often leave — so will they.

If you're in a group of successful pros, the responses can be quite the opposite. They usually don't need anything from you, so they tend to be interested in more than just your resume. Nevertheless, the pressure to "be someone important" is ever-present in Tinseltown. You will be tempted to "act important," whether that means reciting your bio after every "hello" or creatively constructing your credits to sound more successful. Actually, I encourage some creativity in self-marketing (as long as it's still true) especially if it gets you past the dreaded "What do you do/what have you done?" and onto more substantive conversation. Just don't let it morph into B.S. and you'll be fine.

The thing to remember is that you're more than the title on your business card — you can do more and be more. And even if you had no job, no resume, and no fancy letterhead, who and what you are in your core is infinitely more interesting and valuable than anything you could ever engrave on 20 lb card stock. Trust that. Be that. Even if you give the traditional response when asked those introductory questions, silently respond with the truth:

"I'm an instrument of cosmic consciousness and creative genius, and I'm working on awakening to my full potential, developing enlightened entertainment, and transforming the planet in the process. Want to join me?"

Or something like that.

The Pearl of Other People's Opinions

Most people are susceptible to the opinions of others. But nowhere is this more of a jugular issue than in the entertainment industry — a business that often lives and dies by opinions. Where else can the fate of a project you've labored on for months — even years — be determined by one night (opening night reviews on Broadway) or one weekend (most movie releases)? Where else can notorious, even criminal, behavior create such a buzz it makes you *more* famous? Where else is there an entire industry within an industry devoted to proliferating mass opinions for sheer pleasure (tabloid magazines)?

As we've already discussed, the only opinion that matters is the one you have of yourself — or, more accurately, the one your Higher Power has of you. And the only control you have on reviews is in the quality of your work. (Even that may not matter, since many reviews are merely the opinions of people less knowledgeable about your work than you, people with hidden agendas, people sometimes so jaded by overexposure to bad material that they have very little constructive objectivity left.) A real professional — especially an enlightened entertainer — doesn't put too much stock in unsolicited criticisms. They're too busy living their vision to invest time and energy into destructive things.

It's still a good idea to be open to some feedback, however — 360-degree feedback if possible. If you're grounded in a strong sense of self, or at least have the tools to process input, feedback can fulfill a valuable function. From this perspective, you can listen to what others say, not to determine your ultimate value, but to discern your inner voice — those parts where you may have blind spots. How is this possible? There's only One Voice speaking through many mouthpieces. It requires practice, an ability to sort through opinions until you find the pearls. But if you don't take it personally, you can tune other people's feedback like a radio and create a direct link to the divine broadcast.

No matter what anyone, or any institution, thinks about you, it can never hinder, block, or deny the fulfillment of your divine purpose.

Regardless of the feedback, always remember that another person's opinion has no power over you. No matter what anyone, or any institution, thinks about you, it can never hinder, block, or deny the fulfillment of your divine purpose. There is only One Authority governing everything — and Its opinion of you is already locked. You are Its Beloved in whom It is well pleased. And nothing you do, or don't do, will ever change Its Mind.

Flow with the Go: Recognizing Opportunities

Some folks are so busy looking — or waiting — for the *right* opportunity that they miss other opportunities that could get them where they want to go. It's easy to get such a firm picture in your head of who you are, what you *should* be doing, where and with whom — that you are blind to the myriad ways in which the universe is trying to fulfill your heart's desire. There isn't just one way to make your dreams come true. There are infinite possibilities; infinite combinations of people, places, and events; infinite mixtures of thoughts, feelings, and actions. And every time you think you know how things *should* look, you literally collapse all of infinity into a finite pinprick of limited possibility.

For example, if you're a screenwriter, maybe you think the only way you can make money writing, and advance your career, is by selling a script or getting hired on some studio assignment. Because of that, when a lesser or seemingly unrelated opportunity comes your way, you either don't see it or brush it off as "not for you" or "beneath you." Sometimes it really isn't for you. But other times, maybe more often than you think, it's a special delivery from the divine — and you slam the door in the messenger's face.

For example, when I started out as a screenwriter, people began asking me to read their scripts and give feedback. I was reluctant. I didn't think I was qualified and, honestly, I didn't want to "waste" my time. But eventually I wore down and accepted. And after doing it for a while, the thought occurred that I could actually *charge* for script reading. I brushed it off as silly, "not for me," and continued to crank out my own scripts and read other people's at no cost — while toiling away at a day job waiting tables. Still the thought persisted, the messenger kept knocking on my door. Again, I wore down, accepted the call — and started charging to read scripts. And they agreed to pay me. Over and over! Then told their friends to hire me too!

I was a bit shocked and didn't entirely believe I deserved it, but I was learning to go with the flow. Or "flow with the go" as Dr. Michael Beckwith says. And before I knew it, I was able to quit my "day job" and make a living consulting on other writers' scripts while working on my own. But it didn't end there. Some clients liked what I had to say so much they hired me to rewrite their scripts and, in some cases, write them from scratch — at a much higher fee. In other words, I was now being paid as a screenwriter — my original goal.

I started out avoiding and denying the opportunities in front of me because I wanted to focus on getting paying work as a screenwriter — and *I knew best how to achieve this.* After much struggle and resistance, I let go of my ideas of how things *should* happen and just said "yes" to the universe. This resulted in an adventure I never could have imagined — and a six-figure income script doctoring and screenwriting. And that was just the beginning. This directly led to other opportunities, other relationships, script options, script development deals, and staff writing jobs. It also led to me creating a best-selling book on screenwriting and script consulting — *I Could've Written a Better Movie Than That!* — which led to more writing gigs and book deals, including the book you're holding in your hands right now.

I can't tell you how many times I almost said "no" to a party, a meeting, a prospect — that ended up yielding career-changing, cash-infusing, soul-inspiring opportunities. On one hand, life is so hearty and durable, and on the other hand it's so fragile; precariously perched at the edge of each moment, ready to fall into a chasm — or take flight. The universe is a complex thing. It really is a mystery. And regardless of all the planning we do, we can't know what's around the bend. But Universal Intelligence does. Once we set our intentions and do the groundwork, if we are willing to "go out of our mind," and "flow with the go," we'll find a host of invisible angels winging to our aid. And as we continue to say "yes," the path will lead us closer and closer to the fulfillment of our heart's desire and true purpose.

Many people have asked me, "How do I know if an opportunity is right for me?" That's something each individual must discover for themselves. But there are a few characteristics of an opportunity worth investigating:

1. **It has luminosity**. It glows, radiates, stands out from everything else in some way. I'm not talking a burning bush necessarily. Just that the opportunity, the place, the person, or the communication catches your attention more than usual.

2. **It interests you.** There's something about the person, place, or thing that intrigues, inspires, or at least makes you curious. (But because it seems like a tangent, "impossible," or "not for you," you don't think you should pursue it.)

3. **It scares you.** It makes you nervous to even consider it. You want to go for it, you want to say "yes," but you're afraid you'll fail, make a fool of yourself...or die.

4. **It's "beneath you."** Maybe you've already worked a lot in your field, so the idea of auditioning for something out of *Backstage West*, writing a script on "spec," or directing a play instead of a feature sounds like a step backwards. However, there's something about the situation that seems to "call" to you.

What opportunities are you letting pass you by because you don't think they're for you? Scan your life and ask yourself if there are things you *could* do if you were willing to step outside your comfort zone, take a pay cut, take a risk (even risk your pride), or go that extra mile. Try to inquire into at least one opportunity per month that you would normally brush aside. Maybe it's going to a party you usually wouldn't, or sending in a picture and resume for a job you normally wouldn't audition for. Look for where life is opening doors, giving you green lights — then "flow with the go" and see where it leads you.

Divine Justice: Calling on Faith Before Calling Up a Lawyer

In this highly litigious society, the temptation to sue someone — anyone — is spreading like a virus. In the entertainment industry, many people have either caught the suing sickness or they're terrified of being a victim of it. Besides being a waste of time and energy, it erodes trust and respect in the entire community. I'm not saying there isn't a time for upholding your legal rights. What I'm suggesting, however, is adopting the idea of "divine justice." The universe is already an orderly and just system. It doesn't require a battle to restore harmony. In fact, inequalities in our life are usually not because the scales *outside* of us are out of balance, but because the ones *inside* are.

It comes down to the core idea of "Oneness" again. We've talked extensively about this, from various perspectives. But it bears repeating. There's nobody out there but you. If you're engaged in any kind of battle, it's really with yourself. I know this is a huge, ugly horse pill for some of us to swallow, but it is, in fact, the way things really work. If there is only One Life Force (and quantum physicists are now confirming this, naming it, among other things, the "unified field theory"), then there isn't anybody else to battle with. The only place separation exists is in our own mind. So while you may fight the good fight, and even win the battle in court, you will, more often than not, lose the war.

And what is that war? The war on duality — and all the pain and suffering this combative consciousness causes us. This war can never be won by fighting, only by surrendering. And while surrendering may make you appear weak temporarily — even cause you to lose some material good momentarily — it will ultimately make you stronger, more empowered, and capable of manifesting your destiny. More often, however, the act of true surrender — and the transformation it produces — causes you to win both "out there" and "in here." Gandhi brought the British Empire to its knees without firing a shot, throwing a punch, or submitting a subpoena — and he was a lawyer!

Again, I'm not saying you'll never use the legal system. There may be an appropriate time to go to court and make your case. Using legal action may be the way the universe is accomplishing its purposes through you. However, when done consciously, it is quite a different experience. You're not going to court to "get something," "make them pay," "exact revenge," or "lock them up and throw away the key." In your soul, you know you already have it all, that all is well, that your legal "opponent" is really the divine in disguise, and that the case is really about the Karmic Law being fulfilled. From this perspective, you can actually sue someone *and* love them. I'm not kidding! In this way, you're not perpetuating any more separation or creating any more karma.

The consciousness with which you do something is *always* more important than what you do. It is, in fact, what largely determines the outcome. But don't try to fool yourself or the universe, acting like you're more enlightened than you really are. You may be able to put on a show for judge and jury, but there's a Higher Court that always hears your case. If you're still harboring a sense of "us" and "them," the evidence will ultimately be brought to light and you'll be sentenced to hard time in a prison of your own making — one where the only key to freedom will be your own awakening.

So the next time you feel compelled to call up your lawyer, call on your faith first. Ask how this situation is calling you to grow, how it's revealing your own inner struggles and injustices. What qualities would you have to embody to be okay with it? How would you have to change to have compassion and forgiveness for the other person, rather than anger and a desire to "get even" or "get your fair share"? Again, I'm not saying you won't have your day in court. But if you do the inner work, the "you" standing there when the sentence is handed down will not be the same person who filed the complaint.

From Competition to Cooperation

In the West, competition is considered a constructive quality. But the fact is — and this will likely stir up controversy — competition is one of the most "destructive" forces. At least most forms of it. The reason is that, at its core, competition is based on the idea of a "winner" and a "loser"; someone has to be "lesser" for someone to be "better"; if someone gets "a lot," someone has to get "a lot less"; if someone becomes a star, it diminishes *your* chances; if that writer, producer, or director gets a two-picture deal, your odds decrease. It's an either/or scenario. There's a finite pie and the idea of "there's more than enough to go around" is just "pie in the sky." *Lack and Separation,* not Abundance and Oneness, is the premise on which most competition is based.

This is, quite simply, a lie. And it has perpetuated more greed, violence, poverty, and destruction than almost any other force on the planet. While it's true that we live in a finite material world, our ability to manifest is infinite. Even without getting into metaphysics, this world is so plentiful with an abundance of every conceivable resource, that if we used our imagination, if we opened our hearts, minds, and eyes, we would discover that there is, indeed, more than enough to go around. Food is rotting in storehouses while people starve in the streets. There are libraries in every city with enough information to render a free education for all who seek one — yet vast swaths of society remain uneducated, complaining that they don't have the resources. Billions of dollars a year are wasted in government bureaucracy, money that, if freed up, could transform society. I could go on and on with examples like this. But let's look at the entertainment industry, where so many people claim there isn't enough opportunity...

There are over 200 TV channels (and counting), even more radio stations (and counting), hundreds of feature films made a year (and many hundreds more purchased and put into development), over 100,000 books published a year, unlimited cyberspace with unlimited potential for creative productions and dynamic, profitable, purposeful communications, every cell phone and PDA is becoming a mini-entertainment center with a whole line of product all its own, airplanes are installing mini-entertainment centers with content needs all their own, video games are not only becoming ubiquitous but increasingly story-driven (thus, needing storytellers to assist in their development, voice their characters, etc.), hotels are becoming amusement parks filled with "entertainment value" and a need for entertainment-minded people to fulfill that need, and corporate America is now hiring people with degrees in filmmaking, creative writing, and other artistic abilities to bring a more creative, narrative approach to their products and services. (GE recently hired a poet!) We are entering an "entertainment culture" where everything is becoming about the "entertainment experience." (Whether this is a good thing is beside the point — at least the point I'm making right now). The fact is, there is much more demand than there is quality content — especially quality *conscious content.*

But there's an even deeper problem with "competition" as we currently express it in this industry and beyond. Besides being another huge waste of time, energy, and resources (think of how much talent and treasure is spent, and how much mediocrity is mass-produced, in trying to beat the other guy), it perpetuates a belief and experience of lack and limitation that erodes our ability to progress. Many say that competition is good for growth; that it forces people to give better quality and service in order to stay on top; that without it we wouldn't become better. I disagree. Sure, competition, as a force of society, drives some to give more for less — especially those who might otherwise seek to take advantage of others. But it's primarily a force of fear, based on a premise of lack. And the seeds of fear always bring forth a harvest of limitation. Simple cause-and-effect.

If we dig deeper, we see that it's not competition that causes growth (not evolutionary growth), any more than fear causes us to protect our children. We might be afraid they'll get hurt or be unhealthy if we don't do the right things — but that's not the fundamental driving force. The real power behind true progress is, quite simply, love. We love our children. We want to provide a better life for them. That love, that vision, is what inspires and compels us to do what it takes to achieve that. Likewise, when you look into the heart of any truly outstanding business, successful artist, or top entertainment professional, you'll find the same love at work; a love of their art or craft, a love of their business and the product or service they provide; a love of themselves and their own expression; a love of their clients, prospects, audience, and people in general. To the extent that this love is corrupted by competition, to that extent the business, the product, and the prospect suffer.

In our core, we do better, give more, and reach higher because we are inspired by the divine within us to actualize our greatest potential and the greater potential of humanity.

This, finally, is the only genuine competition: *To be better than our former selves — to be the very best we can be.*

Think about it. Do you need to be driven by a desire to beat the other guy in order to succeed? Wouldn't it be more effective to just strive to be the best you can be? In the economics of energy, isn't it more "cost-effective" to put all your energy into your performance rather than wasting it in resistance against a so-called opponent? To me, it's simple math. And then there's the Oneness Factor again. If we're really all one — and we are — who is there to compete against? The short answer: nobody. There really isn't. And all our energy of competition only serves to perpetuate the experience of "otherness" and all the baggage that comes along with it. It saps our creative strength, eats up our vast resources, renders us relatively impotent, and degrades our fundamental character. Rats in a rat race are still rats no matter who wins!

When you align yourself with the principle of oneness, get out of the game of competition, and into the flow of cooperation, you are in league with the infinite power of the universe. It's not an easy world to walk in at first, but the rewards are well worth it. Not only do you have greater peace of mind, more creative energy, and a sense of connectedness with all of creation, but you become more immune from the body blows, blocks, and other opposing forces of the game — because you're no longer on that playing field. As Einstein said, "Arrows of hate have been shot in my direction many times, but they did not touch me, because they came from a world I no longer inhabited."

If You Bill It, They Will Come

As you embrace the business of show, there are many things you can do to "make it official." Exactly how this looks depends on your particular talents and skills. If you're a producer, taking your business seriously might look like getting cards, renting an office space, joining professional networks, soliciting scripts. If you're an actor, it might look like taking acting, voice, or personal marketing classes. If you're a writer, it might look like getting all the necessary equipment and tools for your trade, joining a professional writers group, creating an official office space (even if it's in your home for now), and making sure all your scripts are presented in the most professional format possible.

In all of these cases, you'll engage in some form of advertising and marketing, you may develop a team of professionals (lawyer, agent, manager, accountant) and incorporate yourself. And in all of these, I encourage you to keep a clean, orderly workspace. A cluttered office (or car) is a sign of a cluttered mind. And, whether you're aware of it or not, that clutter is sapping precious psychic energy from you. Get rid of what you don't need. Create a system that allows you to maintain a clean, professional space. If you can't muster up the emotional courage to dive into that experiment in chaos theory called your office — hire someone else to do it.

Bottom line, professionals act, dress, train, and equip themselves like, well, professionals. There are obvious benefits to doing this. For one, you'll appear more professional — and by extension, more successful — to your potential clients/buyers. Think about how you size someone up when you're considering them as a potential employee or partner. If they drive up in a broken-down car, stumble out in an avalanche of fast-food containers, looking like they just rolled off a park bench, how likely are you to give them your vote of approval? On the other hand, if they present themselves in a professional (or at least presentable), outgoing, confident manner, it boosts your confidence in them. I'm not saying this will get you the job — but it will at least not *prevent* you from getting it. This goes for how you present your script, your resume, headshot, demo reel, whatever.

Never give them a reason to say "no."

But there's an even bigger principle at work here. When you *prepare* like a professional, *act* like a professional, *speak* like a professional, and *do business* like a professional (whatever "professional" looks like in your field), you send a powerful message to the universe — especially the universe within you:

I AM a professional.

And the universal law responds in the only way it can — by reflecting back to you what you're projecting into it. The result is that life seems to "magically" support your profession. Opportunities start showing up. Seeming miracles happen.

As discussed in the section, "Play the Part Until You Get the Part," it's one thing to say you're a pro, but it's another thing to align your words, actions, and environment with it. It's not just that actions speak louder than words, it's that words without action lack power. Faith without works is dead. The alchemy of manifesting your dreams requires that you not only believe but *act on that belief.* It's about being in integrity with yourself. If you're thinking one thing and saying another, or saying one thing and doing another, you're out of integrity — and can't hold the energy to manifest your potential.

> It's not just that actions speak louder than words, it's that words without action lack power.

If you claim to be, or aspire to be, an actor, writer, director, producer, musician — whatever — you must live like one. I'm not saying to go rent an office and run a $10,000 ad in the *Hollywood Reporter.* But ask yourself what actions you would take if you knew you were supported by the Universe. Then begin taking those actions. The same is true if you find yourself saying lots of affirmations and prayers and none of them are manifesting. "God helps those who help themselves." Turn your prayers of beseeching (you know the ones, late at night, on your knees, begging for mercy, a new mate, or rent money) into prayers of proclaiming the highest truth about you — then act *as if* they are being answered!

Treat your work like a real business. Read books on business, time management, and self-mastery. Oh, and read that little book your bank gave you — the checkbook. Learn how to balance it. Read a financial statement. Invest. Keep records and receipts of what you earn and spend. Not only will this help you become conscious of your finances — and any limited thinking you have around abundance and wealth — it will come in handy at tax time when you can use that information to save thousands! You may not use most of this, but it will bleed into your subconscious, affirming and strengthening your sense of being a pro — and sending the same message to others in your field.

Where does all this hit you? Check in with yourself. Is this topic bringing up a sense of excitement and possibility, or frustration and repulsion? Does it make you come alive, or put you to sleep? Any limited thoughts or feelings you have about this is the resistance you're using to prevent a breakthrough. Make a note of it. Pray or meditate on it. Create an affirmation to neutralize it. Write a song or scene about it! This is the work of conscious living — this is the world of an Enlightened Entertainer.

It's About the Work: Dealing with Success

Take time to celebrate the victories. Don't steamroll over them on your way to the next project. Not only does all work and no play make Jack a dull and sometimes unemployed boy — it also makes him an unhappy and, ultimately, soul-impoverished boy (even if he has boat-loads of money). On the flipside, don't get attached to and identified with your achievements. If you look back too long, you may not turn into a pillar of salt, but you'll run into the side of a mountain, careen off the road into a ditch, or stall on the highway.

I know one writer who sold a script that got produced years ago. He collected every bit of paraphernalia associated with it, and when I would talk to him, all he did was reminisce about that "big sale." He didn't seem to notice that he hadn't completed a script since. He was so stuck in his past victory that it completely obscured his future vision. Last I heard he was working a "regular job" selling insurance and had left the business. I've known many writers, actors, directors, and executives who suffered from the same syndrome. It's like the graying football captain who still talks about the big game he won in high school, or the middle-aged prom queen who keeps her corsage in the freezer and takes it out often to relive "the good old days" — while the rest of her potential remains frozen.

Life doesn't tarry with yesterday. It keeps moving forward. Every time the planet revolves around the sun, the nature of things is a little different, a little more evolved. If you're not evolving with it, life is literally passing you by. Celebrate your successes, by all means. Throw a party! Then wake up the next morning, take a couple Alka Seltzers (or the homeopathic alternative), meditate, pray — and get back to work!

Your Body of Work: Living a Healthy Lifestyle

I won't spend much time on this, but it's crucial to being a productive professional in this business. If you're an actor or performer, and depend on your looks and physique, this point may seem like a given. But if you're a writer, producer, or executive — and do a lot of sitting — you may be limiting your body of work by not working on your body. The fact is, the work you do, in whatever capacity, takes a lot of energy. It may seem like you're only using your brain, but that brain is connected to your body and it functions based on the overall health of your being. There are scores of studies linking clarity of thought and the ability to function at higher levels with the quality of food and exercise we get. Maybe you already know this. The question is, are you living it?

I'm assuming you want to create a career as a conscious entertainment professional that lasts a lifetime. To do that, and do it with gusto, you need to be in the best shape of your life. So take care of this vital instrument you've been given — your body. Exercise. Eat well. Take vitamins (because of topsoil erosion, most of our food is lacking in nutrients). Stay well-hydrated. Meditate (or do some other form of soul-connecting practice). Have lots of play and recreation (re-creation). And, of course, get plenty of rest. Your muse will thank you — with a greater surge of creativity and the energy to see it through.

Getting Karmic Points on the Deal

When you walk a path of cooperation and generosity, seeking the good in every situation, and taking full responsibility for your experience instead of blaming it on people and circumstance — you enter into a rarified atmosphere where the law of *grace* is activated. From this attitude and altitude of consciousness, you transcend many of the lesser laws set in motion. The so-called "rules" don't apply to you as much. In the midst of a recession, your business booms. When others are complaining that there aren't any parts out there, you'll be playing the role of a lifetime. You'll book jobs without auditioning (even if you're not a star), get writing gigs without showing a writing sample, and get hired on the spot without flashing a resume. Even more powerful, past mistakes will no longer have much — or any — effect in your present. It will often feel like your limited past was just a dream you've awakened from. The whole law of karma or cause and effect will be increasingly nullified — like your cosmic "rap sheet" has been torn up.

> It won't matter how much time you've wasted, or how far off the path you've wandered. In a holy instant, you'll get your life, your career, your passion, and your purpose back again!

One of my favorite biblical statements says that "I will restore to you the years that the locust hath eaten." In other words, all the mistakes you've made, all the things you think you've lost — will be restored as if you never missed a step. If you think your ship has sailed, that your window of opportunity has opened and closed, you'll find another window opening and your ship parked at the curb. It won't matter how much time you've wasted, or how far off the path you've wandered. In a holy instant, you'll get your life, your career, your passion, and your purpose back again! This is grace. These are the good karmic points you get on the deal when you negotiate with your spirit.

Acts of Courage: "Get a Life!"

I'm obsessed with the entertainment industry. I love the "biz," the people, and the work. But, as I've already indicated, there's nothing more boring than someone who has nothing to talk about except their work. What's more, you need real-life, not just reel-life, experience if you want to create work that resonates beyond the borders of Tinseltown.

Take an inventory of all your interests — rock climbing, bird watching, coin collecting, taxidermy — then take time to explore at least one in depth this month. It will expand your horizons, open up vistas of creativity — even make you more interesting at parties!

Check-In

Many ideas in this chapter might have hit up against strong beliefs about your role in this business — and the path to success. Take a moment to reflect over the material. How do you feel about it? Don't accept answers like, "Fine," "It was good," "I didn't have a problem with it." These are tricks of the ego to masquerade feelings of resistance.

Be aware of your beliefs about the "professional" role of an artist or executive. Are the ideas in the chapter conflicting in your consciousness? Is there some confusion? If so, that's a high state on the path. It means that two seeming disparate ideas are trying to "fuse" together but are locking horns, so to speak. Just let them be. Rest in that stew. Let it simmer. Contemplate it. Know the truth about yourself and work. As these ingredients combine and congeal, something new will be revealed that is neither; something cooked fresh from the fire of your soul, spiced with the wisdom of experience.

Enjoy the meal!

TEN ~

Building Business Relationships

"Respect yourself and others will respect you."
— Confucius

Finding Your "Guardian Agent"

The experience of finding and working with an agent (or manager) is a pretty sore subject for some. Most of us have horror stories. You hear the same old complaints — the agent isn't doing enough, they're not returning my calls quick enough, they don't understand me or my work, I'm just a commodity to them, they can't get me an invitation to a major Hollywood funeral — and everybody's going to be there! But the job of an agent (or manager) is no walk in the park either. They have their own terrible tales of clients gone mad. I know, because I've been one of those clients! The real problem is not just finding the right agent (or the right talent if you're an agent), it's about releasing the limiting ideas around this issue and developing a more soulful relationship to the process.

In terms of getting an agent, there's the old Catch-22: It's hard to get an agent if you haven't had significant work, but it's hard to get work without a significant agent. (This is not the "truth" just the experience). For some, the path to an agent is a rough road, littered with the bodies of those who have succumbed to the elements. There are many techniques to finding an agent, and there are plenty of books that have covered this ground. What I want to deal with here is the inner aspect of this relationship.

In truth, our experience with "representation" is a reflection of how we "represent" ourselves. People basically treat you the way you treat yourself — or the way you've trained them to treat you (which is also based on how you treat yourself). This is no different with your agent/manager relationship. If you think they're going to be your mother, your father, or your savior, they will betray you. If you think they'll be the answer to all your dreams, not only are you dreaming, but you're in for a rude awakening. Like our other meaningful relationships, we often use our reps to fill a hole inside of us — a hole only we can fill. If you have a rep right now and are feeling less than empowered — like you work for them instead of the other way around — that's a sure sign that you've made them your "salvation" or, at the very least, your "solution."

On some level, this means you don't feel entirely worthy, capable, or talented enough. Deep down, you don't really believe in yourself or your work. Having an agent is a way to "prove" to yourself that you're worthy, to quiet the inner voice of self-doubt. But it's only a band-aid. And it can put you in a compromised position as the "talent." Likewise, if you're a representative with a client who seems "needy" of your approval or validation, and you play into their weaknesses, you're enabling your client, creating a dependent (co-dependent) relationship — and it will likely cause you many problems as well.

Many of us are still trying to resolve our childhood issues with the authority figures in the business (and elsewhere). We're seeking mom and dad's love and approval; we're trying to plug the large leak left by a life of soul-draining self-loathing, trying to heal the weeping wounds from a life of self-flagellation. But the problem is, *it will never work.* Even if you get a good agent who believes in you and your work, you won't believe them! At least not for long. And if you get a less-than-savory character representing you, they'll likely take advantage of your weaknesses — intentionally or not.

When I used to counsel people on personal issues, and we got onto the subject of how to attract the right mate, they often had a laundry list of qualities they wanted their "perfect partner" to possess. After they laid out the list, I would ask, "Are you the kind of person who would attract this kind of partner? If you were them, would *you* be interested in you?" This was often a conversation stopper. They would tilt their head, look at me with furrowed brow, and ask, "What are you trying to say, I'm not good enough?" To which I'd respond, "I don't know, *are you?*" Sometimes they would have a knee-jerk response of "I'm too good!" But more often, they would grow quiet, as they realized that if they were that proverbial perfect partner they would most assuredly *not* choose them as their mate. So what's the best way to find your Guardian Agent — that rep that is just right for you? *Stop looking.* At least let go of any attachment to the outcome. Instead, focus on developing yourself (inside and out) into the person who would attract the rep you want.

We don't get what we *want*, we get what we *are*. As Marianne Williamson once said, "How can you expect someone to spend the rest of their life with you if you can't stand to spend one night alone with yourself?!"

> We don't get what we want,
> we get what we are.

How can you expect an agent to be a passionate advocate of you and your work, if you aren't a champion of yourself? Honestly ask yourself, "Would I represent me if I was a top-quality agent?" Or, "If I was a producer or financial backer, would I invest millions of dollars and/or put my career on the line for me (as an actor, writer, director, etc.)?" Then be honest. *Really honest.* If the answer is "no," "probably not," or "I don't know," ask yourself why. And listen carefully.

This is usually an illuminating — if painful — process. And a huge step in becoming the "right person" for the "right partner." Now you can see, right before your inner eye, the thoughts/beliefs/feelings causing your limited experience of this agent/talent relationship. In truth, you're not just causing it, the sum total of these beliefs and feelings *are* the relationship — because you can only be in relationship with your own perceptions. From this perspective, it isn't a mystery why you haven't attracted the right agent or manager, why you can't keep them when you do, or why your current rep provokes dark fantasies that make the movie *Swimming with Sharks* look like a sweet relationship film.

The "bad news" is you can no longer blame anyone else for your conditions. The "good news" is you can no longer blame anyone else for your conditions! You're not a victim, lost in confusion and uncertainty. You know where the real work is. It's not about going to the latest pay-to-pitch meeting or agent scene night, getting agency labels from Samuel French and sending out another two hundred agent query letters — it's about working on your beliefs until you become the greatest champion of yourself and your work. It's about becoming so centered in your vision and validity that you don't need to be validated by anyone. It's about "representing" yourself with such confidence and self-assurance that you wouldn't hesitate to pick up the phone or walk in the door of any office in town.

In other words, you need to first agent yourself. The way you want the agent to think about you and your work, *you* must first think about yourself and your work. You must believe so completely that nothing an agent says or doesn't say (which is often more painful), and nothing anyone in the "biz" says or doesn't say can shake you from your center of creative confidence. In truth the Guardian Agent is an Angel within you. And as you embrace it, you'll honor, respect, and hold yourself and work in such high esteem that you'll attract representation that mirrors that.

From this empowered position, you don't *need* an agent or manager to qualify you or your work. But you may choose to hire one. Did you catch that? I said "hire" one. I know we rarely experience it this way, but the truth is that the talent is the employer in the agent/talent relationship. That doesn't mean your agent or manager is your employee, but it does mean you're not *their* employee. It's best to view it as a partnership, where two equally valuable talents come together to benefit each other and the greater purpose of their work. From this place of personal power, you're no longer worried about losing your agent, because you know you've got the goods and can always find another partner.

If you're an agent or manager, don't resent me for saying this. Besides being the truth (come on, you know it is, even if you hate to admit it), it's also a good thing for you. It puts your role in its proper perspective. It empowers everyone to authentically fulfill their role. You're not your client's mother or father, you're not their therapist or priest — you're their representative. That doesn't mean you can't provide a personal touch, guidance, direction, and even comfort and moral support — in fact, this can be the "added value" you bring — but it means you aren't responsible for healing their inner child. It also means you can enter into a deeper relationship with your client, unfettered by the personal projections that often bog down the affair, siphoning off energy that could be put to better use creating, selling, and building a prosperous, purposeful career.

I can hear some of you saying, "This is all a nice idea in theory, but it's not realistic. The fact is the talent *needs* the agent to be credible in this town. The agent is in the position of power, the position to accept or reject us, so the talent has to subordinate themselves to the reps or they'll never find someone to represent them." This may be the status quo, but it's not the truth. So the question is, are you going to continue to live a lie just because it's the most expedient path, or are you going to take the road less traveled? Are you only interested in comfort and convenience, or are you ready to stand for the truth and set yourself (and others) free to fulfill the greatest potential.

The fact is, the reps need the creators. Without them, they have nothing to sell — no scripts, no actors, no directors, no nothing. Sure, some agents and managers have enough talent in their "stable." And some reps deal primarily with stars. But there are many good agents and managers who are in need of a regular stream of fresh talent. If that's you, you're their lifeblood. Heck, you're their light bill! You're the hope of making their car payment, paying their mortgage, funding their kid's private school and, God willing, getting them a regular table at the Ivy (or whatever the trendy spot *du jour* is).

Now, to turn this upside down, let me speak to the agents and managers. From a metaphysical perspective, you don't need the talent any more than they need you. They're not really the source of your livelihood and light bills (but don't tell them I told you), your spirit is.

In truth, you're immune from all the manipulations and tirades of talent that threaten to undermine your own confidence and capacity to perform at your highest potential. There will always

> You never have to sacrifice your integrity or sell your soul for a project.

be another script, another actor, another director, another package. You never have to sacrifice your integrity or sell your soul for a project. *Never.* You are at your strongest — and most beneficial to others — when you know this.

If I've totally confused you, that's a good sign. Remember, confusion is a high state. The fact is, both perspectives are true. As the talent, you must know that you are completely self-contained and don't need anything from anyone; that the full power, potential, and substance of the universe is within you. Likewise, the representatives need to know the same thing. From this place, you are two whole and complete individuals, entering into a relationship not to *get* something from each other that you are lacking — but to give, share, and be of service to each other, the entertainment industry, and the global audience. When it comes to relationships — personal or professional — two halves do *not* make a whole. What's more, two wholes coming together in conscious relationship create a synergistic partnership that is capable of seemingly miraculous things.

Always Give More Than Is Expected

Generosity. That's a word not commonly associated with the entertainment industry — or many other industries outside of the nonprofit sector. But if there's one thing that builds trust and respect in a relationship quickly, it's being generous. I remember once meeting a producer for coffee and paying the bill. By the look on his face, you would've thought I just saved his child's life! He couldn't believe that someone bought *him* coffee — let alone a writer! It colored the whole tone of the meeting. I didn't make a deal that day, but I was on fire creatively, on top of my game. Something had opened up inside of me. That small act of giving had given me so much more in return. And that incident stuck with me. It showed me how little acts of generosity really can go a long way.

I've since bought a lot more coffees — and lunches and dinners — for others. Maybe sometimes my ego is involved, trying to "work the system," but mostly I do it because it just feels good to give. It's our nature. As the sayings go, "Always put the universe in your debt" and "try to outgive God."

Always put the universe in your debt.

Of course, you can never accomplish this in a universe of infinite abundance and unbounded givingness. The universe abhors a vacuum, so it always fills the space you're creating by giving of yourself — resulting in you always having more to give. But it's still fun to try!

This concept is even more powerful when it comes to working relationships. The inclination for some people in this business is to go into a job situation already on the defensive, expecting the other party to take advantage of them, ask for more than they're paying for, or give less than they promised. Some people might say, "Well, yeah, that's because it's true. It's called protecting yourself." I think it's called something else: "cynicism." I'm not suggesting you go into relationships with your eyes closed, but go into them with your heart open. Give everyone the benefit of the doubt. Declare their innocence before assuming guilt. Give more than you're paid for, more than they expect. Give your all. Every audition. Every pitch meeting. Every project. No matter how big or small. Hold nothing back! And the universe will literally seek out ways to bless you.

It's easy to be a "clock watcher," to "give as good as you get." But all this does is perpetuate an experience of lack, limitation, and distrust. There's a reason why Oprah is so successful — and it's not just luck or fate. That woman works her tail off, not to mention being incredibly generous (most of which you never hear about). She gives 110% in everything she does — even though as the creator of a media empire she could get away with a lot less. Paul Newman is another example, as are two-time Academy Award winners Hilary Swank and Tom Hanks. Ironically, in a business that seems to represent the heights of

selfishness and narcissism, if you analyze the lives of the most successful people (not tabloid success, but real staying power), you'll find
many who share these qualities of generosity — generosity of heart,
spirit, time, talent, and treasure. They didn't get where they are, and
win the love and respect of many, by withholding. They got there by
giving their all, thinking of others, extending a helping hand, and
exuding a generative aura wherever they go.

If you're an actor, next time you're at an audition and find your natural inclination is to withhold information or encouragement from
your fellow thespian, try instead to treat them as you would like to be
treated. Put aside competitive thinking and act like a generative being,
like someone who knows there is only one of us here and more than
enough to go around. Sincerely desire that they receive all the good
that life has to offer, and offer your help if there's a need for it. If
you're a writer, the next time you work on a project for someone, try
to give a little more than they expect, a little more than you're being
paid for. Whatever position you find yourself in, become aware of the
"natural" tendency to protect your turf and withhold your good — *and
do the opposite!*

Keep the universe in your debt. Try to outgive God. Every time you
meet someone, bring some kind of gift — whether it's a card, a flower,
a trinket, a kind word, a compliment, or even a silent blessing. Buy
that producer coffee or lunch — and watch the look of shock on his face! Give an aspiring artist a few moments of guidance, direction, or inspi-
ration. Every day, in every way, ask yourself, "How can I be a

> The most powerful way to build relationships is by being in service to one another.

bigger giver?" The most powerful way to build relationships is by being
in service to one another. Give it a shot. And watch as the windows of
heaven open up and pour forth a blessing too big for you to receive.
Then give that away too! Because the good never ends — it's infinite
and inexhaustible.

Your Enemies Are Your Allies

I've spent a lot of time laying the groundwork for these spiritual principles, using clever and (hopefully) entertaining ways to bypass the ego and convey the essential truth of this path. If you've read this far, and done the work, you're a spiritual warrior. So I'm just going to give it to you straight now: The people who cause you the most pain and suffering are your greatest teachers, your true "gurus," your real "soul mates."

Think about that producer who promised you the moon, then basically mooned you; that best friend and fellow actor who stole your girlfriend *and* your part; that acting teacher you entrusted with your soul who berated and humiliated you in front of the class (or still does); that executive who weekly makes you want to pull a *Swimming with Sharks.* What do all these people have in common? They're showing you where you still harbor anger, self-doubt, limitation, fear — they're exposing the areas where you most need to grow. They are, in fact, giving a gift, specially wrapped for you! This is similar to the shadow work, but on a deeper level. We're not merely talking about people who "push your buttons," but people who make you want to pull a trigger!

These core issues are like the "fatal flaw" of the hero in a story. These are the issues that can bring us down, prevent us from fulfilling our purpose. And they are often triggered by the villains of our own show. These *forces of antagonism* — people, organizations, or the "way things are in the biz" — can cause us to dig deeper, peel away our onion skin, and expose our white hot center, or make us retreat in fear and anger. If we "refuse the call" to adventure, the antagonistic forces will grow, claim more territory, and force a face-to-face battle. If we "answer the call," and recognize that the "bad guys" are our *spiritual sparring partners*, providing the playing field for personal growth, we'll find allies (seen and unseen) coming to our aid, guiding us to be true heroes on our journey.

Take a deeper look at the relationships that cause you pain and give them a new meaning. Instead of being the "cause" of misery and failure, make them the "opportunity" for growth and fulfillment. Ask yourself what lessons they're bringing, what gifts they're offering, what qualities they're asking you to embrace. Maybe that raging producer is reflecting your unexpressed anger. Maybe it's a call for you to grow in compassion and understanding, patience and tolerance. Maybe it's a call to reclaim your confidence, making you immune to the opinions of others. From this perspective, going to work becomes like going to the gym to work out your mental, emotional, and spiritual muscles.

You don't have to like or agree with this principle. But you dismiss or deny it at your peril — because it's operating in your life. If you ignore it, you'll continue to find yourself working for the jerky boss, raging director, flaky actor, lazy writer, etc. Even if you move, break up with your partner, or change jobs, you'll find the same people populating your life — just wearing different costumes! Haven't you noticed that? Well, what — or more accurately, "who" — is the common denominator in those relationships?

Acts of Courage — "Love Thine Enemy"

Pick someone you perceive has hurt you the most in this business or in relation to it (maybe you had a parent, spouse, or other family member who didn't support you). Take a moment to get still, eyes closed, and reenter your sanctuary. You're safe here...

Invite this person into your space and ask them, "What do you really think of me? Tell me the thing you think would hurt me the most." What you're after here is an uncensored, on-the-nose negative statement. No subtext here. In other words, they might say, "You're worthless — you'll never amount to anything!" As they talk, just breathe through it.

Be aware of how you feel. Did what they said cut you deeply, hurt you, enrage you? If so, that's good. Because what they told you is what *you* are telling yourself. If it hooked you at all, it's what you believe on some level. That's why they're in your life, to mirror your darkest beliefs, challenge the "fatal flaw," and force you to heal it. Tell them you no longer need them to play the part of the "enemy." You got the message. Thank them for this gift of awareness, release them from the projection, and send them on their way.

Now you know what your real work is. It's not fighting *them*, it's confronting this flawed belief in yourself, uprooting it through your spiritual practice, and planting new, empowering truths in its place. As a final act of release and a supreme affirmation of spiritual maturity, do something this week to honor and thank that individual for playing their part in your Divine Drama. It can be an anonymous gift of flowers, a card, a show of support on one of their projects, or an offering of help. Let your spirit guide you.

Check-In

These check-ins have been about more than asking you questions to prompt you, they're about creating a habit to *check-in* with yourself — on a weekly, daily, moment-by-moment basis. So, are you feeling a more intimate relationship with your spirit/muse?

You've been asked to do some difficult work — especially in this last chapter. If you don't see the "big changes" yet, trust that seeds are being planted. Some may take time to blossom, some may burst forth eighty feet tall like a bamboo tree. Just continue to work the soil of your soul, and your harvest will come in its season.

PART VI
Lights, Cameras, Take Action!

ELEVEN ~

Creating a Career Plan

"He who fails to plan, plans to fail."
— Proverb

Playing "The Procrastinator"

How do you feel when you think about planning your life — or, for that matter, planning anything? Does it send chills up your spine, strike terror in your heart, make you cringe? Does it evoke a sudden urge to take a nap, take a drink, pull into a drive-through, or pull a drive-by? Does it make you sad, angry, even depressed? If you're a highly right-brained person, or you've been wounded in this area, odds are you experience one or more of these reactions when you think about, or engage in, planning of any significance.

Some might just write you off as a procrastinator. But I won't pass such a shallow judgment. Indeed, you might be playing the *role* of the procrastinator. But underneath it, you are working overtime, expending enormous energy — to keep yourself stuck in place. And why did you create this defense mechanism? Perhaps you grew up in a home that was strictly organized, your days regimented, your whole life run by the clock and the calendar. Perhaps you had a left-brained, anal-retentive parent. Maybe you were always warned to "think about your future" and "plan ahead." And when you brought home that masterpiece made of Popsicle sticks, it was regarded with apathy at best, disdain at worst — and you were told to do something "more productive" with your time.

These types of childhood experiences could cause you to become rigid, obsessive-compulsive, and self-critical — especially if you believed you had to become like your parent to get their love. But they could just as easily cause you to rebel, to resent any form of structure, to yearn to be "free" (which was defined as doing anything you wanted, when you wanted, without any regard for the clock, calendar, or compass).

On the other hand, you may have grown up in a household without *any* structure. A household where you didn't know what time — if ever — dinner would be served, where you didn't know what time — if ever — your parent(s) would be home, where you didn't know whether you were coming or going! And eventually you didn't even care. Maybe you had a parent who was emotionally unstable, needy, always on the verge of falling apart. In that case, you may have created a defense mechanism that required you to become a surrogate adult/companion, to "get it together" and "hold it together." If you didn't, the family would fall apart. It was life or death. This could have made you a type-A workaholic to varying degrees. Or you could be a "recovering workaholic," averse to any structure for fear that it will bring out the monster in you again.

Then there's the possibility that your chaotic, controlling, or out-of-control childhood didn't cause you to become either a "control monster" or a "free spirit" but to shut down and become apathetic. Your senses and spirit dulled. Your light dimmed. It wasn't worth confronting your overly critical parent or risking the wrath of your inner critic. In this scenario, we won't find you ordering your life like a drill sergeant or dancing naked in the moonlight, but sitting in that warm, well-worn spot on the couch. Instead of being a controller, you'll *hold* a controller in one hand, beverage of choice in the other, a whole script of well-rehearsed excuses for why you're not doing more tucked in your dirty shirt pocket. In this case, your idea of planning is how far ahead you program your TiVo.

The possible mixing and matching of scenes and scenarios is endless, but the results are the same — you're not able to productively and peacefully plan a purpose-driven life. The point of these descriptions is not to make you feel bad about yourself, but to help you become aware of the unconscious forces that may be working against you. If anything I've said resonates with you on any level, investi-

> If you're thinking, "I don't have any problem putting together a plan," you might be right. But you might also be in denial.

gate it. Get honest with yourself. If you're thinking, "I don't have any problem putting together a plan," you might be right. But you might also be in denial. Just take a look at your life. Does it have structure? Is it unfolding according to a conscious intention — or does it look more like an experiment in chaos theory where you're waiting for some pattern, any pattern, to emerge?

The Spiritual Planning Paradox

As a "spiritual" or "creative" person, you might think planning is an act of will, a weapon of the mind; that it goes against the principle of living a surrendered, spontaneously creative life. The fact is, planning isn't the problem. It's just a tool. In the hands of a person coming from fear, need, or greed, it *can* be lethal — holding the spirit hostage and killing creativity. In the hands of someone who knows they're safe, secure, and supported by a loving, friendly universe, planning becomes a positive process to express the divine potential within them. Planning, praying, and playing are no longer mutually exclusive.

The truth is, the Plan is already perfected within you — just as the oak and its pattern is already programmed within the acorn. But, unlike the acorn, you have the ability to think independently of your circumstances. You have the ability to go against your inner impulses — which is really the Plan speaking to you. And, over time, this may have caused you to become somewhat unconscious of your divine design, deaf to Its guidance. To reverse this requires a degree of discipline. You must not only become conscious of the Plan (or, more appropriately, the Pattern of Potential) within, but also strengthen your ability to stay tuned to it and act accordingly. This, in a nutshell (or acorn shell), is what the tool called Planning is about. When used consciously, it provides a means of excavating the buried pattern within, articulating it in practical, applicable terms, and executing it moment by moment, day by day. It gives your human senses a map of your soul's landscape that you can regularly refer to in order to stay on track and on purpose.

Eventually, planning becomes second nature. In fact, you can reach a point where you're so tapped into the Inner Plan that you require little or no outer plan; you become so self-empty that you're a channel for the divine design to unfold perfectly in present-time. You do and say things that don't make total sense in terms of normal linear, spatial living, but which turn out to be exactly what needed to happen for certain events to occur in the

> You can reach a point where you're so tapped into the Inner Plan that you require little or no outer plan.

so-called future. Life becomes synchronistic, serendipitous. You find yourself getting off the freeway because of an inner "urge," going somewhere you've never been before, and running into a long-lost friend — or soul-mate — and experiencing something that propels your life and career forward. Your plans, then, become a staircase leading to the launch pad from which you blast out of the orbit of earthly limitations and into the rarefied atmosphere where miracles are everyday occurrences.

Your future plans are really a part of God's *now*. And if you can sufficiently live in that pure connection, you can do away with a lot of planning (you'll still have to do some because you live in a world operating in time and space). But until you reach that enlightened state — and you'll know it when you do — planning is still a viable tool for harnessing the power of your purpose and putting it into action. So let's dive right into our planning session, where we will take all that we've learned and put it into practice.

Priority Planning

What is something you could do that, if done regularly, would make a huge positive difference in your entertainment career (and life)? Your answer will give you an indication of what is truly important, a top-shelf priority, in moving you forward. In the following pages, we'll discuss what the "top-shelf" priorities and ultimate goals are in your entertainment career and, using your Mission Statement as a compass, construct a five-year, one-year, thirty-day, and one-week "flight plan" to get you to your desired destination. (Some of this material is similar to the planning section in my previous book, *I Could've Written a Better Movie Than That!*, with appropriate modifications.) I know you're eager to get to work auditioning, writing scripts, making movies — whatever — but you'll get there much quicker and with fewer obstacles if you have a clear road map, with well-defined goals and specific action-steps to achieve them. So let's get to it!

5-Year Vision

What are your big goals in the entertainment industry, financially, creatively, in terms of your overall career? Take a moment to re-read your Mission Statement. Reflect on it. Then go through the visioning process again (as described earlier) and ask your spirit to reveal the greatest possibility for your career and a plan to achieve it. Take as much time as you need to do this. If sufficient material isn't revealed, give your soul permission to soar and imagine where your life and career could go five years from now.

Are you an A-list writer, actor, director, or musician? Are you traveling the globe, performing, making movies, music, or mega-deals? Are you making six figures a year? Seven figures? Eight figures? What about your colleagues? Are you working with the A-list of the industry? Are the projects you're working on being produced, becoming hits, winning awards, changing people's lives? Let your imagination run free. Don't force it in any particular direction. Instead, ask yourself, quietly, over and over, "What do I really want to accomplish with this work over the next five years?" As answers come, write them down. List your goals: financial, career, personal creativity, whatever comes up.

Look at the list. Which goals are aligned with your mission statement? Write those on a clean piece of paper. Which goals can you accomplish in the next five years? Pick ones that are achievable, but a stretch. If you choose goals that feel impossible, your mind won't engage them because deep down you'll know it's a pipe dream. If you pick goals that don't feel challenging, your mind will go soft and, again, will not engage with the level of passion and conviction you need. Write these goals on a clean sheet of paper.

Study the list again. Are these goals aligned with your mission? If not, adjust them so that they are, or consider adjusting your mission if you feel strongly about the goals.

5-Year Vision Statement

Now you're going to put these five-year goals into the form of a present-tense statement.

Example

"My name is John Doe. It is January 1, 2012. I am a highly sought-after screenwriter and filmmaker, creating critically acclaimed, commercially successful film and TV projects that touch millions around the world, adding massive value to their lives.

I am financially secure. I have enough passive income coming in from residuals on produced film and TV projects that I don't have to work at all — freeing me up to do only what I love, and help others do the same.

I am peaceful, confident, and comfortable in my own skin. Everything is working as planned — and even greater than I imagined. I'm on purpose, on track, and deeply grateful for all I have — and it's just the beginning!"

Yours doesn't have to look like this. You may only use one line, or write it in iambic pentameter. Do what turns you on. Literally. It must inspire you — which means to receive the "breath of God" — or you won't have the spiritual oxygen to follow through.

Okay, get comfortable, pull out your notebook, and start writing. Don't worry about grammar or spelling. After you've written it quickly, you can go back and polish it. And don't just make a dry shopping list. Let your creative energy and passion pour into this document. You might even want to turn on some music that gets your juices flowing.

Remember, this is just a "coat" you're trying on for now. If it makes you feel like you need to call Queer Eye for the Straight Guy (or Straight Eye for the Queer Guy, depending on your preference), then take the darn thing off and make a new one!

1-Year Vision

Now you're going to take your five-year vision and create a one-year plan. The first step is brainstorming (or "soul-storming") all the different ways you could achieve your goals. Not just the way it's been done before. And not just the way the "business" says it's done. Think outside of the box office. There's no "right" or "wrong" here, just possibilities (remember how Spielberg broke in?). You could also use the visioning exercise again to catch the divine idea more clearly.

List at least twenty ways to accomplish each five-year goal. Write until you have nothing left — then write some more. That's where the mind stops and the magic starts.

Say you have the goal of being a top actor. Here are some ideas that may be on the list:

- Work on every student film you can (increasing the chances that one of those directors or writers will go on to become a success and take you with them)

- Perform in regular scene nights (or create your own event) open to industry professionals (agents, producers, directors)

- Query agents/get an agent

- Write an article about agents or producers, allowing you to interview them and build relationships with these "gatekeepers"

- Make your own movie and star in it (with the latest digital cameras and computer software, it's becoming easier and easier to make movies)

- Get the Casting Breakdowns and get submitted for every part you're right for

- Put ads in *Variety* and *Hollywood Reporter* — or billboards on Sunset like Angelina (It didn't make her a star, but if you have talent you never know!)

- Save the life of an A-list director — or his dog. When he asks how he can repay you, tell him you want to be in his next movie!

Reality Check

Obviously, some of these actions are more doable than others, and some are just plain silly. While we'd all like to be as brave as Spielberg, most of us aren't likely to break the law to "break in." So take a few moments and narrow your list for each five-year goal down to the things you could do without getting arrested, killed, or forced into seclusion.

Narrowing It Down

Now that you have your list of realistic, but challenging, choices, pick the one sub-goal you'll actually go for (for each of your five-year goals). This should give you a sense of what must come "before" you can achieve your five-year goal.

Reverse Engineering Your Goals

Work backwards from each sub-goal to the step you must take to accomplish it. Let's say your goal was to make a movie. Before that, you'd need to secure locations and equipment. Before that, you'd have to round up a cast and crew. Before that, you'd have to raise the money, sell your script, get an agent, or some variation thereof. Before that, you'd have to write a script or obtain one. Before that, you would need to develop an idea for a script or seek out writers. Get it? Do this until you have the one-year goal. Repeat this process for each five-year goal you came up with.

Go with the Flow Chart

One way to organize this information is to create a *Flow Chart*. Take a piece of legal-size paper and turn it on its side. Make a box in the upper right hand corner and write your 5-year goal inside. (If you have several five-year goals, stack them on the right side of the page.) Draw another box to the left of your five-year goal and write the sub-goal inside. Draw an arrow from the left box to the right box to indicate direction. Work this backwards until you get to where you are now. (You could also use a dry-erase board.)

This gives you a visual "map" of how to get from where you are to where you want to be.

1-Year Vision Statement

As with your five-year goals, you're going to put your one-year goals into a present-tense affirmative declaration. To help you tap into the deeper recesses of your unconscious, try writing it using your left-hand (if you're right-handed). To further free yourself and open up to potentially surprising insights, turn on your favorite dance music, get down and funky or wild and crazy, then sit down and free-write without thinking. Now combine all three versions into one compre-hensive, richly textured 1-Year Vision Statement.

30-Day Vision and Action Plan

We're closing in on the starting line. We began with the end, and we're almost to the beginning. Pretty soon, you're going to have a list of things to do *tomorrow*! Just as before, you're going to "soul-storm" ways to achieve your one-year goals, narrow them down to the "doable" ones, then work backwards until you have your 30-day goals. In addition, you're going to articulate the "actions" you'll take to accomplish these. So if your 30-day goal is to have a first draft of your script, some of your actions might be:

- Research my story idea (online and in interviews)

- Read a few screenplays and watch a few movies in my genre

- Outline my story (as a beat sheet, treatment, or index cards)

- Write five pages a day

You should now have a detailed list of things you can do to achieve your 30-day goals which, when accomplished, will move you toward your one-year goals which, as you achieve them, will drive your with increasing momentum toward your five-year goals.

But wait, there's more!

1-Week Goals

You're a pro at this by now. As you've probably already guessed, your task is to take your 30-day goals and work backwards to the tasks you could do in a single week. If, when you're done, you realize you would need to work 25 hours a day to accomplish everything in a week, re-engineer your 30-day plan to be more realistic.

1-Day Goals

You know the drill. Work backwards from your one-week goals to create a list of what you can do *tomorrow*. Don't freak. If you've followed the process, you should have a list of doable tasks, not Herculean ones. If your to-do list makes you want to binge on bundt cake or drink yourself to sleep, don't panic. Just go back and rearrange your goals until you have a one-day plan that causes maximum inspiration and minimal perspiration.

Keeping a Daily Schedule

Part of being a pro is being organized. There are many theories, it's not one size fits all. Some people create meaningful work and enough momentum to succeed by collapsing at 5 a.m. after a night of partying, rolling out of bed bleary-eyed at noon, and "getting around" to work some point between reading the paper and hooking up with a friend for sushi. But most of us need more structure to get the most out of what we've got.

Keeping a regular schedule and having routines has another benefit besides just greater efficiency. When you do something with relative regularity — like sitting down to write or meeting a rehearsal partner every morning — your unconscious mind begins to gear up and work before you do. A subjective groove is cut. Often you don't even need to warm up — your energy and thoughts pick up right where they left off the day before.

> When you do something with relative regularity... your unconscious mind begins to gear up and work before you do.

Weekly vs. Monthly Planning

Some time-management techniques advocate weekly versus monthly planning. I think it's good to plan at least one week ahead to manage your time and priorities effectively. But the one-month overview gives you greater perspective and allows you to track larger projects. It's up to you, but I say do both. (You could even create a quarterly calendar to be aware of the bigger vision, like a whiteboard in the writing room of a TV series, where they track the arc of the whole season.) Chart your month and/or quarter for the bird's-eye view. Focus on one week at a time. Okay, grab your planner or PDA — and go!

Acts of Courage: "Just Do It!"

This exercise is simple but, for many people, difficult. Identify a project or goal that is near and dear to you — one you know would make a big difference in your life and career — but which you have avoided starting. Then get to work on it — *now*. That's right. Put down this book, pick up that project, and dive in! Forget all of the reasons why you can't start, and just *begin*. Do it for at least 20 minutes, but longer if you are inspired. If you're really "courageous," commit to it for at least 20 minutes every day this week.

What are you still doing here? Get cracking!

Check-In

How are you? If you're frustrated, scared, or numb, don't fret. This is where the rubber hits the road, the pencil hits the page, and many hit a wall. We've had fun philosophizing about changing the world, doing the inner-work, even taking a few outer actions. But the hardest part for some — especially those new to a spiritual path — is coming down from the mountain top. But come down we must, carrying the tablets on our back, etched with a purpose-driven plan: To bring a bold new vision of soul into the rough-and-tumble business of show!

TWELVE ~

Becoming an "Enlightened Entertainer"

"For attractive lips, speak words of kindness
For lovely eyes, seek out the good in people
For a slim figure, share your food with the hungry
For poise, walk with the knowledge you never walk alone
If you ever need a helping hand, you'll find one...
At the end of each of your arms."
— Audrey Hepburn (in an interview for a fashion magazine)

Character Arc

I don't know about you, but this has been quite a journey. Maybe it has opened up a new paradigm of what's possible on this path of entertainment. Or perhaps it has confirmed what you've known all along. You've been asked to identify your limited beliefs around show business, create new ones, and tap into not only your personal vision — but the Big Picture for entertainment and its impact on the planet. You've worked on healing your broken art, developing your character, mastering relationships, embracing the "business" of show, putting a real plan together — and a whole lot more!

If you've done the exercises in this book, you have no doubt made some deep inner changes. If you've just been reading it casually, soaking up the information, many seeds of growth have been planted — and they are working in the deep soil of your soul. Either way, it's unlikely that the person who picked up this book is the same one reading it now. Perceptions have shifted. Ideas have been born. Energies are moving. Change is afoot!

But this work isn't about theory, it's about results. If all it did was inspire and motivate you for a time before going back to "business as usual," that wouldn't be enough. Of course, this work is ongoing, and this book is a manual to be reflected on and applied over and over. Nevertheless, I want you to see real, lasting changes: starting today.

What follows are the belief worksheets you did in the beginning (at least, I hope you did!). And now you're going to fill them out again. The same rules apply. Don't think about your answers; just write the first thing that comes to mind.

See you in a little while!

Entertainment Industry "Belief" Exercise #1

Rate the statements from 1-10 (1 = "totally disagree," 10 = "totally agree")

___ Hollywood is a closed system

___ You can't create good art unless you're struggling/suffering

___ It's wrong to create art (write scripts, act, etc.) to make money

___ Actors/artists are flakes/self-centered

___ Writers are low on the totem pole

___ It's almost impossible to "make it" in the business

___ Striving for success will corrupt you/ruin your relationships

___ You have to take a lot of rejection to make it

___ You have to pay your dues

___ It's too good to be true

___ It's all in who you know

___ The business is corrupt/full of greedy egomaniacs

___ I don't want to be a star

___ Stars don't have any freedom

___ It's not important how successful you are, as long as you do your art

___ Realistically, chances are I'll never make it

___ I'm probably not good enough to make it

___ It takes a lot of luck to make it

___ Very few ever make it

___ I'm not good-looking enough

___ I'm too old

___ I'm too young

___ I missed my chance — and you only get one

___ I'm too late in the game — you have to start young

___ You have to sell out to make it

___ Most actors/artists are below the poverty level

___ I have the potential to be successful — all I need is a break

___ If I "make it" some people won't like me

___ If I "make it" I'll be stalked, or worse

___ You can't have a family/marriage AND be successful in this biz

___ Entertainment people are totally screwed up

___ You can't make it doing your true passion

___ I'm just not talented or smart enough

___ I didn't go to the right school

___ If you don't have friends/family in the biz, you'll probably fail

___ I don't like selling or promoting myself/my product

___ Auditioning/submitting is too much of a hassle

___ Most of the good opportunities are already gone

___ You need to have a good agent

___ Trying to make it is too much work — it's really not worth the struggle

___ You need something else to fall back on

___ It's much more difficult to make it as a woman

___ It's much more difficult to make it as a minority

___ If I make it, I might get addicted to drugs or alcohol

___ Nobody knows anything in this town

Entertainment Industry "Free-Association" Exercise #2

Complete the following statements:

The entertainment industry is _____

The entertainment industry is _____

The entertainment industry is _____

Being a success in the "biz" is _____

Being a success in the "biz" is _____

Being a success in the "biz" is _____

Artists/entertainment industry people are _____

Artists/entertainment industry people are _____

- The reasons I can't or may not become successful in the "biz" are:

- Some of the negatives about being successful in the "biz" or going through the process of trying to become successful are:

- My greatest worries, fears, and concerns regarding the entertainment industry and my experience in it are:

- The worst thing about this business is:

Great work!

Now take the original worksheets and compare them with these new ones. How have your beliefs changed? Have they become more positive, optimistic, and expansive? Or are there areas where they have become even more fearful and constrictive?

Change is a dynamic thing. It rarely moves in a continuous, uphill fashion. The key is to look for "movement." As you do this work, it will likely bring up old, unresolved issues. This can result in a temporary increase in pain and struggle around certain areas. And that could cause your responses on these exercises to seemingly get worse. However, these old wounds and repressed energies are coming up because the work you're doing is "flushing them out." Keep doing the work, and they'll begin to clear. I guarantee it!

In the areas where there is upward growth, ask yourself why. What have you let go of or embraced to facilitate this transformation? What do you need to do in order to maintain or increase the progress in this area? Do you need to adopt new beliefs or habits, or let go of some negative ones still hanging on for dear life?

Don't just dash off these worksheets and move on. Contemplate your answers and the shifts that have happened. Meditate on them. Journal about them. Create affirmations or pray on them. It's all more grist for the personal growth mill.

State-of-the-Heart Entertainment

"Fifty years from now, we're going to be inside the movies," Steven Spielberg said. "We're not going to be looking at them from the outside. A good movie will bring you inside of itself just by the sheer brilliance of the director/writer/production staff. But in the future, you will physically be inside the experience, which will surround you top, bottom, on all sides."

I believe he's right, in terms of the technical evolution that entertainment will undergo. But I believe there's another evolution — or

As we grow into a more conscious community of artists and entertainment professionals, we will not only create the possibility for the audience to be inside the entertainment experience, we will create an entertainment experience that lives inside the audience... and transforms them from the inside out.

revolution — in the works. A revolution of meaning. As we grow into a more conscious community of artists and entertainment professionals, we will not only create the possibility for the audience to be inside the entertainment experience, we will create an entertainment experience that lives inside the audience — and transforms them from the inside out.

In the near future, we will live in an Entertainment Culture. Almost everything we do or see will be packaged with "entertainment value." You won't just go shopping, you'll have an "entertainment experience" as you buy body scrub. You won't just watch TV, you'll interact with the programming and buy things you see on screen. You won't check into hotels, you'll check into theme parks with rooms. You won't have separate computers, TVs, phones, or MP3 players, you'll have all-in-one devices that allow you to listen to music, watch film and TV, surf the net, chat with friends, and check your bodily vitals! We will be a completely wired world. All geared toward entertaining us. Entertaining us to death, some might say — if not literally, then mentally, emotionally, and spiritually. As the Pink Floyd song says, we will become "comfortably numb."

At least that's one possible outcome.

State-of-the-art advances in media and communication will make this future a *physical* inevitability, but its mental, emotional and spiritual impact are still very much in our hands. We can create a media machine of mass distraction — or one that provides mystical direction. We can create entertainment that anesthetizes us into unconsciousness or wakes us up. We can live in an ever-increasing hi-tech, low-touch society, or use technology and media to bring us into a more intimate relationship with ourselves, each other, and Life itself. The wired world has given us a global brain. Enlightened Entertainment can connect us to a global heart and, yes, even our soul.

> We can create a media machine of mass distraction — or one that provides mystical direction.

Remember, the word "entertain" contains two seemingly contradictory meanings: "to divert or amuse" *and* "to contemplate or hold attention." Radical moralists and religious fundamentalists might say we should get rid of the amusement part and pound people into submission with the "lesson," while bottom-line business minds shake their heads at our hearts and tell us to call Western Union if we want to send a message. I don't believe it has to be an either-or decision. In fact, the true fulfillment of *entertainment* — by its very definition — requires that we embrace *both* aspects of it. We need the "medicine" to heal us, but the "sugar" sure helps it go down. Without sugar, the medicine is bitter and we'll do anything to avoid it. But without medicine, all we're eating are sugar pills! Besides making us spiritual diabetics with fat egos, all that sugar will eventually taste as bitter.

We're at a crossroads. A choice point. A tipping point. We can choose to ignore the mystical dimension of media, or put this awesome, ever-evolving entertainment industry back in the service of the soul. That choice — I believe — will determine to a great extent whether we become more self-actualized and awakened with every click

> We're at a crossroads...
> We can choose to ignore the mystical dimension of media, or put this awesome, ever-evolving entertainment industry back in the service of the soul.

of the mouse, jab of the joystick, frame of film, channel surfed, and song downloaded, or if we become lulled into an ever deeper slumber of ignorance, fear, and separation.

That's a Wrap!

We've come to the end of this particular quest. But it's just the start of your Hero's Journey. I'm sure you have questions, but hopefully you've also received answers. Perhaps you still have real concerns, nagging doubts. My hope is that this material has given you enough faith to continue moving forward and doing the work.

In one respect, this book asks you to embrace a radical path; one that seems to go against many "rules" of the business — even the human experience. But, in truth, this work is the most *natural* thing, because it's based on natural principles, on your true nature. Trust that. Release the resistance, and watch the fear and confusion fall away as well.

We can put the *soul* back into the show. We can become the sacred, empowered village again, sitting around the virtual tribal fire, the light flickering in our eyes — dancing, singing, laughing, crying as one — while the enlightened entertainers weave myths and parables, holding up a mirror that reflects our humanity, reveals our potential, and inspires us to fulfill the great destiny for which we were born.

If you've read this far, the tribal fire is already burning in your heart. The question now is: Will you let it burn out, or stoke the flames with conscious attention and deliberate action, until the light consumes you, and your glow illuminates the way for others?

You're not alone. There are many of us on this path and various groups emerging to support you and distribute finished works. Check out the Spiritual Cinema Circle, where you can get conscious films delivered to your doorstep, or *EnlightenedEntertainer.com*, where you can fellowship with like minds and get the support you need to succeed.

And if these groups don't meet your needs – create one that does! Then work with the ideas in this and other books. Support each other in being your best selves. And hold each other compassionately accountable for getting the job done.

I know there is a magnificent purpose for which you were born, and for which this entertainment industry came into being. For your sake — and all of ours — live it fully!

Stay connected. Stay committed. Stay inspired. Sing your song and tell your story — as if your whole life depended on it!

Peace & Abundant Blessings.

Derek Rydall

About the Author

A professional actor, screenwriter, singer/ songwriter, and author, Derek Rydall is also a licensed spiritual therapist and founder of *EnlightenedEntertainer.com* and *Scriptwriter Central.com*, one of the fastest growing online firms for screenwriting and script consulting services.

Derek has coached thousands of artists, professionals, and individuals from many walks of life, including Fortune 500 companies — helping them uncover their creative potential, find their authentic voice, live a more prosperous life, and fulfill their higher purpose.

The nephew of legendary film director Don Siegel (*Dirty Harry, Escape from Alcatraz, Invasion of the Body Snatchers*), Derek has been in show business most of his life. His diverse experience — on stage, in executive suites, in front of and behind the camera — gives him the unique ability to understand storytelling and entertainment on many levels, and allows him to give his clients that extra edge that takes their project to the next level!

As an actor, Derek has starred in several films and TV shows. As a screenwriter, he has been on staff for Fox and Disney, developed projects for Universal, RKO, United Artists, Miramax, Nicolas Cage, Deepak Chopra, and a number of other production companies, as well as working one on one with many writers, producers, and executives from around the world. (He has sold, optioned, or been hired to write over 20 scripts.) As a playwright, he co-wrote and starred in *Welcome Home Soldier* (the longest running drama in L.A. history). As a singer/songwriter, he has performed around the country. And as an author, he has a screenwriting book, *I Could've Written a Better Movie Than That!*

As a result of Derek's consulting, clients have turned novels into scripts, made six-figure writing deals, secured millions in financing, obtained major distribution, won multiple awards, and been hired to executive produce, direct, and star in their movies!

Derek currently resides outside Los Angeles with his wife, two children, and cat.

~~~~~~

Derek is available for speaking engagements, conferences, lectures, and workshops on how to walk a more prosperous, productive, purposeful path in the entertainment industry (and everyday life), how to create more meaningful material, and a host of other topics on writing, creativity, and spiritual practices. His presentations are both enlightening and entertaining, as he brings his audiences to a new level of understanding, inspiration, and motivation.

For more information please contact him at:

Derek Rydall
THE ENLIGHTENED ENTERTAINER
25852 McBean Parkway, Suite #133
Valencia, CA 91355-3705
661.296.4991

www.DerekRydall.com   *derek@derekrydall.com*
www.EnlightenedEntertainer.com   *derek@enlightenedentertainer.com*
www.ScriptwriterCentral.com   *derek@scriptwritercentral.com*

EnlightenedEntertainer.com

A cutting-edge community, dedicated to empowering artists and entertainment professionals by equipping them with the spiritual tools and techniques to make their everyday walk in the business a passionate, purposeful adventure — and inspiring them to produce material that has a positive impact on the planet.

HERE ARE JUST A FEW THINGS YOU'LL FIND:

- **The Enlightened Entertainer Workshop**
- **The Enlightened Entertainer Newsletter**
- **Star Paths Mentoring Program**
- **Wisdom of the Stars**
- **Reel-Life Lessons**

AND A LOT MORE!

Stop by today for hundreds of dollars in free gifts!

www.EnlightenedEntertainer.com
derek@EnlightenedEntertainer.com

MICHAEL WIESE PRODUCTIONS

Since 1981, Michael Wiese Productions has been dedicated to providing both novice and seasoned filmmakers with vital information on all aspects of filmmaking. We have published more than 70 books, used in over 500 film schools and countless universities, and by hundreds of thousands of filmmakers worldwide.

Our authors are successful industry professionals who spend innumerable hours writing about the hard stuff: budgeting, financing, directing, marketing, and distribution. They believe that if they share their knowledge and experience with others, more high quality films will be produced.

And that has been our mission, now complemented through our new web-based resources. We invite all readers to visit www.mwp.com to receive free tipsheets and sample chapters, participate in forum discussions, obtain product discounts — and even get the opportunity to receive free books, project consulting, and other services offered by our company.

Our goal is, quite simply, to help you reach your goals. That's why we give our readers the most complete portal for filmmaking knowledge available — in the most convenient manner.

We truly hope that our books and web-based resources will empower you to create enduring films that will last for generations to come.

Let us hear from you at anytime.

Sincerely,

Michael Wiese

Publisher, Filmmaker

www.mwp.com

FILM & VIDEO BOOKS

Cinematic Storytelling: *The 100 Most Powerful Film Conventions Every Filmmaker Must Know* / Jennifer Van Sijll / $24.95

Complete DVD Book, The: *Designing, Producing, and Marketing Your Independent Film on DVD* / Chris Gore and Paul J. Salamoff / $26.95

Complete Independent Movie Marketing Handbook, The: *Promote, Distribute & Sell Your Film or Video* / Mark Steven Bosko / $39.95

Could It Be a Movie?: *How to Get Your Ideas Out of Your Head and Up on the Screen* / Christina Hamlett / $26.95

Creating Characters: *Let Them Whisper Their Secrets* Marisa D'Vari / $26.95

Crime Writer's Reference Guide, The: *1001 Tips for Writing the Perfect Crime* Martin Roth / $20.95

Cut by Cut: *Editing Your Film or Video* Gael Chandler / $35.95

Digital Filmmaking 101, 2nd Edition: *An Essential Guide to Producing Low-Budget Movies* / Dale Newton and John Gaspard / $26.95

Digital Moviemaking, 2nd Edition: *All the Skills, Techniques, and Moxie You'll Need to Turn Your Passion into a Career* / Scott Billups / $26.95

Directing Actors: *Creating Memorable Performances for Film and Television* Judith Weston / $26.95

Directing Feature Films: *The Creative Collaboration Between Directors, Writers, and Actors* / Mark Travis / $26.95

Eye is Quicker, The: *Film Editing; Making a Good Film Better* Richard D. Pepperman / $27.95

Fast, Cheap & Under Control: *Lessons Learned from the Greatest Low-Budget Movies of All Time* / John Gaspard / $26.95

Film & Video Budgets, 4th Updated Edition Deke Simon and Michael Wiese / $26.95

Film Directing: Cinematic Motion, 2nd Edition Steven D. Katz / $27.95

Film Directing: Shot by Shot, *Visualizing from Concept to Screen* Steven D. Katz / $27.95

Film Director's Intuition, The: *Script Analysis and Rehearsal Techniques* Judith Weston / $26.95

Film Production Management 101: *The Ultimate Guide for Film and Television Production Management and Coordination* / Deborah S. Patz / $39.95

Filmmaking for Teens: *Pulling Off Your Shorts* Troy Lanier and Clay Nichols / $18.95

First Time Director: *How to Make Your Breakthrough Movie* Gil Bettman / $27.95

From Word to Image: *Storyboarding and the Filmmaking Process* Marcie Begleiter / $26.95

Hitting Your Mark, 2nd Edition: *Making a Life – and a Living – as a Film Director* Steve Carlson / $22.95

Hollywood Standard, The: *The Complete and Authoritative Guide to Script Format and Style* / Christopher Riley / $18.95

I Could've Written a Better Movie Than That!: *How to Make Six Figures as a Script Consultant even if You're not a Screenwriter* / Derek Rydall / $26.95

Independent Film Distribution: *How to Make a Successful End Run Around the Big Guys* / Phil Hall / $24.95

Independent Film and Videomakers Guide – 2nd Edition, The: *Expanded and Updated* / Michael Wiese / $29.95

Inner Drives: *How to Write and Create Characters Using the Eight Classic Centers of Motivation* / Pamela Jaye Smith / $26.95

I'll Be in My Trailer!: *The Creative Wars Between Directors & Actors* John Badham and Craig Modderno / $26.95

Moral Premise, The: *Harnessing Virtue & Vice for Box Office Success* Stanley D. Williams, Ph.D. / $24.95

Myth and the Movies: *Discovering the Mythic Structure of 50 Unforgettable Films* / Stuart Voytilla / $26.95

On the Edge of a Dream: *Magic and Madness in Bali* Michael Wiese / $16.95

Perfect Pitch, The: *How to Sell Yourself and Your Movie Idea to Hollywood* Ken Rotcop / $16.95

Power of Film, The Howard Suber / $27.95

Psychology for Screenwriters: *Building Conflict in your Script* William Indick, Ph.D. / $26.95

Save the Cat!: *The Last Book on Screenwriting You'll Ever Need* Blake Snyder / $19.95

Screenwriting 101: *The Essential Craft of Feature Film Writing* Neill D. Hicks / $16.95

Screenwriting for Teens: *The 100 Principles of Screenwriting Every Budding Writer Must Know* / Christina Hamlett / $18.95

Script-Selling Game, The: *A Hollywood Insider's Look at Getting Your Script Sold and Produced* / Kathie Fong Yoneda / $16.95

Selling Your Story in 60 Seconds: *The Guaranteed Way to get Your Screenplay or Novel Read* / Michael Hauge / $12.95

Setting Up Your Scenes: *The Inner Workings of Great Films* Richard D. Pepperman / $24.95

Setting Up Your Shots: *Great Camera Moves Every Filmmaker Should Know* Jeremy Vineyard / $19.95

Shaking the Money Tree, 2nd Edition: *The Art of Getting Grants and Donations for Film and Video Projects* / Morrie Warshawski / $26.95

Sound Design: *The Expressive Power of Music, Voice, and Sound Effects in Cinema* / David Sonnenschein / $19.95

Stealing Fire From the Gods, 2nd Edition: *The Complete Guide to Story for Writers & Filmmakers* / James Bonnet / $26.95

Storyboarding 101: *A Crash Course in Professional Storyboarding* James Fraioli / $19.95

Ultimate Filmmaker's Guide to Short Films, The: *Making It Big in Shorts* Kim Adelman / $16.95

Working Director, The: *How to Arrive, Thrive & Survive in the Director's Chair* Charles Wilkinson / $22.95

Writer's Journey, – 2nd Edition, The: *Mythic Structure for Writers* Christopher Vogler / $24.95

Writer's Partner, The: *1001 Breakthrough Ideas to Stimulate Your Imagination* Martin Roth / $24.95

Writing the Action Adventure: *The Moment of Truth* Neill D. Hicks / $14.95

Writing the Comedy Film: *Make 'Em Laugh* Stuart Voytilla and Scott Petri / $14.95

Writing the Killer Treatment: *Selling Your Story Without a Script* Michael Halperin / $14.95

Writing the Second Act: *Building Conflict and Tension in Your Film Script* Michael Halperin / $19.95

Writing the Thriller Film: *The Terror Within* Neill D. Hicks / $14.95

Writing the TV Drama Series: *How to Succeed as a Professional Writer in TV* Pamela Douglas / $24.95

DVD & VIDEOS

Field of Fish: *VHS Video* Directed by Steve Tanner and Michael Wiese, Written by Annamaria Murphy / $9.95

Hardware Wars: *DVD* / Written and Directed by Ernie Fosselius / $14.95

Sacred Sites of the Dalai Lamas– DVD, The: *A Pilgrimage to Oracle Lake* A Documentary by Michael Wiese / $22.95